Kavru

May you have
a career as glorius
as Rajnikenths

Love
Dinuy

RAJINIKANTH

Also by Vaasanthi

Amma: Jayalalithaa's Journey From Movie Star To Political Queen
Karunanidhi: The Definitive Biography
The Lone Empress: A Portrait of Jayalalithaa
Cut-outs, Caste and Cine Stars: The World of Tamil Politics

RAJINIKANTH

A LIFE

....

VAASANTHI

ALEPH

ALEPH

ALEPH BOOK COMPANY
An independent publishing firm
promoted by Rupa Publications India

First published in India in 2021
by Aleph Book Company
7/16 Ansari Road, Daryaganj
New Delhi 110 002

ISBN: 978-93-90652-10-5

1 3 5 7 9 10 8 6 4 2

Printed and bound in India by Parksons Graphics Pvt. Ltd.

Contents

Prologue[1]

The sight of the jostling crowd in the narrow streets of Royapettah leading to Woodlands theatre in Chennai is alarming. Sadanand Menon, arts editor and film critic, is bewildered as he observes the scene unfolding before him. He has managed to get a ticket for the first show of Rajinikanth's film *Enthiran* (2010) through a fan club member. He has to go through the fan clubs since tickets for the first three days for all the shows are block-booked for the members.

There is a glint of wonder and disbelief in Menon's eyes as he narrates this experience.[2] The show is at 4 in the morning. It is 3.15 a.m. and still dark when he reaches the theatre but is astonished to see thousands of fans already assembled there. There is a huge cut-out of Rajinikanth outside the theatre, supported by scaffolding that he hopes will not fall if there is a strong wind. The nearly eighty-foot-high cut-out is designed in vibrant hues to match a still photograph from the film. The fans carry garlands, plates with camphor, sweets, and pots of milk with great solemnity. They place ladders against the cut-out, a few climb up to the top—they seem experienced at it—and pour milk over the cut-out, adorn it with flowers, light the camphor to the sound of bells as one does before a deity in a temple. They climb down and distribute the sweets offered to the cut-out as prasad to the ardent fans.

Sadanand knows that the fans truly believe this pre-release

---

[1] My descriptions of Rajini are drawn from his various press interviews, speeches, and accounts from his friends.
[2] Interview with the author, Chennai, 17 Aug 2018.

ritual of theirs will ward off the evil eye and assure the film's box office success.

Ritual complete, the fans rush inside the theatre at 3.50. And the theatre turns into a carnival. The fans dance to songs from old Rajinikanth movies. Then precisely at 4 o'clock, they get a signal that the film is about to start. 'There is total silence in the auditorium, a hush that explodes when the letter 'S' appears on the screen. Screams and thunderous applause greet each letter that follows: U, P, E, R, S, T, A, R. Then as the word RAJINI appears, the auditorium erupts—the filmmakers have discovered that this is the way to get the audience elated, by simply announcing the name Rajini like bullet shots, one letter after another, Ra, Ji, Ni—kaa, nth. With each of those shots, the audience goes into ecstasies. And then with the first appearance of the hero, there is complete pandemonium. 'People dancing in the aisles, whistling—some completely drunk,' says Menon. 'It's a strange atmosphere, bizarre.'

Bizarre it certainly is. So what explains this incredible appeal?

'He is the original subaltern hero,' says Menon. 'He resonates with people from the marginalized communities. He has constantly played the outsider belonging to the deprived class. [In] most of the superhit films of his, like *Velaikkaran* (1987), where he plays the role of a servant in some upper-class household, Rajinikanth could become very convincing, as one belonging to a marginalized community. The earlier heroes like MGR and Sivaji also played such roles. They were unconvincing, they were just role-playing, but in Rajinikanth's case, he could become very convincing, therefore the resonance happened very fast.'

He explains: 'The history of oppression of the Dravidian race, the sense of subjugation, a feeling of second-class citizenship, the complexes about being dark-skinned, of not really being part of the national mainstream, and a clear whiff of political and cultural marginalization at that point in time were all encapsulated in the character of Rajinikanth and his film persona.'[3] Rajini managed to flip this and make this marginalized character the hero.

Superstar Rajinikanth is not worried about what the critics say about his acting skills or the explanations about his stupendous mass appeal. His adoring fans turn up outside his gates early in the morning just to have a glimpse of him, exchange a smile or a hand shake. They look at him with love and admiration even when they see him without make-up, balding, grey bearded and looking a little unkempt. He has never cared to hide how he looks without the make-up. He wants his fans to understand that what they see on the screen is not the real Rajini. It doesn't dim their admiration. At times, Rajini must feel like a puppet, caught in the magnitude of this admiration. And while acting has been a passion and has brought him success beyond his dreams, that personality feels like a mirage to him. Time and again, he feels the need to get away from it all—and take refuge in the silent mountains. But equally, it appears, something drags him back. Probably a duty to the people who place so much faith in him.

In the world outside, beyond the lanes of Poes Garden where his house is, his fans have gathered in the thousands to celebrate the new release of his film. It is not just the films, new releases that they were waiting for. They have been waiting for his announcement that they thought would put an end to all their miseries. They call him 'Thalaivar'—leader. He had to just say, yes, I accept the leadership. They would make sure that he won and place him on the chief minister's chair. Didn't they realize the audacity it takes to make that announcement in a state that saw the revolutionary atheist Dravidian Self-Respect Movement that was accompanied by chants of 'Thamizh engkal moochu' (Tamil is our breath)? How can he, a Marathi-speaking Kannadiga from Karnataka, even dare to tread on such ground? How did they expect him to be

---

[3]Ibid.

so impudent as to think he could rule the state that gave him shelter and food when he had come with nothing?

Being a superstar is no fun. It bewilders Rajini and frightens him, in fact. He is not able to handle the halo that he has been endowed with; it has overwhelmed him. Once, all he wanted was to play a role, a small role, on the silver screen. Never did he imagine that the screen would consume his being. There are days when he wonders who he is after the make-up comes off. The question is haunting because he cannot forget the past—that of Shivaji Rao Gaekwad who came to Madras from Bangalore, almost like a beggar, in search of a better future. Tried his luck in films. Slept on footpaths and benches, went hungry for days, borrowed clothes from his friends. The doubt nagged him constantly—what did the future have in store for an outsider, dark and uncouth, in an industry that spoke a different language.

He ended up becoming Superstar Rajinikanth. How did that happen? He does not know. And perhaps he should have stopped with that. His passion was acting, cinema. The roles he played and the dialogues he mouthed—they were not his creations. If he appeared convincing, it was due to his acting skill, nothing more. So why did his fans conclude that he could descend from the silver screen and take hold of the reins of a state of 8 crore people, all because of his on-screen popularity and the adulation of his fan club? And didn't he also delude himself of such a possibility for a while?

'He is our God,' asserted his fans. 'He will lead us to a better future because he is a good man.'[4]

They kept pushing him, believing he was their redeemer. At times, that confused him. How could he convince them that their trust was misplaced? He was an actor first and foremost. And beyond that, he knew little. At times he was swayed by the pressure from his friends who were well versed with the politics

---

[4]Based on interviews with the fans, March 2018.

of the state that he still could not understand. He avoided making a commitment, saying that he was waiting for his god to give him a signal. The fans waited patiently for more than two decades. Then suddenly there was a vacuum in the Tamil political arena, the dominating presence of J. Jayalalithaa, leader of the All India Anna Dravida Munnetra Kazhagam (AIADMK), gone with her death in 2016. Also, at the time, M. Karunanidhi, the leader par excellence of the Dravida Munnetra Kazhagam (DMK), was in bed and ailing. (He died in August 2018.) Joining the fans, others from the political realm started prodding him, telling him the time had come for him to make his entry. Judging the mood, the fans chanted, 'Come, Thalaiva, this is the time to enter. You have friends to help you. Your fans will carry you through to victory. Who cares about ideology? All people want is an honest man as the leader. They see that in you. You are a spiritual person. Tamil Nadu needs such a man to cleanse it of the sins committed in the name of reformation. Dravidianism is a myth.'

He was swayed. In hindsight, perhaps he was carried away. While he was still unsure of where this would lead, he was pulled along by all the encomiums and showers of praise from friends raising his self-esteem.

Then one day, in a fit of supreme confidence he declared, 'My entry into politics is certain!' He vowed to cleanse the system, which he averred had become rotten. It is the will of God, that I should now enter politics.... My politics will be different. It will be spiritual politics.'[5]

His ecstatic fans wept and hugged each other and thought they were at the gates of Paradise and that their miseries would end.

The timing was perfect, he was told. A consummate artist, he knew how crucial timing was. But he was still in a daze and wondered how he made such a daring announcement. In

---

[5]'Spiritual Superstar, political war cry: Full text of Rajinikanth's speech', *News Minute*, 31 Dec 2017.

the course of time, he seemed to have started believing that
he could indeed bring about a change, forgetting that his only
qualification was his humongous popularity among his fans. He
was encouraged by the thought that MGR, a popular star with
a huge fan following, had become the chief minister of Tamil
Nadu and indeed had won the election thrice.

A few months later, he declared, 'I am not MGR, but I
can give you a rule like MGR's, just and fair to the poor', as if
he was already the ruler.[6] The auditorium broke into delirious
applause, unaware of what was in store.

After this announcement, three years rolled by, and fans and
supporters failed to see that age was catching up; ailments, surgeries,
and constant health watch had become his routine, though he
continued to act in films, playing the same old swashbuckling
hero. In the political space as well, huge changes had taken place.
Politics is not cinema. The script changes every day. While he
had promised to fight all 234 assembly seats in the state, there
was no clear plan on how he would win a majority. He had to
still assuage his long awaiting fans. He shared his updated plan,
saying that he was not ambitious, wanted no power, did not want
to become the chief minister. It deflated their euphoria but the
fans were still hopeful, not realizing that he was not cut out for
electoral politics. Then came the COVID-19 pandemic of 2020.
How would a seventy-year-old with multiple health issues enter
politics during this time? When the assembly elections were just
three months away, he had still not formed the party. Then came
the news that he would not be contesting the elections after all.
The fans, though disappointed, agreed that Thalaivar's health was
the most important thing, they nodded in sympathy.

Once, in a public forum, Rajini's mentor, K. Balachander, asked
him, 'How did Shivaji Rao Gaekwad rise to become Superstar

---

[6]'Superstar Rajinikanth enters politics, to contest all seats in 2021 Assembly polls',
Economic Times, 31 Dec 2017 and Bharani Vaitheesvaran, 'I am not MGR, but can
give pro-poor rule like him: Rajinikanth', *Economic Times*, 5 Mar 2018.

Rajinikanth? You have reached great heights now. Do you think you can become Shivaji Rao again?'

Rajini answered immediately, 'I have always remained just Shivaji Rao Gaekwad. This fame, wealth, image of Rajini have not affected me ever.'

His mentor also asked Rajini if he would write his autobiography. 'If one has to write an autobiography, one has to be like Mahatma Gandhi, honest and truthful to the facts, not hiding the negative side. I shall write when I get such courage to tell my story truthfully,' he answered.[7]

He also knows that no matter what others say or write about him, none would be able to unravel the whole truth behind the phenomenon he has come to be. He alone knows that.

---

[7]'Can Rajini become Sivaji Rao again? K. Balachander quizzes Rajinikanth', Sun TV Throwback, Sun TV, 14 Jun 2020.

One

H e is dazed, still not sure why he has been knocked full length on the kadappa (hard stone) floor of the kitchen. He looks towards the door, hoping for a rescue. One more blow, Shivaji thinks, could kill him. He lifts his head a little and sees Ranoji bearing down on him menacingly.

'Who do you think you are, rascal?' his father demands as he gathers pace and aims another kick. Now he will definitely undo his belt. This is the end, the boy thinks. I am done for.

Outside, he can hear someone approaching the house at a fast pace.

'Baba, no, stop that. That is enough.'

Shivaji breathes again, thankful for the respite.

'No,' Ranoji stutters in rage. 'The whole neighbourhood is afraid of me, no one dares stand up to me, and look at this fellow, you know what he's done?'

'I know, I know, he's just a child,' Satyanarayana mumbles, barely sixteen himself. 'We will have to put him in a better school perhaps. Or send him in the evening to some coaching at Ramakrishna Math.'

'That will not help. It is like straightening a dog's tail!' Ranoji thunders. 'He is turning into a criminal. The son of a police constable!'

Ranoji is not the sort of man who will let go of his anger easily. He continues to grumble and curse until he has to pause for breath—this boy will come to no good. He has been born to torture me to death.

Shivaji stays on the floor until his father's legs are out of sight. Then he gets up and leaves the room, dragging his aching body to find somewhere to sit. He is thirsty, hungry. Tears hurt like pinpricks but pride holds them back.

'He is born last to take my life out.' Shivaji is disturbed. What does Baba mean by that? He remembers Aayi, frail and sick, yet toiling in the kitchen. That is the hazy image he has of her in his mind's eye. She wasn't the kind to smile either. Other memories crowd his mind: his mother lying on the floor gasping for breath, a blanket covering her from neck to feet. Rushing home from playing to see her dying. Her lifeless body laid on the floor, wrapped in one of her two saris. The vermilion and turmeric paste on her face that seemed to somehow define his mother. The bier waiting outside in the street. The women's wailing that sent a shiver through his young body. People hugging him and crying. He had wondered: how will my life go on without Aayi?

Now he thought: Why did she die? Why did she leave me to be beaten by a man who behaves more like a policeman than a father? The last-born. A curse. Did mother die because of me? He had not even been ten years old.

He had once heard some of the neighbour women say that when his mother was pregnant with him, her face had an ethereal glow, as if she were carrying a divine child. He laughs when he thinks of that. Bullshit. Baba is right. He is a rascal, an incarnation of Shani, Satan. Good for nothing. He will not change. It is like straightening a dog's tail. He laughs again. He must tell his friends. Must catch hold of a stray dog and see if he can straighten its tail. That will be a challenge.

At the thought of his friends, his smile widens, even the pain diminishes. What would life be without them? The joy he derives from the collective energy, passion, and curiosity—every moment is like a voyage of discovery.[1]

His entry into the world one cold night on 12 December 1950

---

[1]Based on incidents recorded in Gayathri Sreekanth, *The Name is Rajinikanth*, New Delhi: Om Books International, 2008.

in Bangalore was, by all accounts most pedestrian. No celebration awaited the birth of a fourth child to a poor couple. Moreover, the child was skinny and dark. Ramabai and Ranoji Rao Gaekwad, a Marathi-speaking couple, residents of Bangalore for a generation and more, were not particularly fair-skinned themselves, but the child was dark in comparison. Ramabai must have been relieved that the child was not a girl. A boy can make his way in the world, whatever the colour of his skin. The older children, daughter Ashwathamma, and sons, Nageshwara and Satyanarayana, were, however, excited about the arrival of their new baby brother.

They named him Shivaji, after the Marathi warrior king. Baby Shivaji kicked ferociously in response—a true warrior indeed, they laughed. The little one's ravenous hunger could not be appeased by Ramabai's frail constitution and she had to resort to cow's milk to feed the child. Soon, he was quite a handful. When Shivaji was just six, Ramabai put him in Gavipuram Government Kannada Primary School near their house. By this time, Ranoji had retired from service and the family had left the police quarters. They moved into a small house in Hanumanthanagar that Ranoji had managed to buy. The 1,000-rupee pension Ranoji brought home was barely enough to feed five people. So, when Ashwathamma was fifteen, she was married off to Ramabai's brother—with a view to cutting back their expenses. Satyanarayana was sixteen when he decided it was his duty to contribute to the home. He had completed his school-leaving certificate exam and took up a daily wager's job. Ramabai was disappointed that he could not study further, but there seemed to be no other option to feed the family. Satyanarayana made ₹50 a month. He later joined the Bangalore Development Authority as a daily wage employee. He also set up a shop at home selling vegetables and grocery items that family members would take turns to look after. This, of course, did not work out as he thought. It was too much of a task for his father and his brothers were neither responsible nor reliable, so he had to close down the shop.

Shivaji admired and marvelled at Satyanarayana's attitude. He was like Bharatha from the Ramayana, denying himself, as if doing penance for someone's sins. He went about his sacrifice quietly, voluntarily, as if it was most natural. Taking on the role of a parent as a teenager, it was as if he felt responsible for Shivaji. It was he who felt the guilt when Shivaji misbehaved. His burning desire was to ensure that his brother was fed and got proper schooling. It was as if he were born an old man.

Shivaji felt sorry for his anna (older brother), who did not know the pleasures of boyhood, the excitement of secretly smoking a beedi with friends; hiding behind bushes and drinking country liquor and making lewd jokes about girls. Before he goes back home, Shivaji hides the smell of the liquor and beedis by chewing an onion.[2]

Satyanarayana is no fool, of course. He knows all about his brother's waywardness. He hears about his encounters with the local thugs, worries that he has fallen in with bad company. He beats him, advises him. His teachers say Shivaji is smart but warn Satyanarayana that all is not well. He is worried that Shivaji will ruin his future and end up a loafer. He admits Shivaji to Ramakrishna Ashram for evening classes in the hope that the school will impart to him morals and basic spiritual values.

Much later in life, when the loafer had become a celebrity, Rajinikanth himself recounted in a TV interview how he had thrashed a notorious goon in the neighbourhood. One day, he was walking with his friend when someone suddenly charged at his friend and beat him up. Shivaji pounced on the attacker and thrashed him with a ferocity that even frightened the friend, who begged Shivaji to stop. Shivaji looked with contempt at the man who lay bleeding on the ground, and dragged his friend away to rest. It was then that his friend told him that the man whom Shivaji had beaten up was, in fact, a notorious goonda and a

---

[2]Sreekanth, *The Name is Rajinikanth*, Chapter 6.

killer. Shivaji was terrified. Once the reality of his situation sank in, he shook off his terror and said, 'Then, run,' and together they ran for their lives. Shivaji feigned a stomach ache and did not leave the house for days. Outside, he could hear the voices of the man's gang members looking for him. He couldn't hear what they were saying but he imagined the worst. On the third day of hiding in his house, he decided that he needed to clear the air between himself and the thug. He went to the goon's den and said to him, 'I am Shivaji. What are you going to do with me? Are you going to kill me? Come on, kill me!' The goon was surprised. It was almost like the climax scene in a film. But the goon looked him up and down and, to Shivaji's surprise, simply let him go. Shivaji, who had expected something else altogether, walked home with a triumphant smile.[3]

In another instance, Shivaji ended up in the police station for getting into a fight. He thought he would be let off when he told them that he was the son of a police constable. The inspector beat him more when he heard that.[4] When Ranoji came to know about his son's exploits, he was devastated. Wondering if he needed to appease the demons that had possessed his son, he consulted astrologers. One of the astrologers took a look at Shivaji's horoscope, scanned it up and down as if in disbelief and finally said that his son would either become a hermit or achieve a very high status in life. Ranoji returned home ruing the two precious rupees he had wasted on the astrologer who was doubtless a shameless bluffer.[5]

After Ramabai died, Ranoji had taken over the kitchen, but it was clear he was unable to manage the task. Once again, it was Satyanarayana who solved the problem by getting married at the age of twenty to fourteen-year-old Kalavathi. She was a cheerful, smiling girl and took over the running of the house.

---

[3]Ibid., Chapter 6.
[4]Ibid., Chapter 9.
[5]Ibid., Chapter 14.

Shivaji felt great affection for his sister-in-law, who was now the provider of food. He was no longer afraid to enter the kitchen and ask for food.

One day, as usual, he came home ravenously hungry. Kalavathi served him his portion of the food but Shivaji was still hungry. When he demanded more, Kalavathi explained that what remained was for her husband, Satyanarayana. Shivaji stubbornly demanded more. His brother arrived just then and when he saw Kalavathi and Shivaji arguing, he asked Kalavathi to feed the boy. It was only later that Shivaji realized that his brother had gone to bed hungry that night.[6]

Hunger became a constant factor in his life. Luckily, there were many temples in the locality, where, after the early morning prayers, prasad was distributed. To make sure you got the blessing you had to wake up as early as five o'clock and get to the temple. The prasad would be mouth-watering sajjige (semolina halwa) made in ghee or pongal. Some days you might get a second helping. At Gangadheeshwar temple, Shivaji was lucky that the priest's son, Somasundara, was his classmate and a dear friend. He would generously give Shivaji a large helping that he would share with his other friends.

Attending the evening classes at the Ramakrishna Math was a different experience altogether—the school was run by monks. There Shivaji was required to do some small tasks, which he did willingly as he would be given buns and milk. He had to attend classes on religion, culture, and history. They also sang religious songs. Kannada actor Ashok, who was Shivaji's classmate at the Madras Film Institute and remains a very close friend, says that it is the impact of the values taught by the Ramakrishna Math that helped Rajinikanth to remain unaffected by the astonishing superstardom that he attained early in life.[7]

---

[6]Rajinikanth recounted this at the silver jubilee celebration of *Padayappa* (1999).
[7]Interview with the author, Bangalore, 10 Jun 2018.

There was something else that Shivaji eagerly participated in. The math put on plays based on epics and myths, and the boys who had a flair for acting took part in them. Shivaji loved this aspect of the math's activities. Because of his eagerness to take to the stage, he was given a small role in the play *Ekalavya* as Ekalavya's friend. Shivaji took his role seriously. His performance was noticed and appreciated by the famous Kannada poet D. R. Bendre, who watched one of the plays.

Shivaji, who had been losing his way after the death of his mother, gained his equilibrium in the math's serene surroundings. The lessons on religion and the group songs in the evening as well as the theatre helped him gradually get over his grief. Kalavathi, with her youthful and cheerful influence, was also a big part of his recovery.

Shivaji was popular among the students because of his gift for storytelling that kept them enthralled during breaks. There were also plenty of opportunities to act in plays—Shivaji began to think that acting came naturally to him. It also gave him immense joy. He felt empowered when the viewers applauded and asked for more. It opened up a world that was sheer magic, where there was no poverty and hunger; a world that was sublime and poetic. He felt anointed, as if he could perform magic.

Temples meant festivals too and there were many through the year. Deepavali was a favourite time of year—it involved sweets, new clothes, and crackers. Shivaji and his friends would somehow manage to get their hands on some crackers. But there was always a question when it came to buying new clothes. Shivaji had only two sets of clothes that had to be washed and worn every day. They were torn and had been darned and mended several times. During monsoon, when the rain wouldn't let up for days, the clothes wouldn't dry. But he never complained or worried about it. One Deepavali, Satyanarayana told him that he had only seven rupees to give Shivaji to buy new clothes. He could either get a shirt and shorts or three sets of kurta-pyjamas. Shivaji thought over it and chose the latter—he got three sets of khadi pyjama shirts.[8] Even today, Rajinikanth wears kurta-pyjama—that has become his style statement.

Satyanarayana was keen for Shivaji to concentrate on his studies and expected him to become a doctor. He firmly believed that his brother was capable of becoming one. If only the fellow changed his habits, stopped roaming around with undesirable friends, and realized his responsibilities, he could do this.

Shivaji was well aware of Satyanarayana's expectations of him and knew that his brother was in for a big shock. He knew that Anna expected the impossible from him, and not for any selfish reasons. He also knew how disappointed his father was by his mediocre performance. He had continued studying at the Kannada-medium Acharya Patashala High School until Class XI, pre-university, as it was called. He was regarded a bright student, good at mathematics. But he found it hard to cope with English which suddenly became the medium of instruction.[9] His father and brother thought that the English-medium education would ensure a prosperous future, but Shivaji was bewildered by the change. He did not understand half the lessons taught. As the exams began nearing, he lost his nerve. He felt deeply ashamed to see the bent back of his father and his ever-toiling brother. Satyanarayana somehow managed to get money for Shivaji's exam fee. He handed over ₹200 and said, 'Pay the fees, do not think of anything else and concentrate on your studies.' Shivaji knew that it was highly unlikely that he would be able to pass the exams. He had to take a decision that day.

It saddened him, even frightened him, to have to take the decision. But he could not continue to cheat his brother and father. He decided to disappear, go away from home. And maybe

---

[8]From Satyanarayana's speech at the Silver Jubilee celebrations of *Padayappa*, Chennai, Dec 1999.

[9]G. Jagannath, 'Tamil Nadu needs a leader, I will fill the vacuum, says Rajinikanth in debut speech', *DNA*, 5 March 2018.

like in the films he has seen, he would come back a rich man, a savukar, and tell them, 'See I made it! Your good-for-nothing fellow!' He imagines that his father will stare at him, mouth open, dumbstruck.

Having made the decision, he left the house and walked briskly to the bus station and got into the bus heading to Madras.

Having watched some Tamil movies, he had an idea that the city would be the Promised Land for him. His first sight of the open sea sent a thrill down his spine. But soon, under the scorching sun, reality took over. He found that he could just not communicate with anyone without knowing Tamil. All his attempts to find a job failed miserably and within a week he had run out of money. His living conditions—sleeping wherever he found a spot—the constant hunger and the relentless heat became unbearable. He had no option but to go back home. He travelled penniless and ticketless in an unreserved compartment and was lucky that the TC never came to check.[10] He knew the kind of reception that awaited him at home and bore it stoically when his brother and father took turns to beat him.

The outpouring of abuse and cursing was a manifestation of their frustration and disappointment. He wouldn't blame them if they wished him dead. He had been a scoundrel. While his brother had sacrificed his youth to take over the running of the family, what a pest he had been. For the first time in his life, Shivaji felt depressed. His father had once said in anger: 'He will be my death!' It had not affected him at all then. Now he understands how hurt his father must have been. He has never seen anyone's father in the neighbourhood or those of his friends ever speak lovingly to their sons. If the son achieved something, they would not show their appreciation even with a smile. If they turned into a wastrel like him, well, hell's fury would pour down on them. It was the father's right to abuse, to thrash. It

---

[10]See Srikanth, *The Name is Rajinikanth*, Chapter 19.

hurt him more when his father kicked away his plate when he sat down to eat, muttering, 'Shameless glutton!'

Shivaji decided that there was no point in continuing such a despicable life. No one was going to miss him. I don't blame you, he thought, looking at the house he grew up in. Goodbye, he mumbled, good luck with your lives. Sorry I failed you.

He walked away briskly and aimlessly. He met a friend who was drawing some figures on the rocky surface of a hillock. The friend greeted him and asked him to wait till he finished drawing. Shivaji did not want anyone to know what he was about to do. He idly looked at the figures the friend was drawing. They were gods and religious figures. Shivaji turned away. Enough of the gods. Enough of all the chanting that he had been doing in the math. There was only hunger that remained. God could not even appease his one paramount need. He wondered what drove his friend to engage himself in such a useless job. He looked again. One of the drawings of a saint captivated Shivaji. He felt a strange urge to look closer. He felt that the lips of the figure moved and he heard a voice. He closed his eyes. What kind of hallucination was this? He must be hungry...thirsty. He tried to call out to his friend but he passed out.[11]

When he came to his senses, everything looked normal again. A sense of calm had descended over him. It must have been a dream, he decided. A beautiful dream. His friend told him the figure was that of Saint Raghavendra.

Shivaji felt it was a message from some unknown saint not to end his life. 'Get up man,' it seemed to say. 'This life is precious. Fight and face it.'

He walked back home with determination. He apologized to his father and brother, and told them that he wasn't interested in studying any further and would look for a job instead. He knew they would be disappointed....

---

[11]Ibid.

Two

....

'There is a job,' a relative said to him, and his heart lifted. Shivaji had tried his hand at carpentry, run errands, carried endless cups of tea as an office boy.... He will do anything to bring home a few rupees, to show that he could stand on his own feet, contribute something to the house. Anna, however, did not look happy. He avoided his brother's eyes and just nodded when Shivaji left the house. This was not what Satyanarayana had dreamt for him. He had really hoped that Shivaji would become a doctor in a smart white coat, a stethoscope dangling from his neck, the whole town singing the praises of his brother's healing touch. Dr Shivaji.

Shivaji was taken to a godown full of sacks of rice. His job was to carry sacks out of the godown and load them onto the truck outside the huge doors. For every sack he would be paid 25 paisa. His heart shrank like a deflated balloon, but Shivaji did not have any other prospects. He cheerfully nodded and began. He hoisted the sack onto his back and carried it up to the truck. There were men thrice his age doing the same work. They were intent on the task, and counted the coins carefully before tucking them into their waistband. For the first few days, his back hurt, skin became sore, but he did not complain. The hours were long, the work drudgery, and it left him despondent. But he was earning some money, a pittance though it was. He had his moments of reprieve—drinking with his friends, escaping to the movies.... But he felt like he was in a bind that he could not extricate himself from.

Sometimes he wondered if ending his life would not have been better. What had made him change his mind? That dream that he had—it was cowardice that had conjured it. He walked listlessly to the rocky hillock. There was no sign of the drawings that his friend had made there. They must have been washed away in the rain. The gods had vanished. As had the saint. He was still not able to fathom the mystery of the vision he had had that day. He did not talk about it to anyone. His father would have resorted to the belt again if he had tried to talk to him. He sat on the hillock and sent up a prayer. Do you really want me to live such a wretched life? I just want a life that I can bear. Nothing more.

After a few months, Satyanarayana told him about a job opening that he had heard of through a relative. It was for a bus conductor's job—Shivaji would have to sit for an entrance exam and obtain a conductor's license. Shivaji was prepared to go to any lengths to escape the drudgery of his current job. Luckily, he cleared the exam. He was twenty years old when he received a bus conductor's badge from the Bangalore Transport Service (BTS). He also received a smart uniform—at last he looked like a decent citizen with a job—a government job—that was respectable. There was light, after all, at the end of the tunnel. No ordinary light that. It would lead him to new friendships, and a new world—full of opportunities and incredible promise.

He joined the transport service on 19 March 1970, the same day as Raj Bahadur. Bahadur was the driver and Shivaji the conductor for the bus route 10A that went from Srinagar to Majestic. Raj Bahadur, whose family hailed from Tamil Nadu, took an instant liking to Shivaji and the men became friends. Shivaji turned the mundane job of a conductor into an art, a visual treat. The way he walked, moved, and tore out the tickets with a flourish, gave back the change with style, and brushed his hair with his fingers—the passengers noticed it all and were amused. He attracted college students, especially the girls. It was rumoured that people waited to catch bus 10A in order to witness Shivaji's antics. Despite all the style and flourish that Shivaji brought to the job, it was gruelling, being on duty from 6.30 in the morning to 2 in the afternoon. But Shivaji did his job with aplomb. It was during those days that he first tried the quirky habit of flipping cigarettes, twirling his sunglasses, and sometimes reciting dialogues from popular films of the day. While the passengers enjoyed the fact that their dull ride was enlivened, Raj Bahadur was embarrassed and admonished him for the mad display. Little did he know that the same theatrics would one day capture the imagination of generations of moviegoers.

Bhaskar Rao was a journalist with the Kannada daily *Samyukta Karnataka* and travelled to work on this bus every day. When he first saw Shivaji moving towards him in his usual style, chanting 'ticket, ticket', he was amused. Shivaji looked like a boy, with his clean-shaven face and quick smile. He had thick, long hair then; Bhaskar remembers that he would stylishly toss his hair. There was something charming about him though he could not be considered handsome. Bhaskar showed Shivaji the bus pass and explained that he did not have to pay cash. Shivaji was curious about the work that Bhaskar did. They happened to bump into each other frequently and developed a friendship close enough to share coffee in the evenings. It was during these meetings that Shivaji would talk about his fondness for acting and for cinema. He was a fan of Rajkumar, the Kannada matinee idol. And he was awestruck by Rajkumar's popularity and fame. Bhaskar could see that he was obsessed with a desire to act. He acted in the plays that the transport company association staged every month. Shivaji once invited Bhaskar to a play in which he was acting but the journalist could not make it. A few days later, Shivaji showed him a photograph of the play. Bhaskar asked if he could publish it in the paper. Shivaji readily agreed. Bhaskar published it with a small caption mentioning Shivaji's name. Shivaji Rao's first exposure in the media had a dizzying effect on him. He bought several copies of the paper and distributed it among his friends. He wanted to see the newspaper office and showed childlike wonder at everything he saw in the press. Bhaskar took a liking to the young man who spoke endlessly about cinema.[1]

Life was fun now, with Raj Bahadur by his side, who, like him, had great passion for the theatre and the silver screen. After his shift, Shivaji went home, had lunch and rested for a while. Evenings were always the best time. Employees of the bus company had formed an association that performed plays regularly. Shivaji would go to Bahadur's house in the evening, drink a big glass of fresh milk that Bahadur's mother gave him—they had a cow— and together they would go to play rehearsals. The rehearsals would take place from 5 p.m. to 8 p.m. in a hall next to the Chamarajpet police station. They would then walk down to the market and have a few drinks.[2]

Shivaji drank the hard country liquor, arrack, while the others preferred beer. Shivaji would open the arrack sachet, pour the contents into a glass, add a pinch of salt, squeeze a lemon into it, dip his fingertips in it and tap his fingers on the table and make an offering to the gods, murmuring, 'Mari, Thayi, Marikambadevi,' and throw it back in one gulp. He also used to drink 'karuvaduthanni', illicit liquor. (Even after he became a star and stayed at the West End or Taj Residency, when he invited his friends over for a drink and a chat, he preferred arrack, saying that he did not get a kick from other liquor, while his friends were served Scotch whiskey.) But he always knew his limits. Bhaskar Rao has never seen him misbehave. The conversation would always be about plays, cinema, and the famous actors of the day. They would watch every Kannada film that was released. Since there were not many Kannada films, they would watch Tamil and Telugu films as well. Shivaji was a great fan of Sivaji Ganesan and M. G. Ramachandran (MGR). Though he did not understand Tamil, he would manage to memorize the dialogue and

[1]Bhaskar Rao, interview with the author, Bangalore, 8 Jun 2018.
[2]Naman Ramachandran, *Rajinikanth: The Definitive Biography*, New Delhi: Penguin Books, 2014, p. 18.

mimic these actors. He said much later at a function in Chennai that it was Sivaji Ganesan's acting that inspired him to become an actor. 'I watched him. Imitated him. He is the reason I am in the cinema industry.'[3] But Bhaskar Rao knew that he was first an ardent admirer of Rajkumar, the Kannada matinee idol and dreamt to reach his status one day. Whenever Rajkumar's films released, fans would start standing in line for the tickets from the previous day. Shivaji would give money to some young boys to stand in the queue to get a ticket for him for the first show.

As far as the BTS Association was concerned, however, Shivaji was the star. He was always given the lead role. Shivaji played the role of Duryodhana in the play *Kurukshetra*, feeling a strange empathy with the character. He was moved by the love that Duryodhana developed for Karna, the underdog. Duryodhana was the bad guy in the story, but people noticed that so far no one had acted the part with such panache and style. Shivaji as Duryodhana lifted the mace with such nonchalance. Duryodhana would walk fast, deliver the dialogue with such speed and anger that he spit fire. He was kind, he embraced a friend who had been humiliated. He was generous, he was human. Duryodhana was not a villain. He became the hero. Shivaji became Duryodhana.

The audience went into raptures, clapped and whistled when Shivaji was on stage. Raj Bahadur was convinced that Shivaji was meant for bigger things. The silver screen, perhaps. Their other colleagues too felt that he would be a different kind of an actor surely, and could become even famous, if he were lucky. Shivaji laughed and thought it was an idler's dream. A risky one too. He was happy that he was acting in the plays they staged and thrilled with the appreciation he got, but there the matter should end. No big dreams, thank you. After all, it had taken a great struggle for him to land this secure government job. He knew

---

[3]'Bus conductor Rajini was a big hit with Bangalore commuters', *Deccan Herald*, 23 Jan 2013.

his friends were speaking out of love for him. Look at those heroes on the screen. Light-skinned, handsome. Who would look at him, dark and rugged as he is? Rajkumar looked like a real prince in whichever role he did. It would be foolish to think of the impossible, to build castles in the air. Forget it.

But Raj Bahadur had sown the seed in him. The lure of the silver screen became an obsession. 'Don't underestimate your talent,' his good friend said.[4] This became a mantra—whispering in his ears even in his dreams. He would wake up thinking: What is the harm in trying one's luck? But he knew what his father's reaction would be. He could visualize the scene. His father's raging fury—'Have you gone crazy? Have you looked at yourself in the mirror? Do you think people will spend their money to see such a face on the screen? This conductor's job is a godsend. A man who is too avaricious, and a woman who is short of temper, can never live a good life, remember. Avarice will bring you down.' Baba's curses, verbal whiplashes—he is used to that. He is also aware that all the anger and frustration were a manifestation of the love Ranoji had for his youngest child—love that he did not know to demonstrate any other way. But Baba has a point. It is a crazy thought. Irresponsible, in fact.

What will I say to the producers when they ask me about my background? That I am a bus conductor? They would probably shoo him away like the lady of the house does to a beggar at the door: *mundakke hogi* (keep moving). They would not be so polite. They will chase me out.

But Raj Bahadur has faith…and a plan, 'You don't go there like a beggar, of course. You have to equip yourself for the job, you fool. Like a doctor or an engineer gets equipped to face their professions. Don't you know that there is a new institute in Madras for film studies, acting, and other skills concerning cinema? You join the institute, get the training. Famous directors

---

[4]Sreekanth, *The Name is Rajnikanth*, Chapter 24.

come there as guest lecturers. It is up to you to create a good impression. I have no doubts about your ability. They will notice you and give you a role.'[5] That was ingenious. Raj Bahadur was smart, a man of the world. Above all, he was a good friend.

This was perhaps too good to be true. But Bahadur didn't indulge in idle words, he was a man of action.[6] He got the application form and made Shivaji fill it up and even paid for the photographs that were needed to be attached to the form. Though the Kannada film industry was thriving, Madras was the epicentre for the South Indian film industry—even Hindi film producers and directors came there for technical assistance, sometimes. Shivaji was filled with doubts and apprehensions about the logistics. It was a two-year course—how was he going to pay the fees? And what would happen to his job? Raj Bahadur knew that was worrying Shivaji. He advised him to take casual leave from BTS, and then take leave without pay once the days of the casual leave were used up. That way he could hang onto the government job in case the plan to enter the world of cinema didn't work.

Satyanarayana, of course, was not convinced initially. But, eventually, he came around. He too knew that Shivaji had tremendous acting talent. He was also aware that acting was Shivaji's passion and thought the poor boy needed to do something that he liked. Besides, the two-year course was education, learning, and any additional knowledge was good. He and Bahadur agreed that they would somehow manage Shivaji's expenses in Madras. But it was difficult to convince Ranoji. An old-fashioned man, he didn't consider films a decent vocation. He was appalled that his vagabond son, who by some luck had landed a government job, wanted to throw it all away to join a field with no security and one in which so many hopes have been dashed. But Satyanarayana

---

[5]Ibid.
[6]Ramachandran, *Rajinikanth*, p. 20.

was firm and said they should not stand in Shivaji's way. He was confident that a certificate from the institute would launch his brother's bright future. Had it not been for the film institute, he would not have agreed to send Shivaji to Madras. Shivaji's application was accepted and he was called for an interview at Madras.

Shivaji felt humbled by this turn of events. The steadfast love and generosity of Raj Bahadur, the magnanimous gesture of his brother—because of his stay in Madras the family may have to forego a meal daily—does he deserve all this? When he left for Madras, their encouraging words and hugs brought tears to his eyes. When he fell at his father's feet, Ranoji mumbled, 'Be blessed wherever you go. Let the gods be with you.' Shivaji set off for this new world with hope and trepidation. Strange people. An unknown language. It was like plunging headlong into a dark tunnel.[7]

---

[7]Adapted from Sreekanth, *The Name is Rajnikanth*.

Three

The heat was a physical blow, he was drenched in sweat and his clothes stuck to him. But there was hope and he could hear some music nearby. Perhaps there was a temple around there. It's a welcome sign, he thought. There were no giant trees along the roads like in Bangalore, nor cool parks. Even the sea looked bleached, shimmering in the heat as if the water might burn to the touch. Madras was a different world. But it was a land of promise.

Be brave, his friend Raj Bahadur had repeatedly said. Believe in yourself, you have talent. Shivaji had his misgivings, though. He remembered his previous trip to the city when he had aimlessly roamed its streets and returned to Bangalore defeated and hungry. But this time he was armed with a letter for an interview. There was a purpose in this trip. He asked around for directions and was directed to the building in a compound cooled by a canopy of green shady trees. *The South Indian Film Chamber of Commerce, Institute of Film Acting*, the board said. Shivaji felt a frisson of anticipation and nerves. While the Film Chamber of Commerce set up in 1938 was primarily engaged with the commercial aspect of the industry, the Film Institute was a new venture founded by people who were interested in good cinema. If selected, Shivaji would be in the very first batch.[1] The aim of the institute was to train students belonging to the four southern states and therefore had different batches for the different languages—Tamil, Telugu, Kannada, and Malayalam. Shivaji would be enrolled in the Kannada batch.[2]

---

[1] Anand Sankar, 'The Dark Knight of Chennai', *Business Standard*, 20 Jan 2013.
[2] MovieBuzz, 'Superstar Rajinikanth: I follow Big B's advice in life!', *Sify*, 22 Nov 2019.

When he found out that S. R. Puttanna Kanagal, the legendary Kannada director, would be interviewing the candidates for the Kannada batch, Shivaji became nervous. He was a great fan of Kanagal's films—*Belli Moda* (1967) and *Naagarahaavu* (1972). As per the alphabetical order his turn came towards the end and he was exhausted with anxiety. The interview was held on the lawns of the building, there was a cool breeze from the sea not very far away, but Shivaji was sweating. Kanagal looked at the plump, dark young man who had sharp eyes and moved briskly. The director could see that he came from a poor home, something that he empathized with, having risen from similar background. He asked Shivaji to relax, and select a favourite piece from any play he liked. Shivaji had already rehearsed a piece from *Thoppi*, Muniyappa's historical play. He sent a silent prayer to the unknown saint and readied himself. Suddenly there was a transformation— in his features, his demeanour, and speech. With a regal gait, he walked up and down spitting words in anger and disdain. When he finished the piece, his features changed again. Kanagal must have been impressed by the audition piece that Shivaji performed with such passion. He must have seen the latent talent and decided that by giving this young man a chance, the Kannada film world may see the birth of a new talent.

The candidates were told that they would be informed of the results of the test by post.

When Shivaji went back to Bangalore, he had no idea if he had made it into the institute. He went back to his job as if there had been no interruption. But his nights were restless and he could hardly sleep. When he finally got the letter informing him that he had been accepted, he nearly broke down. It is a passport to success, to a new life, Raj Bahadur said to him. That only made him want to weep more. Ranoji, though full of apprehension, wished him well. Satyanarayana asked him not to worry about them and promised he would somehow manage to send him money. Shivaji made a mental note of all these kindnesses and hoped he would be able to repay his debts someday. As they had planned, he took casual leave from BTS and left for Madras. His bag was light—one pair of pants, two shirts (his bus conductor uniform), a lungi, a packet of Nanjangud tooth powder, and a comb. He freshened up at the railway station waiting room in Madras and went straight to the institute. He was immensely pleased to see his name among the list of selected candidates on the noticeboard.

The year was 1973. P. R. Ramadas, an academic from Hyderabad who had a Master's in Fine Arts from the US and had also worked in Hollywood (he had a small role in the 1963 Marlon Brando-starrer *The Ugly American*) was the principal at the institute. He had returned to India to found the institute as requested by Telugu actor A. Nageswara Rao and singer Ghantasala Venkateswara Rao.[3] 'Usha Arasu [a graduate of the National School of Drama] was the guide for the batch,' said Ashok. 'There were classes on theory, body movements, language training, acting, and physical fitness with breaks in between for lunch and tea.'[4] There were only five other students from Karnataka in Shivaji's batch. As Shivaji could not understand a word of Tamil, he found it difficult to make friends outside his class.

But there was a more immediate problem—finding a place to stay. With the meagre resources that Shivaji had, it was hard enough to get food. He did not have enough money to rent a room. The first few nights in Madras, he slept on the footpath. Then he stumbled onto Krishnan's mess. It was a tiny hall, just 40 by 80 feet, meant for poor students. They charged a nominal fee for food and stay. Shivaji was happy that he had a roof over his head but the corner spot in the dormitory that he was given was very close to the kitchen. Coming from the cool and pleasant conditions of Bangalore he was already reeling in the heat of Madras and the added heat from the kitchen made it unbearable. Luckily,

---

[3] Ramachandran, *Rajinikanth*, p. 23
[4] Interview with the author, Bangalore, 10 Jun 2018.

his Kannada batchmates Venugopala (who changed his name to Ashok when he became an actor), Ravindranath and Raghavendra (he changed his name to Raghunandan later) came to his aid.

Ashok, a Kannada film actor who is originally from Bangalore, and remains a very close friend of Rajinikanth's, remembers their experiences from this time of life, forty-three years ago. 'Six of us—Raghavendra (who changed his name to Raghunandan), Shivaji, Chandrahas Alva, Amar Mullah, Ravindranath, and I—and three more from Karnataka had applied for admission at the institute. Seven of us were selected. One left and therefore six of us remained. When Shivaji joined the institute, he looked like a ruffian. He was fat, uncouth, and had an air of bravado about him. He would talk roughly and get into fights easily. His transformation from what he was in those days to how he is today is a miracle. Initially, perhaps because of the lack of money, no proper place to stay and being in the midst of a crowd whose language he could not understand or speak, Shivaji was rather disillusioned with the training course.' He said to Ashok, 'What is it they teach here that I did not know? I will just pack up and go back. I need to earn money. I am a burden to others if I stay here.' Ashok told him that it would be foolish to go back. 'In two years, you will get a certificate from here that will be a passport to your future. Be patient.' Ashok understood how he felt. He needed someone to talk to in his language. The Tamil boys made fun of him. It was humiliating.[5]

'We were all frustrated at one point of time or the other. Ravindranath, Krishnaswami, and I—Krishnaswami was in the Telugu batch but was from Bangalore and spoke Kannada—had taken a room on rent in Aminjikarai. It was a large room with a double cot and attached bathroom. The rent was ₹175, which was high for us those days. When I saw how pathetically Shivaji was living, I asked him to come and share with us. He had

---

[5]Ibid.

given an advance of ₹60 rupees for that corner in the mess. They returned ₹30. We all lived together for two years. Slowly, we taught him to become civilized—bought him a toothbrush, toothpaste, made him bathe every day. He survived somehow,' chuckles Ashok. He remembers that Shivaji seemed to have deep faith in Saint Raghavendra. There was a calendar with a picture of Raghavendra in their room. After having a bath, Shivaji would stand before that calendar with his eyes closed.

'The influence of the Ramakrishna Math has been very strong in him. It is that and his deep faith in Raghavendra that have sustained him and kept him level-headed in the midst of unimaginable fame and wealth,' says Ashok.[6]

Sharing a room with friends taught Shivaji to be more disciplined in his personal habits. But food was still inadequate. Most of the money was spent on cigarettes and the occasional drink. Again, help came from another batchmate, Raghunandan. 'We were all from poor backgrounds,' says Raghunandan, who hails from Udupi. 'We all loved cinema, had acted in small plays back home. It was a period of great struggle for all of us. Food was the main topic of our conversation. Where will we manage breakfast, lunch, and dinner were the questions before us, Shivaji, in particular. He was always ravenously hungry. He was unable to bear hunger. I was happy I was able to help my friends to a certain extent. A distant relative helped me get a night receptionist job at Woodlands Hotel in Chennai. I was therefore given a room there and food was free. I would do night duty and go to the institute in the morning. The dining hall supervisor was also from Mangalore. He would pack me thirty-thirty-five idlis in the morning when I left for the institute at 9 o'clock. I would take them to Shivaji and the others. Shivaji's face would beam at the sight of me and he would shout, "Raghu banda, Raghu banda (Raghu has come, Raghu has come)!" he laughs. 'At dinnertime

---

[6]Ibid.

at Woodlands, thirty to forty steel plates with food would be kept ready for the rooms. Some rooms would cancel the food. Since I was in charge of the night shift, those plates could be given to Shivaji and others. They would come to the hotel every night hoping to get food. One day when they came, no plates were available. Shivaji said he was extremely hungry and begged me to find some food. I asked them to wait and after the main staff left, I gave Shivaji the key to the store on the second floor where very costly food items were stocked. The fellows literally ransacked the place and left it dirty, did not even bother to clean the mess. At 5.30 in the morning, I finished my duty and as I was about to go to my room, the security man brought my luggage and said I had been asked to vacate the room. I had lost my job. I went to Amar Mullah's house and told him what happened. He was not surprised; it served me right he said, but gave me breakfast and a bit of advice. I later went to Shivaji's room and gave vent to my anger. Shivaji was shocked and felt very sorry.' Raghunandan smiles, 'It's funny to think of it now, but mere survival was a problem then. Later, I pleaded with the manager at Woodlands, saying it was not a crime to help fellow Kannadigas who were hungry. The manager finally relented and said he would help me till I finished the course but on one condition: "You must not let that kariya (blackie) in."

'Later, after Shivaji became famous, Rajinikanth's financial advisor Murali (brother of Vittal who was in the Telugu batch) held his wedding reception at Woodlands. Rajinikanth was going to attend it. I joked with the manager about what he said about "kariya". He begged me not to say it aloud. "His fans will kill me," he said.'[7]

Shivaji felt that his friends were doing more for him than he could for them. They were more disciplined, kept their belongings neat. They did not smoke or drink as much as he did. He didn't

---

[7]Raghunandan, interview with the author, Bangalore, 8 Jun 2018.

care if he skipped a bath or missed brushing his teeth sometimes. Yet they tolerated him, even cared for him and took his side when anyone taunted him. He still wore the conductor's uniform—he didn't have anything else to wear. Not that he cared. He was never apologetic about his appearance. He would make huge promises at times when he was inebriated, 'When I become a big star, I will not forget you all; I will never forget the past; I will take good care of you.' They would laugh and stop him, 'Saaku, saaku, bidu (Enough, enough, stop).'[8]

During wedding season, they would slip into a wedding hall, pretending to be friends of the groom or the family of the bride. They would have a hearty meal, and come out munching paan, laughing out loud, showing their red-tinted teeth. When it was not wedding season, they would try and come up with some ingenious plan to manage their hunger.

Raghunandan recalls: 'There was a guy named Pradeep in the Telugu batch, he gave us something called Ramarasa, it was not a drug but made of some herbal leaf, they even make payasa (sweet pudding) with it. But when we had it, we would feel like laughing. We would walk to the beach laughing.'[9]

'Once when he was back in Bangalore during the year-end break, Shivaji, Ashok, Ravindranath, Amar Mullah, and I were walking around aimlessly when we ended up at a palm reader, Ramanujam. He started reading our palms and told us about our futures. It's strange but his predictions were accurate. He said Amar Mullah, who was actually the best looking of us all—tall, well-built, and fair—would join an institute and not become an actor. He said Ashok would become a hero but will not become a great star. For Ravindranath and me, he said we would go into the technical side. He looked at Shivaji's palm and told him that in two years he will be the king! Shivaji was angry as we

---

[8]Ibid.
[9]Ibid.

left the place. He scoffed, "We don't know how to get the next meal, and he says I will become king. I am hungry now, man, what do we do?"'

Raghunandan laughs again. 'Strange, isn't it? There were thirty-three students in the institute. Out of that only Shivaji and Chiranjeevi, who was our junior, became successful.'

But that success came at a price. 'Shivaji felt he had lost his freedom because of his fame. One day, we were taking a walk in Bangalore. He had disguised himself as he usually does when he is in Bangalore. There was a big bungalow with a big dog chained to a pillar. Shivaji said, "Do you see the dog, that is me. I am chained like that dog."'[10]

Those two years at the institute were exciting and trying years. Exciting because each day was a lesson, a window to a different and new perspective of the acting craft. Trying, because money was always short. Whatever Shivaji's brother and Bahadur managed to send every month didn't last for more than twenty days. During the weekends, when he returned to Bangalore and went on duty as a conductor, he would make some money by not issuing tickets. That was the only way he knew to make up the shortfall. Many others also resorted to this, but Shivaji was found out and dismissed from the job. He had lost his safety net in case the film industry didn't work out.[11]

The two-year course had exposed him to the best minds of Indian cinema. He was taught, coached, and challenged by veterans who had made a mark in the film industry. One of the guest lecturers at the institute was director K. Balachander. He was reputed for his bold themes and stories that questioned societal conventions. His films rattled the middle-class audience but also attracted them and drew them to the theatres. Balachander's lecture lasted for an hour—the students were mesmerized by his

---

[10]Ibid.

[11]Bhaskar Rao, interview with the author, Bangalore, 4 Jun 2018.

brilliance. Shivaji was greatly impressed by the lecture and wanted to be introduced to the master. He did not know at that time that his life would change forever with that meeting. He had no real strategy. What could he, a Kannada-speaking boy, hope to get from talking to someone who directed Tamil films peopled with actors who spoke chaste Tamil? But it became a burning desire. He begged his lecturer, Mr Gopali, an alumnus of the National School of Drama, to introduce him to Balachander when he next visited the institute. Gopali remembered his request and when Balachander visited the institute to conduct a practical exam at the end of the course, told him that there was a lad from Karnataka in the Kannada batch who was very eager to meet him. 'He seems to be a great fan of yours though he does not know the language well enough to follow or converse.'[12] Balachander good-naturedly agreed to meet Shivaji. Balachander's sharp gaze sized him up instantly. There was something about Shivaji's energy that caught his attention. In his broken Tamil (he knew but a smattering) Shivaji told the director that he had seen one of his films *Aval Oru Thodar Kathai* (1974) three or four times. 'You must learn Tamil,' Balachander said to him.[13] He then moved on to meet the faculty members. 'Spotting Rajinikanth was sheer destiny,' he would often say later.[14]

At the end of the day, as he was walking to his car, he went past a group of students who hurriedly made way for him. Balachander turned and saw Shivaji in that group. Their eyes met and the director was struck by the power in that look. Years later, he told actor Krishnan (he joined Balachander's film company, Kavithalayaa Productions and is known as Kavithalayaa Krishnan) about that chance encounter: 'Our eyes locked. That was destiny. If it had not happened, I may not have cast him in my films at all. He may have gone back to Bangalore and tried his luck in

[12]Sreekanth, *The Name is Rajinikanth*, Chapter 32.

[13]Ramachandran, *Rajinikanth*, p. 27.

[14]Kavithalayaa Krishnan, interview with the author, 17 Mar 2018.

Kannada movies. There was something in the guy's eyes that was inexplicably arresting.'[15] Balachander had an eye for the unusual— whether in the theme of a script or in the persona of an aspiring actor. Shivaji was dark-skinned but with chiselled features and eyes that could reflect diverse emotions—Balachander was convinced that he could mould the actor. He could experiment with this fresh face and get him to play the anti-hero. So far Tamil cinema had seen stereotypical villains. This villain would be different—raw and vicious. He had three projects in mind where he could give this boy a shot. He knew Shivaji desperately wanted to act and would be overjoyed to work for Balachander. He did not know Tamil, true, but learning a language is no big deal for an actor who is expected to have a good memory. Balachander's decision was impulsive, and not only would it change Shivaji's life forever but would change the audience as well. They would shift their allegiance from the fair-skinned romantic heroes to the dark villain; that humble subaltern hero that Balachander had in mind would one day become a cult figure.

For his part, Shivaji was not aware of having made any impression at all. He was happy that he was introduced to the man whose work he admired. But Gopali said that when Balachander said he would keep someone in mind, he meant it. Shivaji was ashamed that he could not even speak one line of Tamil. He had stammered and stuttered in front of the genius who had directed talents like Sivaji Ganesan, MGR, Gemini Ganesan, and many others, including Kamal Haasan.

Shivaji passed the exams and got his certificate. His friend, Ashok, with whom he shared the room, was leaving Madras for Bangalore, having received an offer to act in a Kannada film. The future again became a question mark. Where to stay, where to eat—where will the money come from? Ranoji had been angry and Satyanarayana upset when a letter from BTS informed them

---

[15]Ibid.

that Shivaji Rao Gaekwad had been dismissed from service. They had always known that there was no guarantee that he would become a successful actor. Shivaji was too petrified to face them. He had no other option except to wait for some good luck to knock at his door. But he had no place to stay. Luckily, his friend, Vittal, from the Telugu batch, offered him a room in his house and took care of his food. Shivaji believed that some divine power was surely protecting him. He hoped the same power would also get him a spot in the film world.

He didn't have to wait long. The day he received a call from Balachander's office, he could hardly believe it. He almost became delirious. Vittal was happy for him and wished him good luck, but also asked him to relax or the day would end in disaster. The next day, he stood nervously in front of the famous director, but Balachander put him at ease with small talk and then asked him to act a piece that he was comfortable with. After Shivaji finished and stood silently, Balachander felt that he could definitely do better with a little guidance. However, he said he was offering him a small role in a film called *Apoorva Raagangal* (1975). 'It's small but interesting part,' Balachander told him. 'You must do it,' he continued, 'but you need to learn Tamil first.'[16]

Shivaji agreed at once and bent and touched Balachander's feet. He was still not sure if he had heard right. He was even more stunned when Balachander later said he would give him roles in two more films that he had planned.

He rushed back to Vittal to share the excellent news. Since the film would not start shooting for a while, he left for Bangalore, but with a sense of elation. His first thought was for his friend Raj Bahadur—without his encouragement and generous help, none of this would have been possible. He also wanted to thank his brother for his sacrifices and his belief in him. How was he ever going to repay him? In their family, they didn't express emotions. He

---

[16]Ramachandran, *Rajinikanth*, p. 27.

knew that his brother didn't expect him to express his gratitude. But yet he felt humbled at the thought of the affection that an unworthy fellow like him had received from them. Raj Bahadur's role in this journey was far from over. Originally from Tamil Nadu, Bahadur started Tamil lessons for Shivaji in earnest. When Shivaji returned to Madras, Balachander was surprised that he now spoke Tamil reasonably well, though with a Kannada accent. He was a little worried, not aware that the unpredictable audience would be charmed by it.

Four

....

Shivaji was worried that the shoot would not start on a Thursday. He had come to believe that Thursday was an auspicious day for him. There was nothing to show that it always worked, but he had come to know that it was an auspicious day for Saint Raghavendra, whom he had come to revere. He cursed himself for being so stupid and superstitious but he couldn't shake it off. For the first two days, he didn't have any scenes to shoot since Kamal Haasan, the lead actor, was shooting his scenes then. So rather than hang around on set, he would go outside, sit and smoke. When Balachander came to know this, he shouted at Shivaji: 'Don't you want to learn?'[1] Experienced actors were a treasure trove of knowledge and watching them at work was a way to learn the craft. Balachander's volatile temper was well known. But the master had a point. It was indeed a treat to watch Kamal Haasan in action. Shivaji marvelled at his skill. He put all of himself into the role, into the moment. He made you believe it was real. Kamal had all that a hero needed: looks, talent, and experience. No wonder he was already a big star though he was much younger than Shivaji. But he had had an early start, as a child artist at the age of six. A sense of diffidence gripped Shivaji. How will he survive amidst such talent?

There was a problem with his name, too. Sivaji Ganesan was a famous name in Tamil cinema. He was known for his ability to take on a variety of roles and had a big fan following. Balachander decided that Shivaji needed a new name. He chose the name Rajinikanth—the name of a character from a film he

---

[1]Kavithalayaa Krishnan, interview with the author, 17 Mar 2018.

had directed—*Major Chandrakanth* (1966).

It was a strange feeling to have a new name. That important rechristening happened on an auspicious day—it was Holi, the festival of colours and joy. On that full moon day, a star was born. For Shivaji, it was even more significant because it was a Thursday, and his first shoot had been scheduled for that day. The date was 27 March 1975. For many years after, Shivaji made it a point to meet Balachander on Holi to pay his respects.[2]

For his very first scene in the film *Apoorva Raagangal*, an unkempt Rajinikanth, with an unshaven face and in shabby clothes, was to fling open the gates of a house and enter the compound. 'His very first appearance on the screen was symbolic,' says Y. G. Mahendran, an actor and brother-in-law of Rajinikanth. (Rajinikanth's wife, Latha, and Mahendran's wife, Sudha, are sisters.) 'Not many actors get such an opening. It was as if the doors of opportunity opened for Rajini.'[3] Mahendran's father, Y. G. Parthasarathy, a well-known theatre personality, was the principal of the Film Institute when Rajini was a student there. He had told his son about a student named Shivaji who looked rugged but there was something in him that was different, attractive, and promising.

The other actors in the film had already established themselves: Kamal Haasan, Srividya, Major Sundarrajan, Jayasudha, and Nagesh. It was an unconventional story—considered to be 'revolutionary' by the standards of the 70s. Bhairavi (played by Srividya) is a famous singer. Prasanna (Kamal Haasan) is a much younger man who falls in love with Bhairavi and wants to marry her. But there is a complication he is not aware of—Bhairavi has run away from an unhappy marriage. Her estranged husband, Pandian (Rajinikanth), enters the story only at the end of the movie.

Rajinikanth was nervous during the first few days of filming.

---

[2]Srinivasa Ramanujam, Vishal Menon, 'My name is Rajinikanth', 10 Dec 2016.
[3]Interview with the author, 28 Mar 2018.

The first shot had to be retaken many times. Balachander began losing patience but understood that the new actor was nervous. Rajinikanth had only two lines of dialogue.

'Is this Bhairavi's house?' he asks Prasanna, who is standing on the balcony.

'Yes,' the young man answers. 'Who are you?'

'I am her husband,' he says hesitantly.

Prasanna is shocked—he had no idea that Bhairavi was married. He rushes down to challenge the intruder and it is only then that we see Pandian's face—he looks tired, sick.

Prasanna challenges him: 'What is the proof, can you show me the proof?'

'I can't,' says the intruder, 'but *she* can't forget.'[4]

It was a simple sentence, one that any actor could have performed. But the new face, his unique demeanour—the audience loved him.

'Who would have believed then that the gesture, as he opens the gate, nothing more than a swing of his arms, would mark the beckoning of a new crowd of fanatical admirers never heard of before?' Mahendran laughs. Balachander was satisfied with Rajinikanth's performance and was happy that his instincts had been proven right. He knew that his new find was star material. He said in an interview to the Tamil magazine *Kumudam* that he was introducing in the film a new actor Rajinikanth who he believed had a huge future.[5]

Once Rajinikanth completed his scenes, he went back home to Bangalore. He was Shivaji once again and hated to be addressed as Rajinikanth by his friends. *Apoorva Raagangal* released on 18 August 1975 and was a great success, running for more than hundred days. Shivaji and his friend, Raj Bahadur, went to see the film at Kapali Theatre in Bangalore. Raj Bahadur was overwhelmed with

---

[4]Dialogue translation by author.
[5]Balachander mentioned this during the silver jubilee celebrations of *Padayappa* in Dec 1999.

pride and joy. Shivaji broke down, overcome at seeing himself on the big screen amidst talented and successful actors. Shivaji hoped that this meant he had arrived. No more going hungry, no fear of the future. But in life, and especially in this industry, success could prove to be ephemeral.

His friend assured him that this was just the beginning. Shivaji was not aware that his brother Satyanarayana, who had watched the film in another theatre, broke down too. He could not bear to see his brother die at the end of the film. After seeing Shivaji's brilliant performance, he was relieved, convinced that allowing Shivaji to go to the Film Institute had been the right decision.

Once the film became a hit, Balachander held a big event to celebrate the 100th day of the film's running. Rajinikanth was invited to attend with his family. Satyanarayana and Shivaji boarded a bus to Madras and attended the function, the like of which the duo had never seen before. Shivaji was presented with an appreciation shield. His brother in the audience brimmed with pride. The film went on to win several National Film Awards— Best Feature Film in Tamil, Best Cinematography, and Best Female Playback Singer.

After this, Shivaji sat idle for a while in Bangalore. He was back to his routine of hanging out with friends. Life was fun for a while. But, soon, the silence from producers and directors became depressing. He would get together with Film Institute classmate Ashok and the journalist Bhaskar Rao and discuss what the future might bring. The Kannada film industry was small and dominated at that time by Rajkumar, Kalyan Kumar, and Udayakumar (called the Kumara trio), and Ambarish. In any case, the Kannada film industry was not known to be lucrative for actors. It was quite a well-known fact that S. R. Puttanna Kanagal and G. V. Iyer, who were producers and directors, were not good paymasters. The future looked bleak. Shivaji shuddered at having to go back to the days of being told that he was a good-for-nothing, shameless glutton.

Bhaskar Rao advised him to shift his base to the Tamil film industry. 'Madras is the Mecca for the South Indian film world. Learning Tamil should not be a problem. Balachander has already spotted you. Take this opportunity and stay in Tamil films. You will become famous.'[6]

Before he could act on this, however, Puttanna Kanagal, the man who had interviewed him for admission at the Film Institute, offered him a villain's role in his Kannada film *Katha Sangama* (1976). In *Apoorva Raagangal* he had played a complex character—a man who started out bad, but turned good—not an out and out villain. But he was ready to take on any role. *Katha Sangama* won awards and critical acclaim and, needless to say, the Kannada-speaking audience, too, took notice of Rajinikanth. He had smoked in *Apoorva Raagangal* but it was in *Katha Sangama* that he performed his now iconic trick of stylishly flipping a beedi and lighting it. Although the movie was a big hit, 'Rajinikanth could not click in Kannada cinema,' Bhaskar Rao recalls.

It is strange that Rajinikanth never became a big name in Kannada cinema. He was a Kannadiga (though he spoke Marathi at home), and could speak chaste Kannada and quote from Kannada literary works. Yet his gestures of irreverence and stylish tricks that fascinated the Tamil masses did not capture the Kannada audience the same way. M. K. Raghavendra, film critic and author, says, 'That is because the strong working class that emerged after the social juggling that happened in Tamil Nadu during the Dravidian Self-Respect Movement is not there in Karnataka. Karnataka never saw such a social churning. The Tamil Nadu proletariat is totally different from that of Mysore, for instance, which followed a system of hierarchy, which was never disturbed by a social revolution.... Rajkumar, who was a big star, played roles that projected Brahminical qualities though he was not a Brahmin. In his films, the villains are called Thimmaraju or Kattayya [that are]

---

[6]Interview with the author, Bangalore, 4 Jun 2018.

non-Brahmin names. Rajkumar as a police inspector who tortured these people would have a name like Narasimhamurthy, which represented the higher class. Mysore never saw the social revolution that would empower the masses. In Tamil Nadu there was already a class waiting for an envelope of empowerment—Rajinikanth's gestures seem to suggest nonchalance, power, impetuousness, don't-care attitude. This certainly would attract the masses. The working class which does not have power would like to see the demonstration of personal power.'[7]

Tamil Nadu has witnessed a social revolution the like of which no other Indian state had seen. The Self-Respect Movement, led by E. V. Ramasamy Naicker, better known as Periyar (the elder), began in 1925 as a protest against the hierarchical supremacy wielded by the Tamil Brahmin class that formed just 3 per cent of the population. It gained momentum with a resurgence of Tamil pride and Tamil chauvinism with claims that the language was older than or as old as Sanskrit and not an offshoot, unlike other Indian languages. It was this combined with Periyar's Self-Respect Movement that led to an anti-Hindi agitation and the downfall of the Congress government in the state in 1967. Periyar believed that 'We are fit to think of self-respect only when the notion of "superior" and "inferior" caste is banished from our land.'[8] He offered a vision of a bright future without the need for God. Though the general public did not take his atheism seriously, his speeches challenging caste hierarchy caught the attention of the middle, lower, and the subaltern classes. Until his death in 1973, he relentlessly continued speaking on this issue.

R. M. Veerappan (RMV), film producer and Dravidian politician (of the AIADMK), admirer of MGR, producer of the superhit Rajinikanth movie *Baashha* (1995), was a follower of Periyar in his youth. Now a believer, he says, 'Neither the Alvar

---

[7]Interview with the author, Bangalore, 20 Jun 2018.
[8]E. V. Ramasamy, Round Table India, 24 Dec 2011.

nor the Nayanar saints,[9] not even Saint Vallalar[10] of the last century said there was any difference among human beings. But [even they] could not change the mindset of the people. Periyar in his crude way churned the society in a manner no one else could...'[11] The churning was so effective that it culminated in the demolition of the Congress in the state. The Dravidian parties—Dravida Munnetra Kazhagam (DMK) and the All India Anna Dravida Munnetra Kazhagam (AIADMK)—are both offshoots of the Dravidian Movement started by Periyar. These two parties have been ruling the state for more than sixty years. The non-Brahmin class—upper, middle, and lower—gained a voice.

It is in this atmosphere—the air filled with irreverence to caste and class hierarchy that Shivaji Rao Gaekwad entered Tamil films—with his anti-hero image, nonchalance, defiance of authority, and rakish smile.

Again, it was Bhaskar Rao who predicted during those uncertain first years that Rajinikanth would become a superstar. He had written a review of *Katha Sangama*. The piece had been short and needed four more lines to fill it out. Bhaskar Rao hastily added what came to him. He wrote, 'Here is an actor with such talent that it should not surprise anyone if he becomes a superstar one day.'[12]

Actors who were baffled at the way he stormed the field could only attribute it to 'sheer luck' or the fact that he was 'blessed'. Rajini *was* lucky in a sense. His arrival coincided with a massive change that the Tamil film industry was undergoing in terms of production, content, and storytelling. Tamil commercial cinema was dominated by MGR (who also belonged to the DMK), Sivaji Ganesan, Gemini Ganesan, Jaishankar, and such others. From

---

[9]Tamil poet-saints of the sixth to eight centuries. The Alvars were devotees of Shiva and the Nayanars were devotees of Vishnu and his avatar Krishna.

[10]A Tamil poet-saint of the nineteenth century.

[11]Interview with the author, Chennai, 2004.

[12]Interview with the author, Bangalore, 4 Jun 2018.

the 1950s till the early 70s, films that projected the resurgent
Dravidian symbolisms and party ideologies with melodramatic
acting and theatrical textual Tamil scripts dominated the scene.
The Dravidian Movement used films and film songs sung and
acted by MGR, the hero, to take its ideologies to the masses.
The audience lapped it all up during the period that was charged
with and inspired by revolutionary ideals. MGR always played
the do-gooder, a protector of damsels in distress, a non-smoker,
and a non-drinker. His promoters envisaged his characterization
with a view to projecting him as a future chief minister of Tamil
Nadu. He became a symbol for the party. MGR fan clubs were
created to muster votes.

The DMK came to power in 1967, and later when the DMK
split and MGR formed his own party, AIADMK, in 1974, there
was no longer any need to use cinema to take the ideology to
the masses. Veteran actors MGR and Sivaji had outgrown their
romantic hero roles. Even their most ardent fans were tired of the
same old plots with heroes giving sermons about good behaviour.

By the time Balachander came on the scene, the cinema-going
public was ready for a whiff of fresh air. Balachander was born
into a Brahmin family in Nannilam, a small town in Thiruvarur
district. He completed his graduation and joined the Accountant
General's office in Madras as a clerk. A theatre enthusiast, he had
been writing plays with themes that interested the middle class.
He was not part of the Dravidian movement. The movement had
empowered the backward classes. And now a vibrant middle class,
aware of equal rights and gender issues, was ready for a conscious
questioning of traditional mores and values. Balachander was able
to capture the shifting mood of the audience and write plays that
spoke to them. His characters were bold, irreverent, and asked
pertinent questions. The dark actor was not always the villain and
the fair one was not an angel. There was no age taboo for love.
He painted prostitutes as prisoners of circumstances and not as
social outcasts. The woman was no longer just the loyal faithful

wife who did not cross the threshold of her house.

His plays were huge draws and when he ventured into cinema, his films were box office hits.

It was at this time that music maestro Ilaiyaraaja and director P. Bharathiraja also entered Tamil films. They set new trends in music composition and storytelling respectively. Bharathiraja shifted the lens outside the studios and set his stories in the countryside. Theatrical dialogue backed by ideological underpinnings was replaced by colloquial banter. For the first time, the urban audience could smell the freshness of the village air and hear the chirping of the birds. This is when Rajinikanth entered. His entry marked a clear break from the conventional fair-skinned hero who was a paragon of virtue. Rajinikanth was dark, he smoked and drank on-screen, and could play dark characters and get away with it. His rawness and irreverence made him a hero of the subaltern.

Sadanand Menon says, 'With Rajini, Tamil cinema, and by extension, Tamil society learnt to be kosher with being "bad". It was no longer something that someone was going to make them feel guilty about. Rajini taught Tamil society to abandon platitudes about Rama as maryada purushottam and accept the possibility of a Ravana or a Duryodhana actually being good. When Rajini stared directly back into the camera...and hissed out the lines from the corner of his mouth, executed his side-winded walk of electric energy, tossing his tousled hair, he became the new and manifest example of hitherto suppressed expressions of desire, no matter how risky or preposterous it seemed.'[13]

The most conspicuous difference that the audience saw in Rajinikanth was his unbridled energy. After that initial lull, Balachander cast him in three films: *Anthuleni Katha* (Telugu, 1976), *Moondru Mudichu* (1976), and *Avargal* (1977) in quick succession. It ensured that the film-going public didn't forget him. In the year 1977, Rajinikanth acted in fifteen films, and didn't play

---

[13]Interview with the author, Chennai, 16 Mar 2018.

the hero's role in all of them. Unlike other actors, Rajinikanth
enjoyed playing the villain and stole the show with his off-beat
portrayals of these dark characters. All the films were hits and
Rajini began to be considered lucky by producers.

Y. G. Mahendran got to know Rajini well when they worked
together on the Tamil film *Bhuvana Oru Kelvi Kuri* (1977), directed
by reputed director S. P. Muthuraman. Mahendran found that
Rajini was an intense person who did not speak much. He was
very respectful to his seniors—even to Mahendran, who was a
senior in the profession, and also because he was the son of his
former principal. Mahendran noticed that Rajini would listen
carefully to suggestions given by everyone, but he would take
only what he thought was right for him. He knew right from
the beginning that he could survive in the field only if he stood
out. Mahendran remembers how an experienced senior actor, P.
Sivakumar, tried to coach him on how to deliver a line. Rajini
listened and nodded, but finally delivered the line in his own
style. 'People think he is a director's actor, but he often went
beyond the brief. Muthuraman allowed him the freedom. That
is why the pair clicked so well.'[14]

Muthuraman has been associated with the legendary AVM
Studios that has produced over 170 films in Tamil, Telugu,
Kannada, Malayalam, and Hindi since 1955. He started there as
an assistant in the editing department and went on to become
a successful film director. Sitting in his modest office room at
the AVM Studios compound, he remembers his reaction when
he first saw Rajinikanth on the screen in a villain's role. Actors
who played the villain followed a set formula—they had a loud,
sinister laugh, rolled their eyes, and gritted their teeth. But Rajini
played it very differently and with a style that had not been seen.
Muthuraman was impressed. When it came to casting Rajinikanth
for *Bhuvana Oru Kelvi Kuri*, he cast him for the hero's part and

---

[14]Y. G. Mahendran, interview with the author, Chennai, 28 Mar 2018.

made Sivakumar the villain. He was convinced that Rajinikanth was capable of bringing something unique to the character. The two main characters were not straightforward—the one who came across as the villain was, in fact, the good guy while the one who seemed to be the hero was the villain. Muthuraman felt that making Rajinikanth appear to be the good guy would ensure that the audience would be surprised. Sivakumar, who had always played the good guy, was disappointed when he came to know that he would be playing the villain. But Muthuraman convinced him that it would work. The film became a box office hit.

'Mind you, at that time, Rajinikanth was not able to speak two sentences at a stretch in Tamil,' laughs Muthuraman.[15] Rajinikanth was a little nervous when he saw that he had to speak lengthy dialogues in the film. Muthuraman put him at ease, telling him to prepare as much as he could and then act in his own style. This freedom and belief that the director showed in him allowed Rajini to reach 'the next level' in his acting career. Muthuraman believes that if A. V. M. Chettiar (founder of AVM Productions) had been alive, he would not have accepted Rajinikanth, because Chettiar demanded perfect rendering of Tamil. But it was Rajinikanth's Kannada-tinged Tamil and the speed with which he delivered his lines that became a style statement. Muthuraman and Rajinikanth worked together in twenty-five films, with Rajinikanth playing a variety of characters. *Bhuvana Oru Kelvi Kuri* was not only a commercial hit, Rajini's acting in it also received critical acclaim.

Sivakumar's friends felt that he should not have agreed to take on the villain's role. But 'it was destiny', he says. 'I told them so. Rajinikanth was destined to shoot up in popularity due to that role. No power on earth could have changed that.'[16]

But it was not sheer luck or divine grace that was the reason for his success, says Muthuraman. It was hard work and total

---

[15]Interview with the author, Chennai, 27 Mar 2018.
[16]Interview with the author over phone, May 2018.

involvement in the work he did. Unless he had absorbed the story completely and internalized it, he would not act. His popularity was the direct result of his dedication to the craft.

Muthuraman admits that directors like him did indeed include songs and scenarios that they knew would appeal to the fans— the speed and unique gestures. Unlike in earlier years, this was not done to curate his image. Instead, it catered to aspects of Rajini's persona that the filmmakers knew the fans loved. The 1980 film *Murattu Kaalai* directed by Muthuraman had a song with these lyrics:

> Pothuvaa en manasu thangam,
> aana oru pottiyinnu vanthuvitta singam
> (Usually my heart is like gold
> but when there is a contest it becomes fierce as a lion)

And in the 1989 film *Raja Chinna Roja* had this:

> Superstar yaarunnu ketta kuzhanthaiyum sollum
> (If you ask: 'who is the superstar?', even a child will tell you)

Once when the cast and crew were driving to a location for an outdoor shoot, a group of schoolchildren from Classes V to XII blocked the road, forcing the vehicles to stop. 'They had come to know that Rajinikanth would be in that group. "Stop the vehicle, we want to see Rajinikanth!" they shouted. Such was his appeal. He had caught the imagination of children as young as six.'[17]

Rajini's fans would request the theatre manager to play the songs again and again. This was very different from MGR's popularity. MGR's image was built very carefully and systematically as a viable political leader. Rajini had no political ambitions when he first entered films. He wanted to work as much as he could,

---

[17]Muthuraman, interview with the author, Chennai, 27 Mar 2018.

act in as many films as possible, take every opportunity that came his way and make money. He began working non-stop. The recognition that came early in his career was intoxicating, blinding. He worked like one possessed. Work became an obsession. A disease, an affliction...till the mind went berserk.

Five

....

The phone rang. Muthuraman looked at the clock—it was 3 a.m. He had returned from the studios half an hour ago and was preparing to go to bed. The phone stopped ringing, then started again. Muthuraman was tired, but what if it was an emergency? He answered. It was Rajinikanth.

'Yes, tell me, what's the matter?'

Rajinikanth's anxious, hurried voice said, 'Nothing, sir, was my shot okay today?'

That evening the unit had wanted to wrap up at 9 p.m. The last shot was not satisfactory. Muthuraman decided it could be shot again the next day. But Rajinikanth insisted on getting it done that night no matter how long it took. He felt that he would lose the mood, the momentum. The shooting continued and finally it came out perfect. They had finally packed up at 2 in the morning.

Now that Rajini had called about the next day's shoot, Muthuraman was annoyed but answered calmly, 'Of course, don't you know I would not okay the shot if I was not satisfied?'

'Yes, sir, but I just wanted to make sure. I can't sleep if I'm not certain it went well. What will be the shot for tomorrow, sir?'

Muthuraman exclaimed in exasperation. 'You want to know now? I will tell you tomorrow. Now go to bed.'

'I can't sleep, sir. If you tell me briefly, I can be better prepared for tomorrow, sir.'

There was urgency in the voice, an insistence. Muthuraman knew Rajinikanth by now. This man would not let him sleep if he didn't comply. He briefly told him what he had planned for the next day.

'Thank you, sir.' Muthuraman put the phone down, thinking how strange this man was.[1]

Rajinikanth was always in a tearing hurry as if there was no tomorrow. He was always anxious. Muthuraman knew that when a situation was explained to him, Rajini internalized it fully. He needed to digest the scenes and dialogues. Only after that could he perform. It was hard work.

By this point, Rajini was already famous. He had had thirty-six releases in two years. Another twenty films were on the floor. Many of the films that he had so far done were hits. Directors and producers felt he had the Midas touch. He was aware of this. But unlike other stars, Rajini did not demand any special facilities at the shooting spot. Many actors, even the most junior ones, demanded special food from five-star restaurants. Muthuraman had seen it all. But this man from Bangalore was different. Once when they went for a four-day outdoor shoot, Rajinikanth came as he was—no luggage, no change of clothes, not even a toilet kit. When Muthuraman asked him about it, Rajini told him he didn't need anything. 'As soon as we land, there will be the studio lungi to wear and then of course the costume for the shot. There will always be a comb, I can get some toothpaste and soap anywhere.' 'He managed like that for four days,' Muthuraman remembers.[2]

'There was once a shoot in Pollachi for *Ranuva Veeran* (1981) in a rice mill. There was some problem in the rice mill and they asked us to stop shooting. I went inside to sort out the matter. That took a while. When I came back to prepare for the shot, we couldn't find Rajini. My men went in search of him and found him sleeping on a mound of paddy sacks. The place was hot. I scolded my men and asked them why they didn't give him a mat and ask him to lie down under a fan. Of course, they had

---

[1] Interview with the author, Chennai, 27 Mar 2018.
[2] Muthuraman, interview with the author, 27 Mar 2018.

no idea that he was sleeping on the sacks. We woke him up and I asked him why he slept here—it would hurt his back and skin. Rajini dismissed this concern and told Muthuraman: "Before I worked as a conductor I worked as a coolie in a godown. I used to carry paddy sacks on my back. My skin is used to it and my back to the load."[3]

Muthuraman was stunned by the humility and simplicity of this man who had attained unimaginable fame and success. And had earned a lot of money. Even today, Muthuraman says, he has no airs.

Another time, Muthuraman remembered, separate vans were being provided for the leading stars. They had their make-up done there; they could rest and eat in privacy. The producer A. V. M. Saravanan was particular that Rajinikanth be given a good van. But Rajinikanth would have none of it. He said he was happy with the old system and continued to have his make-up done in the common room, ate with everyone, and slept anywhere he found a spot.

Bhaskar Rao, the journalist, happened to meet Rajinikanth during the production of the Tamil remake of the Kannada V. Ravichandran and Anant Nag-starrer *Shanti Kranti* (1991) in Bangalore. Rajinikanth was the hero in the Tamil version titled *Nattukku Oru Nallavan* (1991). Bhaskar Rao was surprised to see that Rajinikanth was not in the van assigned to him; instead, he was sitting on a chair outside, holding an umbrella, waiting for the shot. During this shoot, Rajinikanth invited Bhaskar and some other friends like Ashok to his hotel room in the evenings. When they got together, Rajini would order Scotch whiskey for them while he had his favourite local arrack. He would tear open the sachet, pour the drink into a glass, add a dash of salt and squeeze a lemon—always offering it to the gods first—and then drink it in one gulp. Bhaskar still remembers that Rajini was warm and

---

[3]Ibid.

friendly and never lost his cool even when inebriated.[4]

But there was another side of him that was unsavoury and puzzled those who witnessed his erratic behaviour. It started showing during the peak of his activity, within two years after his first film. Many directors and producers asked Muthuraman how he managed Rajini as he had not had any problems with the actor during the twenty-five films they worked on together. Muthuraman explained that Rajinikanth was hyperactive and worked non-stop, without eating or sleeping at regular hours. He advised patience and tact.[5] Not everyone was willing to be as forgiving as Muthuraman. Thirty-six releases in two years, many of the films runaway successes, was a stupendous, incredible achievement. There was a lot of jealousy among the actors, seniors and juniors alike, that a man from Karnataka, who was still not fluent in Tamil—an ordinary looking, dark-complexioned fellow—should have won accolades that perhaps were due to them. To their mirth and glee, his behaviour became a point of gossip, inside and outside the industry. Word reached the press and there were reports of his wild misconduct almost every day. It was said that he had slapped a reporter and that incident turned the press against him. He lost his cool when reporters mobbed him and became irritated by the blinding camera flashlights; besides, half the time, he could not understand them. He shooed them away rudely, and this was seen as arrogance by the press that was used to being treated well, even pampered by the film world. His detractors said that success had gone to his head, that he needed a rap on the knuckles, and that he behaved badly because he was 'mental'.

While there was a lot of resentment and gossip within the entertainment industry, it made no difference to his popularity with the filmgoers. They didn't read newspapers or magazines.

---

[4]Interview with the author, Bangalore, 4 Jun 2018.
[5]Muthuraman, interview with the author, 27 Mar 2018.

Even those who did read the reports did not believe them. But his behaviour worsened, worrying his friends. Rajini began to behave badly in public places, including in hotels and on flights— throwing tantrums, getting into arguments, embarrassing fellow artists on a flight abroad. It became a regular occurrence on the sets; there were reports of him becoming uncontrollable, getting into fights, physically assaulting people.

Had Shivaji Rao Gaekwad changed? Shivaji had to be aware that he was behaving strangely. He wanted to focus on the task and it annoyed him when there was an unwanted interruption. He wanted to be left alone. He could not step out onto the street. The press always managed to sniff him out and they pressed him with various questions: You said this, you said that. He would dismiss them: So what? What is it to you?

He was always angry and irritated—he could not understand why. Part of it must have been the fear that stemmed from his early life. He wanted to show the world that he was somebody. He was scared of falling asleep—what if he missed an opportunity that came his way? He would have felt happy, felt important, that there was an offer or request from a director or producer every day. It would have erased the fear that he was a nobody, a fear that had gripped him when his father and brother berated him.

When he first started acting, his father had told him, 'If you earn money (clearly, his father still doubted his ability to make a living from this field) you must first buy a house. You will at least have a roof over your head, a kitchen to cook your food. It will be an asset to fall back on.'[6]

These words came back to him every night when he returned to the room he had rented at a friend's place. He was paid ₹15,000 per film, while even a modest house would cost several lakhs. He came across one in Nungambakkam (where The Spring Hotel now stands) which cost ₹24 lakh. It was way beyond his

---

[6]Raghunandan, interview with the author, Bangalore, 23 Jun 2018.

budget but he liked it so much that he did not want to let go of it. He paid an advance and told the seller that he would pay the rest in eighteen months. That debt hung like the sword of Damocles over his head. To make the money needed to buy this house, he had no other option but to work day and night. He set himself a punishing schedule. Between 1978 and 1979 he worked in multiple shifts in multiple languages—Tamil, Telugu, Malayalam, Kannada, and Hindi. He would shoot during the day and travel at night to shoot for another film the next day. This relentless travel and work started clouding his brain. Once when he had to speak at a public event in the midst of this maddening schedule, the organizers were embarrassed when he mixed up all the languages in the course of a five-minute speech. He knew it was a disaster. But he could only blame the organizers who had insisted that he speak a few words. There were vicious headlines the next day and whispers doubting his mental stability. Luckily, Shivaji could not yet read enough of the Tamil script to read these reports. He was not interested in what was being written or said.

It was strangely during this descent into violence and a desperate need to keep working between 1977 and 1979 that some of his best performances were seen. Starting with Muthuraman's *Bhuvana Oru Kelvi Kuri*, he went on to act in Bharathiraja's *16 Vayathinile* (1977), M. Bhaskar's *Bairavi*, J. Mahendran's *Mullum Malarum* (1978) and several other films that revealed the extent of his talent and originality in delineating the character beyond the director's conception of it. After watching *Mullum Malarum*, Balachander wrote Rajini a letter saying, 'I am proud that I introduced you as an actor.'[7] It is a letter that Rajinikanth still cherishes.

The period was not merely the most productive but also saw his popularity hitting incredible heights. He sailed through

---

[7]Kavithalayaa Krishnan, interview with the author, 23 Mar 2018.

it all like a robot, unmindful of the physical strain, focused on the job. He was a different man in front of the camera. There seemed to be a symbiotic relationship between Shivaji Rao and the camera. Shivaji receded, Rajinikanth became a blur, and he merged with the character. He was aware that the audience were his gods; the producers told him that he had to appease the gods, keep them happy.

But he had shut himself away from the outside world, so much so that he was bewildered one day to see a forty-foot cut-out of himself at Chennai's Plaza Theatre announcing the release of *Bairavi*. There were huge posters all over the city, he was told—they had his photo with the words 'Superstar Rajinikanth'. The film had been directed by M. Bhaskar and produced by Kalaignanam. The distribution rights had been given to one Kalaipuli Dhanu who was an expert in marketing. He had defied an objection from the corporation commissioner and put up the huge cut-out. Rajinikanth was embarrassed and told the producer that it was not right to call him Superstar when there were veterans like Sivaji Ganesan and others. But they pacified him saying it was all part of publicity for the film. And it worked. People thronged to the theatres repeatedly and the film became a big hit.

The moniker Superstar came to stay. His fans adopted this title enthusiastically. Overnight, Rajinikanth became an icon. Dhanu printed more posters for Bangalore. They had the words 'The greatest Superstar Rajinikanth in *Bairavi*' in big, bold letters. Shivaji didn't want to know if his father saw the posters. If he had seen them, he would most likely have distanced himself from the man on them: 'Athu yaaro, nanna magaa illaa, (That is someone else, not my son), he would have said.

Rajini did not realize that he was becoming increasingly socially disconnected. It was a dangerous metamorphosis. He was ashamed when his mentor Balachander admonished him and asked him to behave. He knew he had to calm down, but could not.

He was in the grip of some unknown demons. Of the directors who worked with Rajinikanth during those difficult years, only Muthuraman and Balachander were able to 'manage' Rajinikanth. According to Kavithalayaa Krishnan, 'Rajini would keep quiet only in the presence of Balachander.'[8] Pushpa Kandaswamy, Balachander's daughter, recalls the unique bond that her father had with Rajinikanth. It was not just a relationship between a mentor and his protégé. It was something more than that. 'Appa felt responsible like a parent for Rajinikanth's behaviour.' Her father understood that Rajini was a simple man. His greatest ambition was to get a chance to act and earn enough money to lead a good life. He could tell that the sudden fame and superstardom that he achieved within such a short span of time affected his mind deeply, almost fragmenting it. Balachander was agonized when Rajini would ask him in desperation, 'Why did you introduce me to films? Why did I become so famous?' The young man did not know how to strike a balance between his stardom and normal life.[9]

Things came to a head during the filming of V. Sasi's film, *Allauddinum Albhutha Vilakkum* (1979). It was shot simultaneously in Tamil and Malayalam and was Rajinikanth's first Malayalam movie. He wanted to do his best. Kamal Haasan played the role of Allauddin, Rajinikanth was Kamaruddin, the commander of the armed forces of Baghdad, and Sripriya played Jameela. Rajini was very aware of the presence of the extraordinary actor Kamal Haasan on set. That very likely led to him feeling that he was being ignored, sidelined. This idea consumed him. Sasi was bewildered. He did not know how to handle him. He immediately contacted Balachander and told him that there was a crisis. Pushpa remembers that when Sasi called and asked for Balachander's help, 'Appa went immediately to the spot and cajoled Rajini, "I'm with you. Don't

---

[8]Interview with the author, Chennai, 23 Mar 2018.
[9]Pushpa Kandaswamy, interview with the author, Chennai, 9 Jan 2019.

be scared. I am here for you." Appa's presence had a dramatic sobering effect on him.'[10] It was as if Rajini was mesmerized by this mantra.

Rajini wanted Balachander to be the clapper to every film of his, no matter who the producer was. The mentor was an important figure at every phase of his protégé's life. Pushpa says that it was almost like a father holding his little boy's finger, helping him take his first steps. 'That relationship was very beautiful.'[11]

Balachander was worried that Rajini's violent behaviour would be misconstrued, and it was, as was evident from the negative reports that kept appearing in the gossip columns. Both Balachander and Sripriya recognized that Rajini needed immediate medical attention. Balachander had to work very hard to persuade Rajinikanth that he needed to go to the hospital. He was admitted in Vijaya Hospital where he was put under medical care for nearly two months between the end of 1978 and the beginning of 1979. The doctors said he just needed rest and sleep. For the first few days, sleep eluded him—he had trained his brain to go without sleep. But, slowly, he learned to calm down and his system came back to normal. It was nearly a spiritual experience for Rajini. Recalling those days S. P. Muthuraman says, smiling, 'The story of Allaudin proved to be metaphorical. At the end of the movie Jameela, Sripriya's character, rescues Rajini's character Kamaruddin from quicksand. In real life, Sripriya was one of the first people who saw that Rajinikanth needed help and reached out a hand.'[12]

After his recovery, Rajini read out a list of names at a public event and thanked them for having helped him during those difficult days. Strangely, Sripriya's name was missing. It's possible that he was so confused at that time that he had not been aware of her role in helping him.

---

[10]Ibid.

[11]Ibid.

[12]Interview with the author, 27 Mar 2018.

After this stay at the hospital, the Superstar returned, born again. Fresh, his energy doubled.

He still had the magic touch. The name Rajinikanth became synonymous with the word 'success'. He could not be stopped.

Six

Surya was about twenty years old when he became a die-hard Rajinikanth fan, and at sixty, he still remains an ardent one. His eyes become misty talking about those days, forty years ago.

'I first saw his film *Kuppathu Raja* (1979). I was struck by his style. I was completely captivated by it. The way he walked, his actions, everything was superb. He would rotate a knife on the tips of his fingers. Somehow, he would twist it so that he held it by the handle. It may have been a trick of the camera, but it seemed so real. I was fascinated. It was his style that attracted me.'[1]

Surya was a school dropout. He told his father that he was not interested in continuing his studies, so his father found him some odd jobs to do. A Chennai man, Surya is now in charge of one of the several Rajinikanth fan clubs in the city.

Forty years ago, Surya and other fans would gather at the gates of Rajinikanth's Poes Garden home early in the morning every day. And through the years, generations of fans have continued to throng his gates. He was friendly and warm. When he came out, he would approach them and speak to all of them. Sometimes, when he was relaxed, he would sit on the swing in his veranda and chat with them. He used the respectful 'vaanga' to address them. Even though he was not all that fluent in Tamil, the fans understood his staccato speech. No other actor could match his speed, energy, and grace. The fans felt that other actors held themselves a little aloof, as though very aware of their own superiority. They were stars, unreachable. Thalaivar, on the other hand, was so simple. He would approach them without any make-

---

[1] Interview with the author, Chennai, 28 Mar 2018.

up and they felt as if he believed that he was not that different from them. He exuded so much energy, and so much warmth, that they felt he was a man they could trust. They would do anything for him. Die if necessary.

Fans clubs get preference for the first shows of Rajinikanth's films. The fans deposit money at the clubs, and tickets are purchased for all the shows of the first three days. Earlier, tickets used to be distributed somewhere in central Chennai, then at R. K. Lodge. Rajinikanth later took a place on lease next to the Hotel Palmgrove premises. Tickets were distributed from there for a while. But when Rajinikanth constructed a wedding venue, Raghavendra Kalyana Mandapam in 1989, the fan clubs found a permanent spot for ticket distribution.

The fan clubs have been accused of having hiked ticket prices. Surya denies that as absolutely false. 'Not a single rupee more than the ticket price was charged,' he declares.[2] The fans ensure a full house on the first three days. Even a flop film breaks even. It was during Rajinikanth's most frenetic period—between 1977 and 1979—that the fan clubs sprang up all over the state. Rajini had no idea about them because he was working nearly twenty-two hours a day and slept for less than two hours.[3]

Surya says they didn't think they needed their hero's permission. 'Does anyone need the deity's permission to offer flowers to it?' That was the logic they applied in forming these clubs that were proof of their affection and admiration. They would pool together money for banners, posters, and flags. They also started rituals where they decorated the cut-outs with flowers, bathed it with milk, and prayed for the film's success.

Rajadurai[4], 'pettai rowdy' (rowdy of the hamlet) as he is known, doesn't feel any shame in admitting that he once stole

---

[2] Ibid.

[3] S. P. Muthuraman, actor Sivakumar, and, Y. G. Mahendran in various interviews with author.

[4] Name changed.

his wife's jewellery to fund the Rajini release ritual. 'Don't tell my wife,' he winks at his friends. He tells us about a Tamil saint who stole things to offer his deity Shiva. 'This is for a cause,' he asserts. 'To show my love for Thalaivar. My wife's money is mine, after all,' he reasons.[5]

This spontaneous fan movement was something that even MGR had not enjoyed. The detail that could have gone against Rajini—his outsider status—combined with the fact that he had no specific caste-identity worked in his favour. That was the advantage that MGR and Jayalalithaa had too. As Rajini's star was on the rise, MGR passed away in 1987. MGR's fan club organization had been deliberate and planned. He had been active in politics before he started acting in films. And the fan clubs were created with the specific intention of promoting his name and image and later to mobilize election campaigning and fundraising. MGR's fan clubs had functioned as part of the DMK and, as anthropologist Sarah Dickey writes in her revealing study, 'the fan club work added substance to his image'[6]. MGR himself said the fan clubs and the party were not distinct.[7] The clubs had no dearth of finance. The cadres went about collecting 'donations' which was protection money in reality.[8] When Musiriputhan, an MGR mandram (club) chief, was asked if fan club funds had been subjected to an audit, he responded, 'Who keeps track of what goes into a temple hundi?'[9]

The importance of MGR's association and identification with the DMK can hardly be underestimated. The reason for his tremendous success cannot be attributed primarily to his convincing on-screen portrayals of the invincible good guy. Several

---

[5]Interview with the author, Chennai, 28 Mar 2018.
[6]Sarah Dickey, 'The Politics of Adulation: Cinema and the Production of Politicians in South India', *Journal of Asian Studies*, Vol. 52, No. 2, 1993.
[7]Vaasanthi, *Cut-outs, Caste and Cine Stars*, New Delhi: Penguin India, 2006.
[8]Dickey, 'The Politics of Adulation'.
[9]Ibid.

film stars have tried their luck in politics—Sivaji Ganesan, for instance, who was arguably a better actor and as popular—but none were even remotely as successful as MGR was. The mystique of MGR rested on the fact that his film and political careers were closely intertwined 'in a remarkably symbiotic manner'[10] that created for him an unbeatable image as folk hero. Interestingly, the projection of MGR as a superman became a political necessity for the survival of many in the party. A lot was to be gained by sustaining the aura.

With MGR's passing, a lot of his fans moved to Rajini's fan clubs. By 1996, there were over 50,000 Rajini fan clubs spread all over Tamil Nadu,[11] much more than MGR ever had. Today, there are Rajini fan clubs in China, Japan, and Malaysia. Even the fan club members themselves have lost count of the number of clubs.

Though Rajinikanth is not identified with a particular caste, his fan clubs are built along caste lines.[12] Professor S. V. Srinivas points out: 'It's interesting to note that though Rajini's appeal cuts across all sections of the society, the clubs tend to veer round their own peer groups, caste, and neighbourhood. The fans are investing something of their expectations in the star. Especially in a star like Rajinikanth. It is possible that the fans are bringing something to the star like they did to MGR. There is some manipulative exercise by the star and the lower class buying into his logic and believing in the man who is not working in their interest.'[13] Srinivas believes that the fans don't necessarily expect to gain political power through Rajini. But they want their contributions to be recognized. When organizational restructuring took place in the

---

[10]M. S. S. Pandian, *The Image Trap: M G Ramachandran in Film and Politics*, New Delhi: SAGE Publications, 1992.

[11]Sowmya Rajendran, '50,000 Fan clubs, Millions of Followers: The Universe of Rajni Fan', *The Quint*, 31 Dec 2017.

[12]As noted by producer Rinku Kalsi, in the documentary *For the Love of a Man* on Rajini's fan clubs.

[13]Interview with the author, Bangalore, 18 Jun 2018.

clubs once Rajini announced his decision to enter politics, many fans left because their work had not been recognized. But they don't join any other fan clubs; they remain Rajini fans.

Rajinikanth's screen persona is far larger than anyone can imagine. In the words of Sadanand Menon, his audience base that 'turns him into a humungous cultural totem-pole' is nearly incomprehensible. But as Menon also notes that 'in the past few years, film after film starring Rajinikanth has flopped, despite the huge euphoria and media build-up preceding it. It was almost as if the fans did not need to see the films anymore.'[14] As far as the fans are concerned, though, their god cannot die. He needs to be resurrected. They would reinstate him, transfer power from his screen persona to the real man. When Shivaji Rao stepped into the tinsel town of Madras, he was unaware of the politics and the social history of the state. He might have had some understanding of the Dravidian movement, but was not interested in politics. His sole aim was to make a living using the talent that he believed he possessed. But despite all this, he became a symbol of political power in the eyes of his fans. They have been trying to persuade him to enter politics. They have fought for their leader on the streets with Kamal Haasan's fans. When the fights descended into ugly brawls, Thalaivar got to know about it, lost his cool and said: no more fan clubs. At least, no new ones. Rajinikanth avoided confrontations and certainly didn't want to butt heads with Kamal, who was, and remains, a good friend. Surya says that they stopped forming new clubs in the early 90s because it became unwieldy. According to him, it was also rumoured that Jayalalithaa, who was the chief minister at that time, became suspicious of Rajinikanth's political ambitions and that the Intelligence Bureau had carried out secret investigations regarding the fan clubs' funds and resources.

But ever since Thalaivar announced that he would be making

---

[14]Interview with the author, Chennai, 16 Mar 2018.

his foray into politics, in 2017, the fan clubs turned themselves into the Rajini Makkal Mandram (Rajini People's Club) so as to include those who were not part of the fan clubs, but would like to join once Rajinikanth started his own party. Thalaivar himself had given the fan clubs the go-ahead to register all the unregistered clubs. Surya says it was mind-boggling how many hundreds of people were coming forward to join the mandrams. He processed at least 2,000 applications every day. He was surprised by the number of women, who had never been a big part of Rajini's fan base, coming forward to join the mandrams. According to Surya, this was because 'Everyone is having a hard time now. There are problems in day-to-day affairs—at the ration shop, school admissions, in getting a job, rising prices and so on. They feel Thalaivar, when he comes [to power], will set things right.'

And how will he do that?

'He will. Just wait and see. Hundred percent!'[15]

Hectic activity began in every district to form new mandrams. The office bearers were meticulously chosen and specific duties were allotted to them. Their duty was to work towards building the structure and getting it ready to face election. Rajinikanth told them that if they had their own political ambitions, and came expecting to get posts of power, they would be shown the door. The district heads reiterated that they were not looking for political power or posts. They were responsible citizens. They would abide by the principles set forth by their leader: 'unmai, nermai, kadamai'—truth, honesty, duty. Their only desire was to ensure that their leader became the next chief minister of Tamil Nadu. They knew that he would take care of them. He was their Krishna who will lift the Govardhan hill and provide protection from the torrential miseries they had been suffering.

In 2017 December, Rajinikanth had announced his intention to form a political party and contest the assembly elections in

---

[15]Interview with the author, Chennai, 28 Mar 2018.

2021. He asked the fans not to join any political debate in the meanwhile. He asked them to do the work, the rest would follow. Three years later when the COVID-19 pandemic hit most unexpectedly, it became highly doubtful if he would meet his promise at all. All film shoots were stopped, the lockdown stretched on for months, and he informed his directors that with his delicate health would not begin shooting till the vaccine was available. The Rajini Makkal Mandram went quiet as did the actor.

In keeping with Tamil Nadu's penchant for political leaders who were once actors, Kamal Haasan launched his Makkal Needi Maiam in February 2018. The careers of these superstars—friends and competitors—have run on parallel tracks. Kamal had started working in films as a child artiste, so although he is four years younger than Rajini, he has seniority in the industry. They were both lucky to have had Balachander as their godfather and mentor. They acted together in many films at the beginning of Rajini's career. They were appreciative of each other's talents and generous in their praise for the other. Rajinikanth was very aware that he was not the artist that Kamal was. He realized early on that he could not compete as an actor, so he 'changed his route'.[16] They acted together in eighteen films in the early years of Rajini's career. Later, when they both became considerably famous, they mutually agreed that they would no longer appear together in films. They needed their own space to grow. Besides, casting both giants in a film would place a very heavy burden on the producers and the stakes would be unrealistically high.

The actors have remained friends, respecting each other in public and private. When Rajinikanth toyed with the idea of starting his own party, there were speculations about whether they would join together. Political analysts began debating who between them had the winning chance if they didn't. As film stars, they have never criticized each other. But politics was a different game.

---

[16]Muthuraman, interview with the author, 27 Mar 2018.

Seven

Once Rajinikanth came back to work after his medical treatment, his schedule slowed down considerably following his doctor's advice. He was also more relaxed as his financial situation had become more stable. Before this he had been frenzied with the need to earn money to buy the house for which he had made a down payment. His father's words about owning a house giving him a sense of security had always been at the back of his mind. Despite the health setback, he had managed to buy that house. The day that Rajini became a home owner is etched in his memory. He shared this moment during the opening of the Spring Hotel. He was so happy that he had purchased a property with his own money that he sat on the compound wall and smoked a 555 and had Vat 69 instead of his usual Wills cigarette and McDowell's whiskey.[1] Balachander was the first person he informed. He showed the director around his property and fell at his feet and sought his blessings.[2]

His mentor had always advised him, 'Don't run after happiness. It is not something you can chase. Happiness comes with tranquillity. Tranquillity comes when you have someone to love you, care for you, share your moments of joy and sorrow. Friends will not be there with you forever. They have their lives, their worries. You need someone as your partner in life.' Balachander's sermon became a constant refrain after Rajini returned from the hospital. 'Look for a good, intelligent wife, madaya!'[3] His

---

[1] Remarks made at the opening of Spring Hotel, 'The Spring Hotel Launch', 10 Apr 2010, available here: https://www.youtube.com/watch?v=-w5u25yrzZw
[2] Ramachandran, *Rajinikanth*, p. 101.
[3] Kavithalaya Krishnan, interview with the author, 23 Mar 2018.

mentor took the liberty to scold him, call him 'madaya'—idiot and admonish him, like he was his father.

Rajinikanth would smile in response. Who would marry an idiot? Back in Bangalore, he had had many girlfriends, a couple of them quite serious, according to Bhaskar Rao. But, in retrospect, that had been fun and nothing more. He was around many women—his co-stars—he laughed, joked, and teased them, but he could not think of any of them as a life partner. And he knew that none of them would consider him as their partner either. They might even discuss his family background, call him uncouth, even immoral. He lived life recklessly—and his art and life were inseparable from cigarettes and alcohol—traits that disqualified him from being good husband material.

But the professional success continued and he went on to buy his second (and current) home in the posh Poes Garden area in 1980. Sripriya remembers how one day after a shooting schedule, Rajinikanth asked her to hop into his car and drove her to his new house. His pride in this achievement was evident. His neighbours were the who's who of Chennai—the city's top celebrities, lawyers, and industrialists (Jayalalithaa was his neighbour). Rajinikanth made some alterations to the house and named it Brindavan. His brother Satyanarayana came with his family for the house-warming ceremony after which Rajinikanth moved into the house.

Balachander shot one scene of *Agni Sakshi* (1982) in Rajinikanth's house. Rajinikanth had a cameo in the movie, appearing as himself. After the day's shoot was over, Rajinikanth took Sivakumar, who was the lead in the film, to show him around the house. Impressed by the house, Sivakumar remarked that he was happy to see Rajinikanth's remarkable growth in such a short period. 'You've made your parents proud.'

Rajini smiled sadly and said, 'All this money and fame seem to mock me today. I so much wanted to show my father the house. I wanted him to see my films. I troubled him a lot when

I was young. But he loved me dearly and was supportive. I went to Bangalore and wanted to bring him with me to show him the house, and to let him see a glimpse of my popularity. But by then he had lost his sight. I wanted him to come here and live with me, but he feels comfortable only in the surroundings he is familiar with.'[4] Sivakumar was deeply moved.

Between 1975 and 1979 he had fifty-three releases—some of the films had been produced simultaneously in two languages. Several were remakes of superhit Amitabh Bachchan films. The fans had not even been aware that their hero had been missing in action during the time that he was in treatment because his films continued to release during this period: the Telugu film *Amma Evarikaina Amma* was his last release of 1979 in November. After his recovery, *Billa* was released in January 1980. *Billa* was a faithful remake of the 1978 Hindi film *Don*, except transported to the environs of Madras.

Tamil Nadu had witnessed strong anti-Hindi agitation in the 60s. Hindi films, Hindi songs, even news bulletins were banned in Tamil Nadu when the DMK came to power in 1967. It was the only state that showed the news in Tamil at primetime rather than in Hindi. It was only in the late 70s that Hindi films began to get released in the larger cities in Tamil Nadu, but they had limited audiences since people did not understand the language. Theatres were not enthusiastic about playing movies that would not run for over two weeks. The people of Tamil Nadu were not familiar with Amitabh Bachchan and his runaway hits. 'What all of this meant for Rajinikanth's producers was a hit machine named Amitabh Bachchan who was starring in film after film having story lines that could be adapted in other language movies.'[5] Tamil producers felt that those stories could be remade in Tamil with Rajinikanth as the lead. *Billa* was a big hit. It was a turning point

[4]Sivakumar, phone interview with the author, Apr 2018.
[5]Ramachandran, *Rajinikanth*, p. 103.

in Rajinikanth's career, disproving detractors who had claimed 'he was finished'. Rajinikanth did not try to imitate Bachchan. Some film critics even said Rajinikanth's performance surpassed Bachchan's.

It was a time of remakes, especially in the Tamil and Telugu film industry. This trend continued into the 80s. The Tamil film industry regularly remade Hindi, Telugu, and Kannada movies. There was a ready story and script that the producers knew would work. Rajinikanth watched the original films, but interpreted the character his own way. Special Rajini dialogues were added that were about his looks and his trademark speed. For the Hindi remakes, the Salim–Javed script was translated pretty much as it was as the dialogues went with Rajinikanth's on-screen persona. When Rajinikanth spoke those lines with his own speed and intonation, they became his words.

One of the most successful movies he acted in at that time brought out a different side of the actor. Balachander directed *Thillu Mullu* (1981), a remake of Hrishikesh Mukherjee's very successful *Gol Maal* (1979). Rajinikanth was initially unsure about playing a comedic role. But, more pertinently, playing the character meant he would have to shave off his moustache. In a superstitious way, he attributed his success to his moustache. Besides, it was very much a symbol of masculinity in Tamil culture. Without it, he would feel effeminate, defanged. But Balachander explained that the character needed such a portrayal. Finally convinced, Rajinikanth shaved off his moustache and surpassed himself in the role. The audience roared with laughter and came to the theatre again and again. *Thillu Mullu* marked a turning point in his life in another way. It was during the production of this film that he met his future wife, Latha, on the sets. One day during the shoot, he was informed that there was a college student at his door, who had come to interview him for her college magazine. Quite dramatically, like in his films, a young woman, petite, fair, and smart-looking, entered his room with a nervous smile. Shivaji Rao was suddenly very conscious of how he looked—devoid of his favourite moustache.

Eight

Y. G. Mahendran, brother-in-law of Latha, recounts the meeting he set up for her with Rajini.

'I was not aware that she was such a huge fan of Rajinikanth. Since I had acted with him in many films, she pestered me to fix an appointment with the star for an interview that would be published in her college magazine. I found that he had some free time during the shooting of *Thillu Mullu* and organized the meeting after consulting him. The interview went on for more than an hour behind closed doors.'[1]

Y. G. Mahendran has no idea what they talked about. Was it love at first sight? Or did they have subsequent conversations and meetings? In any case, Rajinikanth told Mahendran a few days later that he wanted to marry Latha. Mahendran initially thought Rajinikanth was referring to the actor Latha. He laughed and told Rajini to talk to her directly. When Rajini explained that he was talking about Mahendran's sister-in-law, the latter was taken aback.

Mahendran knew Rajinikanth only professionally. He had seen that Rajini was very respectful to everyone and was humble despite the fame he had achieved in such a short time. Mahendran admired how hard he worked. He could tell that Rajini was aware of his strengths and weaknesses and chose his roles accordingly. This self-awareness combined with hard work was the reason for his success. But he also knew that Rajini had worked himself so hard that he had ended up in the hospital. The matter of Latha's marriage would, of course, have to be decided by her parents, so

---

[1] Interview with the author, 28 Mar 2018.

he arranged a meeting between them and Rajinikanth at their home in Nungambakkam.

Latha's family were orthodox Brahmins. They must have been surprised and perhaps disturbed by this development. They might even have tried to dissuade their daughter from doing anything rash but 'Latha was very firm in her decision to marry him', Mahendran admits. The family knew, of course, that Rajinikanth had had a nervous breakdown. Latha was convinced that she could provide him the care and affection that he needed. Most importantly, she was completely smitten by him. But the negative reports in the media would definitely have given the family cause for concern. For six months, Latha's parents put off their decision.

It was in March 2018, at MGR's birth centenary celebration, that Rajinikanth revealed for the first time that it had been the chief minister's intervention in the matter that had paved the way for his marriage to Latha. He also revealed that some years before he had asked for Latha's hand, during the course of the two-month treatment when he had suffered his breakdown, MGR would call the hospital at least twice a week to find out how he was progressing. MGR also asked Rajini to come and meet him once he had been discharged. It is likely that Rajini shared this information to dispel rumours that had been floating around at that time that he and the chief minister had not been on good terms. When Rajini went to meet him, MGR was happy to see him and advised him to take care of his health. He also advised him to marry a nice girl from a good family. 'Tell me as soon as your wedding is fixed, I shall attend your wedding.' Rajinikanth remembered this and informed him once he had decided to marry Latha. Six months later, MGR asked him what had happened about his marriage. Rajini confided that the girl's family had not given their blessing.

Two days after this conversation, Rajinikanth got word from Latha's parents that they had agreed to the marriage. It appears MGR had called Y. G. Parthasarathy (Mahendran's father and doyen of Tamil theatre) and told him not to hesitate in the matter, assuring him that Rajini was a good man, though a little short-tempered. MGR must have also found out from his sources that Rajini was medically fit. Now that he had the go-ahead, Rajinikanth felt empowered at the thought that he could win the heart of a beautiful, educated girl who spoke excellent English.

After informing his brother, father, and close friend, Raj Bahadur, Rajini had to tell Balachander that he had taken his advice and acted on it. He introduced Latha to his mentor. Balachander congratulated the star and told Latha that she would have to handle him with care and patience. 'He is short-tempered, but a good fellow,' he added, smiling.[2]

Rajinikanth decided to inform the press as well. 'Film News' Anandan was a veteran film public relations officer and film historian. He was an influential columnist for the magazine *Film News*, which gave him the moniker. Anandan began his career by handling the PR for MGR's films. He was later Jayalalithaa's personal public relations officer in the 70s. Rajinikanth requested Anandan to organize an informal press meet at his Poes Garden residence, inviting reporters from just twelve Tamil and English publications. It was organized for 25 February 1981. The journalists were given a press kit that contained a photograph of Rajinikanth and Latha with garlands around their necks. The journalists assumed that the wedding had already taken place. But Rajinikanth informed them it would take place the next day at Tirupati and that he did not want any nosy parkers from the press to land up there.

Someone asked, 'What if someone did go?'

'I will thrash him,' said the Superstar.[3]

The journalists were offended by the rude reply and left in a huff. It was Anandan who had the nerve to tell Rajinikanth

---

[2]Balachander, *Padayappa* Silver Jubilee celebration.
[3]Film News Anandan, interview with the author, 2011.

that he should not have retorted so sharply to members of the press who had come there at his invitation. An apology was issued and the papers avoided mentioning the offensive words used by the star.

The marriage was a very private affair in Tirupati attended by relatives and close friends Raj Bahadur, Ashok, Raghunandan, and Ravindranath. But there was some unpleasantness when two journalists who had attended the press meet showed up and started taking photographs. Although he had apologized for what he said, Rajinikanth had meant every word—he slapped the journalists and broke the camera. They had to run for their lives. Latha, who had already been warned about Rajinikanth, put on a brave face, convinced that what Balachander had said—that he was a good guy—was what was important. Rajinikanth's friends knew that his anger was always short-lived but were embarrassed by his behaviour.[4] Rajinikanth left with his bride to Bangalore to get his father's blessings. A grand reception was held at Taj Coromandel on 14 March.

Once again, life changed for Shivaji in ways that he could not have anticipated. As for Latha, who had been brought up in a very disciplined, conventional Tamil Brahmin household, the change must have seemed unimaginable. But surely a sense of calm and order enveloped the house with an intelligent, sensible woman like her taking control of running it. After all, she had stuck with her decision to marry him even though she knew about his mood swings and unpredictable temper. A fiercely independent person, Rajinikanth had taken the decision to marry rather impulsively and once the honeymoon period waned, he probably felt restricted. Not only did Latha bring her calming presence into his life, but she was also meticulous and disciplined, very different from her new husband who had lived life without needing to check in with anyone. Though he was once again extremely busy with

---

[4]Raghunandan, interview with the author, 23 Jun 2018.

work, there were times, according to his friends, when he felt like throwing up his hands and saying marriage was not for him. He was convinced he was a misfit living in too much refinement that he was not used to. At one time, all he wished for was two square meals a day. Once his hunger was appeased, he only needed a mat and a corner to sleep in. When he walked along the spacious corridors of his well-decorated house now, he sometimes felt like a stranger. It was almost like walking into an Ingmar Bergman film. Watching himself in it! He did not use the many things that surrounded him. There was a tennis court in the house, but he didn't know how to play the game. There was a swimming pool and didn't know how to swim. This life felt heavier and more burdensome than the heaviest paddy sacks he had carried.

This dissonance brought him to explore the spiritual world even more. There were days when he felt like leaving it all and disappearing into the woods or caves. Despite his interest in the lives of sages and sadhus, he could not give up cigarettes or alcohol. He craved non-vegetarian food, chicken in particular. But he comforted himself—he had read autobiographies of yogis who smoked and drank and ate meat. When he confessed to Kamal Haasan that he wanted to renounce everything, give up acting and go away somewhere, the latter seems to have 'cajoled him back to the material world'[5].

At one point he said frankly that he wanted to divorce his wife for no particular reason, says actor Kavithalaya Krishnan.[6] The local papers even printed the story the next day. Latha, now mother of a young daughter, was petrified and approached Balachander. The director immediately admonished Rajinikanth and told him to behave responsibly. Love should make one a better person, he told Rajini. Rajinikanth could not disobey his

[5]Ramachandran, *Rajinikanth*, p. 116.
[6]Interview with the author, 23 Mar 2018.

guru. Next day there was a public announcement that the news about the divorce was false. Soon Latha and Rajinikanth had their second daughter and things settled down on the domestic front. What possibly helped was that the two of them clearly demarcated their professional spaces. They did not interfere in each other's work lives. In 2002, Latha founded a value-based school called The Ashram. Rajinikanth does not get involved in any of the school activities, its finances or management.

When he needs a break, it is said, that he goes to his farmhouse at Kelambakkam, away from the hubbub of the city. There he can be meditative amidst the sylvan surroundings. He also regularly visits Bangalore where he has a modest flat on Race Course Road. The flat is very simply furnished, almost spartan—he sleeps on a mat on the floor and cooks for himself. There, with his friends Raj Bahadur, Ashok, Raghunandan, and Ravindranath, he is in his element. Sometimes they take a trip to a remote spot in a forest. Or they just visit their old haunts in Chamrajpet, Gandhi Nagar, and around Hanumanthanagar where he grew up. He would have to disguise himself, of course. In Bangalore, he travels in auto rickshaws or walks. But what fun he has! He laughs and chats with his friends like he never can in Chennai.[7]

There is something about the air of the city he was born in. He feels a thrill the moment his feet touch its soil. And he feels a sense of belonging when he can speak in the language he knows best. He once had a great desire to make well-known Kannada literary works into movies. *Chikka Virarajendra* by Masti Venkatesha Iyengar, for instance. He could imagine himself playing the nineteenth-century last ruler of Kodagu, who was driven out of his kingdom and met his death in an alien land.[8] Unfortunately, though, the Kannadigas did not care for him. It's sad because they don't know how deep his roots are in Karnataka.

---

[7]Raghunandan, interview with the author, 23 Jun 2018.
[8]Malavika Avinash, interview with the author, Bangalore, 21 Jun 2018.

His friend Ashok also believes that Shivaji is lonely, not just a loner. Ashok recalls something that happened in 1992. 'Shivaji had come to Bangalore for a shoot and came to meet me once the day's work was done. I had a film shoot at Kengeri. He waited for me in my room. When I returned, he was asleep. I went to him and touched his cheeks and called him gently. He opened his eyes, saw me, held my hands, and his eyes suddenly became moist. I thought something was wrong. My palms were still on his cheeks and I asked him what was wrong. He said no one had touched him like that, with such gentle affection.'[9]

Latha once told Raghunandan that her husband was most happy when he was with his friends from Bangalore. To his friends, he is still the simple Shivaji, whose only passion was acting and whose desire was to be certain of his next meal. They know he will never forget the path he travelled or the friends who helped him on the way. And he is aware that they are friends who make no demands on him. Shivaji thinks the most famous stories about friendships pale before the relationship he has with his close group. He and they know that the fame and wealth he has earned by some miracle are a mirage, ephemeral. They often go to Mantralayam, where the temple of Saint Raghavendra is, not only to seek his blessings, but also to cleanse their minds. 'During the shooting of an action film, between shots when he had to wait, I have seen him reading Osho's book,' says Y. G. Mahendran. 'When we went for outdoor shoots, if he came to know about the temples around there, he would always persuade me to accompany him to visit them. At the temple, he would sit in meditation in a quiet spot. There was a streak of spiritualism in him even when he was wild—that always surprised me.'[10]

Rajini and Latha had decided that their children would not be

---

[9]Interview with the author, Bangalore, 10 Jun 2018.
[10]Y. G. Mahendran, interview with the author, 28 Mar 2018.

exposed to the film world. It was only much later in life that the two girls even seem to have watched Rajinikanth's movies. Ironically, both the daughters—Aishwarya and Soundarya—are now involved in the film world as a director and a graphic designer respectively. They are ambitious and have great expectations. Being the father of industry kids is not something that makes Rajini particularly happy. Because the chances of their success or failure will not be determined by the fact that they have anything to do with him as his daughters.

Director Muthuraman says Rajinikanth is very close to his family and enjoys playing with his grandchildren. The entire family sits in the first row during his film events, but a certain distance is maintained. Rajini's trips to America to the Lotus Temple run by Swami Satchidananda Ashram and his trips to the Himalayas are all strictly solo affairs in which no family member partakes. 'Spirituality is like a seed inside him,' Latha said in an interview. 'Maybe he was born with it.' She thinks that is the reason he manages to keep his head firmly on his shoulders amidst the phenomenal changes that have occurred in his life. She knows that his spirituality is his private world and she will not intrude.[11]

Private milestones like wedding anniversaries are celebrated but work always takes priority for him. Prabhu Raja Cholan, the young assistant of director S. Shankar, had an exciting experience of watching Rajinikanth during the photo shoot for the film *Sivaji,* (2007). Prabhu, a fan of the superstar from age six or even earlier, was thrilled to see that his hero was so simple. This was a man who earned 100 crore or more as the rumours went, but had no airs, he would stand up whenever he was introduced to someone, even a junior hand like him in the unit. That day the photo shoot went on endlessly and Rajinikanth complied with all the demands of the photographers without break. When it

[11]'Latha Rajinikanth about Rajinikanth's Spirituality', Thanthi TV, 11 Nov 2018, available here: https://www.youtube.com/watch?v=vFqb7HBj_rc

ended, Rajinikanth got up and said, 'Can I leave now? Today is our wedding day. My wife will be waiting at home.'[12]

But he would make sure to be there when he was needed. When Latha was admitted to Vijaya Hospital for some minor surgery, the doctor who went on her morning rounds was shocked to see Rajinikanth sitting on a chair near the bed, all crumpled and covered by a bedsheet. He must have sat there all night.

Although Rajini's interest in the spiritual was strong and he often wondered about leaving everything to become a hermit, he became a huge commercial success in the totally materialistic world of cinema. In his daily life, he was transformed into a money-making robot, a winning horse in an unpredictable race.

A film could become a commercial success if it was repeatedly seen in A, B, and C centres. These are categories that determine what the viewers enjoy. Category A look for story/content; B enjoy action, and C want to see their favourite hero. It was reported that Rajini's fans saw every film of his more than fifteen times. Muthuraman admits that he was the one that turned him into a commercial hero. 'Certain punch lines were deliberately added to the script and songs were composed to suit his persona.' Muthuraman also realized that Rajini was well suited to action films. Sentimental stories appealed to the women in the audience but action films drew all ages, even kids, if Rajinikanth was in the film. With this view, AVM Productions produced a film aimed at children—*Raja Chinna Roja* that released in 1989. It was the first Indian film that combined live action with animation.

Muthuraman's 1980 film *Murattu Kaalai*, with Rajinikanth in the lead, set the trend for his commercial movies. According to Muthuraman, it was a turning point in Rajinikanth's career. In *Murattu Kaalai*, Rajini plays Kaalaiyan, a farmer. Having played only urban roles until this time, Rajini was a bit apprehensive and unsure if he could portray the character convincingly. But

---

[12]Prabhu Raja Cholan, phone interview with the author, Aug 2018.

Muthuraman was an experienced director who knew the pulse of the rural audience. He knew that Rajinikanth would steal the show. And that is what happened. The story included the sport jallikattu (bull fighting). Film critic Kumuthan Maderya analysed, 'Kaalaiyan's fearless participation in *jallikattu* emphasizes his ferocious masculinity and signals the end of the castrated protagonist in the Neo-Nativity films. *Murattukkalai* has since acquired an iconic status and is considered to be a classic in the genre of action films in Tamil cinema.'[13]

After *Murattu Kaalai,* a new formula for heroism entered Tamil action film aesthetics. In contrast to MGR films that centre on the struggle of the hero to protect the vulnerable, Kaalaiyan's struggle was a personal vendetta. It suited Rajini's rogue persona that was different from the law-abiding MGR hero. Rajini represented the angry hero who would achieve justice for himself and establish a new social order, independent of the state.

Dialogues, punch lines, and lyrics that were written for Rajini gradually took on political connotations even though that was not the intention. The larger-than-life Rajini image was created. He became a force to reckon with. According to Maderya, 'The subversive charisma of the Rajini persona found an especially willing audience among marginalized men.... Rajini's being dark-skinned enabled male fans from the subaltern classes and lower castes in Tamil Nadu, most of whom are dark-skinned, to relate with ease to Rajini's characters.' He quotes anthropologist Frederick Bailey: 'the [masses] see the [the hero] not only as an ideal above them but simultaneously as one of them'.[14] He was turning into their political representative. The Thalaivar.

Muthuraman is proud of having started the trend. Rajinikanth's stock went higher with every film from that point on. Rajinikanth had dreamt of being a character artiste, but turned into a

---

[13]Kumuthan Maderya, 'Rage against the state: historicizing the angry man in Tamil cinema', *Jump Cut: A Review of Contemporary Media, Jump Cut,* No. 52, Summer 2010.
[14]Ibid.

commercial hero. He knew, of course, that these were the roles that made him popular and wealthy. He believed that it was the audience who decided if he had depicted a character successfully. The fact that the audience came back repeatedly to watch the films was clear proof that he had been successful. Often, he would go in disguise to watch his films and would stand outside to listen to the reactions of the viewers,[15] like a violinist who ends his performance and waits for the applause. Muthuraman was careful to give Rajinikanth different types of roles and found that he was able to carry them all convincingly because he was focused and hard working. But, despite that, the actor had been typecast. Rajini wanted to break away from the typecasting and time and again he experimented with something he thought was substantial, noble, like *Baba* (2002), but failed. It was clear that he was in show business, and was not an actor taking part in a play staged at Ramakrishna Math.

His most commercially successful films followed a formula with very similar plots. The distributors wanted a lot of action scenes, fights, and songs because the majority of the audience was the young working class that wanted these elements. The story became less important. The middle-class audience that wanted a strong storyline had shifted to watching television.

But Rajinikanth also acted in films like *Johnny* (1980), *Moondru Mugam* (1982), and *Engeyo Ketta Kural* (1982), which were memorable for his superb acting skills. The last, directed by Muthuraman received several awards—Tamil Nadu Film Fans Association Award for Best Actor, and the Filmfare Award for Best Film in Tamil. The 1980s was also when Rajinikanth made his foray into Hindi films with T. Rama Rao's *Andhaa Kanoon* (1983). The movie also starred Hema Malini and Reena Roy and had a guest appearance by Amitabh Bachchan. Though Rajinikanth was the hero, Bachchan was given prominence in the film's publicity.

---

[15]Raghunandan, interview with the author, 23 Jun 2018.

But the North Indian audience did notice Rajinikanth's cigarette tricks, and his unique acting style, and was impressed. He starred in *ChaalBaaz* (1989) with Sridevi where she played a double role. Many in the Bombay film circles appreciated not just his speed and energy but also his comic timing. In 1991 he starred with Amitabh Bachchan in *Hum*.

The Superstar of Tamil films was not all that well known on the sets of Bombay. He was not like the other male actors. Rajinikanth was very punctual, quiet, and kept to himself. He didn't join the parties that took place after pack up. 'He would sit alone in his room and open a fresh bottle of Johnnie Walker Blue Label, one of the most expensive blended Scotch whiskies in the world. He would have a couple of drinks and he would give the bottle away to a unit hand and open another bottle the next evening. That was the only gesture that pointed to his wealth.'[16]

Apart from *Hum*, 1991 saw three more of his Hindi films being released—*Farishtay*, *Khoon Ka Karz*, and *Phool Bane Angaray*. Rajinikanth, however, cannot claim that he was a big hit in Bollywood. The North Indian audience was used to a different look and accent. They might have wondered how Rajinikanth became such an icon in Tamil films. He could in no way compete with the stars of Bollywood.

It was Tamil Nadu that embraced him totally and with love. Shivaji Rao, who was born in Karnataka and spoke Marathi at home, was always overwhelmed at the thought of it. There were more milestones to reach. Acting in a film directed by the renowned director Mani Ratnam, for instance.

---

[16]Deepa Sahi, quoted in Ramachandran, *Rajinikanth*, p. 132.

Nine

Award-winning cinematographer Santosh Sivan was fascinated by what the camera revealed. The man in the frame had an amazing presence. Even when he was sharing the frame with other actors, it was Rajinikanth who drew the eye. His dark skin took on a beautiful sheen in the golden light of the setting sun. Sivan was amazed by the radiance that exuded from his eyes. Rajinikanth was playing the part of a character named Surya in the film and needed to be associated with the sun visually and metaphorically.

The director of the film was the talented Mani Ratnam. He had an MBA degree and had sort of drifted into filmmaking. It was not a world he was unfamiliar with. His father, S. G. Ratnam, had been a film distributor. Mani's talent was apparent right from his debut film in Kannada, *Pallavi Anu Pallavi* (1983), for which he won the Karnataka State Film Award for Best Screenplay. After that, there was no looking back. His films in Tamil from *Mouna Ragam* (1986) to *Nayakan* (1987) to *Agni Natchathiram* (1988) to *Anjali* (1990) won him national and state awards. *Nayakan*, starring Kamal Haasan, was India's entry to the Oscars in the foreign language category and made it to *Time* magazine's all-time 100 best films list. Mani Ratnam was considered the face of a new generation—English-educated and exposed to the best of world cinema.

When asked about his experience directing Rajinikanth in the lead role in his well-crafted film *Thalapathi* (1991), his eyes start to sparkle, as if the very memory of it rekindled a sense of joy. 'He is the easiest actor I have worked with,' he says, smiling. 'The thing is [when] you cast a big star...there are expectations from his followers. You can't ignore it. It's the elephant in the room. Unless the character is large enough to take in the followers, you don't go to him.'[1]

Ratnam had seen Rajinikanth in *Mullum Malarum* in 1978 and thought he had done a brilliant job. He had met Rajini three or four years before *Thalapathi*. He struck the director as 'a genuine man, a simple, straightforward man who was street-smart...who knew what he wanted. ...his honesty and plain talking was very charming. And he is not trying to please you.'[2] Ratnam believed that if that genuineness could be brought out on-screen, then the battle was won.

Ratnam wanted to ensure that the character that Rajini played would be large enough that his fans would be attracted. So, when he had a story where Rajinikanth could play a modern-day Karna, a character with a dramatic backstory, someone who overcomes large obstacles, Ratnam felt confident that the role was big enough for the superstar's on-screen persona.

'He is the most problem-free actor...' says Ratnam. '...if you want him at a particular time, he will be there. You want him at 4 o'clock in the morning, 5 o'clock, far away from Mysore, where the film was shot, he would be there! It was a pleasure working with him. And he will have thoughts and ideas. And if that doesn't suit you, he has no issues about it, he was willing to be directed. He was willing to let you lead the way.'[3]

Most Rajini films leaned heavily on the persona that the audience had come to love, but this film was different. '*Thalapathi* is also possibly one of the last films that gave Rajini the leeway to act rather than merely perform, and for people who've only seen the later bombastic superstar, this film can be quite the revelation,'

[1]Interview with the author, 17 Mar 2018.
[2]Ibid.
[3]Ibid.

says film critic Rakesh Mehar.[4] This acting talent is on display in the scene where Surya learns that his biological mother had him when she was an unmarried teenager and abandoned him on a goods train. Ratnam agrees that the scene was powerful and a lot of thought went into composing and preparing the shot. Rajinikanth knew that this was the heart of the story. On the day of the shoot, Ratnam and his crew had set up the crucial scene and were ready for the shot. Ratnam explained the shot to Rajinikanth. 'He had to understand that for the first time he comes to know about the truth of his birth. There is disbelief and denial and then an acceptance that comes through... he listened intently and then he said, "I need time. We will do this tomorrow. I need to prepare."'[5] Rajinikanth wanted more time to prepare for the pivotal scene. His performance, Mani Ratnam says, illustrates '...his sharp mind that absorbs and then converts it into performances'.[6] *Thalapathi* was not a typical Rajinikanth film. So, when it worked, it was a great relief. The film was both critically acclaimed and commercially successful. That was the only film, however, that Ratnam did with Rajinikanth. Clearly, he didn't find another role that was big enough for the star.

Despite the success of this film, Rajinikanth went back to his formula films. He would have liked to take on meatier acting roles, but the distributors and fans expected a certain kind of story from him. In his movies, Rajinikanth could never age, could never be defeated—he became the invincible god on the screen. His strength came from the fans just as a stone gets its divinity from the collective devotion of the faithful. The words he uttered on the screen became mantras for the fans. Even before the release of the film, they were eager to hear the punch lines.

Many of these punch lines were about challenging the powers

---

[4]Rakesh Mehar, '"Thalapathi" turns 25: How Mani Ratnam gave us our favourite Karna in Rajinikanth', *News Minute*, 8 Nov 2016.
[5]Interview with the author, 17 Mar 2018.
[6]Ibid.

that be. The political world started watching with more than casual interest to read between the lines. Rajini must have had his doubts. Who was he, an outsider, to comment on the politics of the state or to criticize the administration? But he felt obliged to do so. Perhaps he started believing in his larger-than-life image. He was aware that he was deeply connected to the fans who promoted his image and saw him as their leader. He felt indebted to them. He needed them as much as they needed him.

It was during this time that there were developments in the political arena that had a direct impact on the fan clubs. Jayalalithaa was in power, and there was no dearth of news and controversies. From the day Jayalalithaa assumed office, the changes were perceptible. She took the oath of office as chief minister in the name of God in the Centenary Celebrations Hall of Madras University on 24 July 1991. So far, atheist Dravidian leaders had always taken the oath in the name of Nature and Conscience. As she was leaving after the oath-taking ceremony, K. A. Sengottaiyan, a new member of her cabinet, fell at her feet. Other junior ministers went further and prostrated themselves full-length on the floor. She did not try to stop them. To have these men at her feet perhaps gave her a sense of triumph and gratification. The chief minister started wearing a cape over her sari—there was speculation that she wore a bulletproof vest under it. When a reporter asked her about the cape, all she said was 'I like it'. Journalists felt that there was something regal, almost forbidding about her. She was not very approachable. Something about her made men uncomfortable. Rajinikanth, who had grown up in a conservative family, was no exception.

Initially Rajinikanth was delighted with Jayalalithaa's ascent to power but gradually friction arose between them and eventually blew out of proportion. When Jayalalithaa won the 1991 elections with a thumping majority, Rajinikanth was holidaying in Kathmandu with his wife, Latha. They were extremely happy to hear the news of her victory. Jayalalithaa was very close to

Y. G. Mahendran's family. Soon after their return to Chennai, Rajinikanth and Latha went to Jayalalithaa's house in Poes Garden to congratulate her. Rajinikanth was impressed by her intelligence and the courage of her convictions. He also had a lot of empathy for her, having observed the problems she had faced at the time of MGR's demise.

All was well between them for a while. But it started becoming clear very soon that Jayalalithaa had little tolerance for dissent or criticism. There were rumours of brutal attacks on journalists and others who dared to criticize her.[7] Rajinikanth appeared not to have noticed these reports and rumours. But what annoyed him was getting caught in traffic jams when vehicles were held up for more than half an hour whenever the chief minister's convoy went past. He was irritated by the number of vehicles in the convoy and the power and arrogance they conveyed.

It was at this time that Rajini's fan clubs were on the rise. This caught Jayalalithaa's attention and she started to become suspicious of his political ambitions. People warned her to watch him.

Nearly every morning, a large crowd of fans would gather at Rajini's gates with some complaint or the other. Rajinikanth had left the fan clubs to his trusted aide, Satyanarayana, who now told him a disturbing story. The police were investigating the details of the fan clubs, their numbers, activities, functions, and finances. They were also asking if Rajinikanth was entertaining the idea of entering politics. Some of the fan club members were even taken to police stations and questioned. Rajinikanth was shocked and angry. There were rumours and speculations doing the rounds in the media. Rajinikanth felt he had to clarify the facts in print. He offered to write a series of articles in the Tamil magazine *Thuglak*, edited and run by his friend Cho Ramaswamy.[8] He wanted to

---

[7] 'Of Lathicharge, assault and intimidation: Reporter's diary from Jayalalithaa's times', *News Minute*, 9 Dec 2016.

[8] They were published under the column 'Those Five Functions' between 21 Feb 1996 and 1 May 1996.

justify statements he had made in at various functions that had become controversial and earned the ire of the chief minister. In one of the articles he talked about how he was so worked up about the situation that he spontaneously came up with lines when shooting a scene in *Annaamalai* (1992). Addressing the politician character, he says, 'Look, I am just quietly doing my job. Don't provoke me. If you do, then I will not only do what I say but also what I've not said.'[9] When he said this spontaneously, the entire unit clapped. Rajinikanth wrote: 'When the movie was released the fans knew what it meant and cheered lustily.'[10]

Annaamalai is based on the Hindi film *Khudgarz* (1987), which in turn was inspired by Jeffrey Archer's 1979 novel, *Kane and Abel*. Balachander had asked Suresh Krissna, who had worked as his assistant, and was now working in Telugu and Hindi films, to direct. Krissna's debut film as director was the very successful *Sathyaa* (1988), starring Kamal Haasan. A Tamil born and brought up in Mumbai, he was familiar with Bollywood. He had assisted Balachander on many movies, but had not worked on any of Rajini's films. When Balachander approached him, Krissna had no idea what the project was about. When he met Balachander, he was given the outline of the story and informed that Rajinikanth would be the lead. He was apprehensive about how he would handle the Superstar. This project was very different from any that Krissna had worked on. It was made in a big rush—the script was being written as the film was being shot.[11] Krissna did not even have time to interact with the star and get to know him before they started filming. And, worse, Krissna had not seen any of Rajini's movies. Rajinikanth seems to have had his own

---

[9] In Tamil, the dialogue sounds like a challenge: 'Enna vambukku izhithaa, naan sonnatheiyum seyven, sollathathiuym seyven.'

[10] Translation by the author.

[11] 'Suresh Krissna director of Annamalai, Baasha, Aalavandhan is a huge fan of Amitabh', Bosskey TV, 8 Jul 2016, available here: https://www.youtube.com/watch?v=oBuPXcHjbKc

doubts about the director. He knew that Krissna had directed Kamal Haasan's *Sathyaa*, which was of a different genre.

Nevertheless, the two of them hit it off famously on the very first day of shoot. One of the first scenes was a comic one involving Rajini and a snake. Krissna was fascinated by Rajinikanth's comic timing and was in splits, even forgetting to say cut. Every salute, every action he performed, defined the 'Rajini style'. His movements had an energy that was incredible. Within three days, Krissna says, he became a great fan of Rajinikanth.[12]

As had become the norm, the story had been rewritten, and dialogue and punch lines added with a view to capitalize on Rajini's image. Krissna played up Rajini's popularity with the on-screen titles. The words 'Super' and 'Star' appeared as neon dots, as the film's opening credit sequence was inspired by the James Bond films. Krissna also copied the Bond style for the way Rajini's character, Annamalai, introduced himself. 'I'm Malai, Annamalai,' he would say with a smile. This was repeated by children and adults alike, along with other spontaneous lines Rajinikanth came up with. *Annaamalai* is a rags-to-riches story, a tale of hope for the poor. Annamalai was a saviour who fought for justice. He was real and convincing.

From that point on, Rajini's films were expected to have some political message in the form of an outright attack on the establishment through songs or dialogues. *Annaamalai* is considered to have started the trend although the film did not have any obvious political themes. It projected a citizen's rage against injustice and could be related to any anguish that the viewer had experienced. *Annaamalai* became a runaway success. His fans didn't get tired of watching it, or repeating the dialogue that featured in it.

---

[12]Ibid.

Ten

....

Rajinikanth was agitated. His pride was hurt. His fans were being put through a lot of trouble. And, worst of all, Jayalalithaa suspected him of having political ambition. Perhaps it was hard for her to believe that the fan clubs were not his doing, that they had been formed by the fans themselves with a view to supporting Thalaivar's films. He was not responsible for the myths that had grown around him. Some fans would cheer when they saw him, 'The future chief minister be blessed!' How could he convince the chief minister that these cheers embarrassed him? Nevertheless, he was upset that his fans were being hassled for their senseless prattle.

Rajini could not understand why Jayalalithaa did not ask him directly about the fan clubs. Whenever MGR heard a rumour about Rajini that bothered him, he would call him to ask about it. They were able to clear up the matter with just one call. Rajinikanth called the chief minister's residence several times but did not get to speak to her. He wrote her a letter explaining that the fan clubs were not secret political organizations. He got no response. He got angrier and more agitated.

Jayalalithaa was very guarded; she had learnt early in life that people were not to be trusted. Her arrogance was a mask she wore to find her way through the harsh, macho world of politics. Rajini's anger against Jayalalithaa stemmed in no small part from that sexist place. It's likely that a patriarchal mindset fuelled his irritation. His friends and colleagues called him humble, but when it came to confrontation with a woman, it was hard not to see that his ego was hurt—as a superstar and as a man.

Professionally it was a heady time—*Annaamalai*, which released on 25 June 1992, was running to full houses, and perhaps this made him feel he had the authority to speak his mind. He got a chance a month later to publicly vent at a felicitation function arranged by the South Indian Films Chamber of Commerce to honour Jayalalithaa on 26 July 1992. At the venue, he was disgusted that the ministers were standing with folded hands and bent heads well before she arrived. When he spoke, he took the chance to say what Jayalalithaa had refused to listen to before: he first reiterated that he was not interested in politics. But he then went on to say that if he was destined to enter the field, no one could stop him and that he was not afraid of anyone. He then looked at Jayalalithaa and said, 'You are in a seat of power not because of your effort but due to circumstances. I want to put an end to the rumours that there is enmity between the chief minister and me. I have no enemies. I am my own enemy.'[1]

It appeared that he hadn't thought about how Jayalalithaa would react to this. Or perhaps he did not care. (He wrote later—in the column in *Thuglak*—that he would always say what was on his mind without worrying too much about its impact on the listeners.) The audience was dumbstruck. Jayalalithaa did not react, and ignored him as she left. The fans felt that the Thalaivar had given a fitting reply to the arrogant woman. Soon after this, the police stopped their harassment of the fan clubs.

Rajinikanth turned his attention back to his acting. He knew that no film that followed the stupendous success of *Annaamalai* could be successful, no matter how good the script and strong the performances. But he was in no hurry. The next few releases that followed *Annaamalai* were indeed damp squibs. He produced *Valli* (1993) under his own Rajini Arts banner, directed by his friend K. Natraj, who had studied with him at the Film Institute. Rajini wrote the script, story, and dialogue. Perhaps he felt that after all these years, he knew how everything worked. Or perhaps it was

---

[1]'Those Five Functions', *Thuglak*.

to save money. In reality, this film was a philanthropic venture. He was pained to see that many of his friends who had done the course with him had not had the kind of success that he had. They were still struggling to earn a comfortable living. He wanted to give them all roles in the film.[2] Each of them was given UTI Infrastructure bonds worth two lakh rupees.[3]

The film had all the masala elements that the fans were used to. The story was a parody of the political situation in Tamil Nadu. Veeraiyan, Rajinikanth's character, is an angry, bitter man who has been released from jail, having been convicted for killing his wife's rapist. Once back in his village, he finds that nothing works as it should. Corruption is rampant and the administration undertakes populist measures to keep the people quiet. Veeraiyan now turns activist. He convinces the villagers to demand jobs and refuse the free saris and dhotis that the politicians dole out. He advocates revolution saying that educated youth should replace politicians.

Indian cinema in the 80s and 90s had many such stories. Rajinikanth might have thought they would resonate with the audience and hence make the film successful. But his script lacked the punch that blockbuster script writers could bring. *Valli* was not successful. His own fans didn't support the film the way they usually did. But his friends had jobs for a while and were grateful for the chance they were given.

Y. G. Mahendran says that Rajinikanth has never forgotten those friends from his past life in Bangalore and always tries to help those who stood by him during the early difficult days in Madras.[4] Rajini felt deeply indebted to his friend Raghunandan, who managed to arrange food for all of them during the Film Institute days. Rajinikanth helped his friend buy a house and funded his sons' education. 'He is basically full of compassion,' says Raghunandan, sitting in his modest flat at Yeshwantpur, Bangalore.

---

[2]Malini Mannath, 'Rajini arrives, with a bang', *Indian Express*, 27 Aug 1993.
[3]Ragunandan, interview with the author, 23 Jun 2018.
[4]Interview with the author, 28 Mar 2018.

'When he saw poor people on the footpaths and the roadside, he said he felt guilty for possessing so much material wealth when those people lived with nothing. He once gave me ₹10,000 and asked me to distribute it to the needy in a day. I went round distributing [the money] to roadside vendors and the disabled who were baffled by it.

'When I was without job for a long time, he gave me a beautiful letter of recommendation and asked me to submit [it to] an institute. He came with me in an auto to be sure that I gave it to the head of the institute.'[5]

Those who manage the activities at his Raghavendra Mandapam in Kodambakkam, Chennai, are his friends who have not been successful in their endeavours. At the venue, there is a room with a thatched roof on the terrace of the building. Rajinikanth loves to sit on the floor and eat with his friends like he did back in the day. 'Rajini's sense of loyalty and feeling of indebtedness to his friends is amazing. Success has not gone to his head,' says Mahendran.

Rajini's brother, Satyanarayana, continues to live in his house in Hanumanthanagar that Rajinikanth has renovated and modernized. His other brother, Nageshwara, became seriously ill due to alcoholism and died, though Rajinikanth tried hard to get him the best treatment available. His sister, whose married life was not happy, was widowed with three children and died a few years ago. The other members of the family live their own simple lives. They shun the media and refuse to speak about their celebrity relative, making it clear that the world of the Superstar is not theirs.

According to Rajinikanth's friends, he does not want any publicity about the charitable works he undertakes. He donated money to renovate the school where he studied, but refused to attend any event to celebrate the completion of the work.

---

[5]Interview with the author, 23 Jun 2018.

Kavithalayaa Krishnan recalled that when a crew member died in an accident during the shooting of a film, Rajinikanth met the family and gave them money. The press had no knowledge of this, whereas photos of some other stars appeared in the papers as having been the ones who had given them money.[6]

His loyalty and feeling of indebtedness to director Balachander is legendary. Krishnan, who worked in Balachander's production company, remembers how concerned Rajini once became when he heard that the director was struggling with depression. He went to meet Krishnan on the set and asked for some time to talk. The unit was surprised to see the Superstar walk in. Rajini knew that Krishnan met Balachander every day and wanted first-hand information from him. Krishnan confirmed that Balachander was very upset because of the financial loss that his film *Duet* (1994) had incurred. He went to meet his mentor the very next day and spoke to him for a long time. Krishnan doesn't know what transpired between them. In any case, Balachander recovered from his depression soon after.

A little later, Rajinikanth acted in *Muthu* (1995) for Balachander's production house. The film was very successful. According to Krishnan, he might have worked for free to help his mentor out. But there was not a word about it in the press.[7] There was an inexplicable bond between the two. It could be because of the extraordinary humility of the star towards his mentor and the consequent total trust and affection Balachander developed for his protégé. Rajini would never sit down in front of Balachander. When he heard that the director's car was approaching the set or the studio, Rajini would get up from his chair and keep standing till the car arrived and Balachander emerged from the vehicle. There was a joke that went around that when the director called, Rajini would answer the phone standing up.

---

[6]Interview with the author, 23 Mar 2018.
[7]Ibid.

The success of *Annaamalai* had convinced Rajinikanth that teaming up with Suresh Krissna was lucky for both of them. After a great deal of deliberation, they agreed on a theme that Krissna felt could be crafted into a powerful script and that could be a good follow-up to the success of *Annaamalai*. But when the script was nearly ready, Rajini decided that they would make a comedy instead. Although he had had a couple of other releases in the meantime, he wanted to lower the expectations of the fans about the Krissna–Rajini team so that when the next powerful film was released, it would be compared with this comedy and not with *Annaamalai*. Krissna was not convinced about this.

And that is how *Veera* got made in 1994. Krissna did not like the story at all—it condones bigamy—but it turned out to be a hilarious entertainer. According to Krissna, its success was entirely due to Rajini's brilliant comic sense and timing. The film was remade in Hindi as *Saajan Chale Sasural* (1996) starring Govinda. On the day *Veera* was released (14 April 1994) Rajinikanth announced that he would be producing *Baashha*, based on the 1991 Amitabh Bachchan-starrer *Hum*. The Tamil script, of course, was written to suit not just the expectations of the fans, but also the star's image. 'Rajini's audience was universal—from kids to old people, so you need a careful mix of everything. It's very difficult to write a mass script for the Superstar. He would say his film must reach A to Z audience. You must have everything but in a new package,' says Krissna.[8]

Krissna deliberately made the first half of the film totally un-Rajinikanth-like. When he first narrated the screenplay to the team, they were aghast—there were no action or comic scenes till the interval. Even worse, the superstar gets tied up and beaten. The producer, R. M. Veerappan, was horrified by the idea. But Rajini knew it would work. Rajini as auto driver Manickam is a Good Samaritan who quietly helps those in trouble. But it's

---

[8]'Suresh Krissna director of Annamalai, Baasha, Aalavandhan is a huge fan of Amitabh'.

clear that there's more to him than meets the eye. Over the course of the first half of the film, the suspense about his back story keeps building.

The second half of the film was shot underground in the Golconda Fort in Hyderabad. On the day that Manickam's old identity—that of a don called Baashha—was to be revealed, Rajinikanth looked like a different man.

Despite the strategy that he had employed with releasing *Veera* after *Annaamalai*, Rajini worried that expectations for *Baashha* were very high. The shoot was to take place in the afternoon. Rajini was in his hotel room. Krissna and a couple of others joined him. His transformation had already begun. He switched off the lights and stood before the huge mirror in the room and started rehearsing. He adjusted the muffler round his neck; brushed his fingers through his hair. He walked up and down several times, brows knitted together. There was complete silence in the room. Manickam was turning into Baashha. But Rajini said something was missing. Sundaramurthy, the make-up artist, produced a pair of rimless glasses. Rajini tried it on and said, 'Awesome, I am ready.' When they reached the shooting spot, Krissna impressed on the star that the dialogue that followed had to be forceful and fierce because it was the climax of the scene. The result was stunning.

Baashha ran for more than hundred days. When Krissna watched the first day first show of the film at Albert Theatre, he got goosebumps when he saw the reaction of hundreds of Rajinikanth fans. Twenty-one years later, he experienced it again at Satyam Cinemas when the digitally re-mastered version of the film was premiered. Almost 200 youngsters danced right next to the screen. They had seen the earlier version several times and knew the dialogue by heart. They clapped even before the actor started speaking. It was a unique experience to see that the Rajini magic still worked.[9]

---

[9]Ibid.

It was in this film that Rajinikanth utters the famous line: 'If I say [something] once it's like I've said it hundred times.' This took on a political connotation that was not intended when the line was scripted. But in light of the ongoing feud between Rajinikanth and Jayalalithaa, this is how it was interpreted. Much before *Baashha* was released, they had had more public disagreements.

The government had constructed Film City and preparations for the opening ceremony were on. When Rajini came to know that the film city was to be named after Jayalalithaa—J. J. Film City—he was annoyed. When there were such giants of the film world, such as Sivaji Ganesan and MGR, he felt it was arrogant of her to name it after herself.[10] He boycotted the event. If Jayalalithaa had noticed his absence, she did not react to it. But later she announced that land would be distributed to workers in the film industry. Rajinikanth was happy to attend this function. When he went up on stage to speak, he first congratulated her but then reminded her that it was the poor people who had brought her to power and not the rich, so 'please do good for poor people'. He heard later that Jayalalithaa did not appreciate this.[11]

He blundered again at a function organized by the government in April 1995 to honour actor Sivaji Ganesan for having been awarded the Chevalier of the Ordre des Arts et des Lettres by the French government. At the ceremony, Jayalalithaa spoke highly of the actor. Rajinikanth gave the vote of thanks but added that honouring Sivaji was Jayalalithaa's atonement for what she failed to do when the film city was inaugurated. 'To err is natural. But to correct the wrong done is human.' he said.[12]

He heard from reliable sources that when she reached home, she flew into a rage, kicked over a chair and screamed, 'I will not rest till I finish that fellow. Next time he speaks about me

---

[10]'Those Five Functions', *Thuglak*.
[11]Ibid.
[12]Ibid.

I will show him what I can do.'[13]

Rajinikanth brushed it aside. Her fits of rage, tantrums, and arrogance were legendary. He didn't see any reason to be scared. When he saw people trembling at the very mention of her name, he thought it was ridiculous. But many in the film circle were embarrassed and worried about Rajinikanth's bravado. His many detractors concluded once again that success had gone to his head.

He became busy with the production of the film *Muthu* as he had promised his mentor. Now that he seemed to be in open conflict with the chief minister, rumours were rife about his possible entry into politics. The filmmakers wanted to cash in on this situation and include dialogue to cater to the expectations of the fans. They had started demanding that he enter politics. The script for *Muthu* had this line that is politically loaded: 'No one knows when or how I will show up. But when the time is right, I will be at the right place.' It could be interpreted both as a message to his fans (I'll enter politics when the time is right) and as a challenge and warning to Jayalalithaa (you won't see it coming).

The film was a blockbuster and completed a 175-day run at the box office. It was dubbed into Japanese and became one of the most successful Indian films in Japan. For a long while, the Japanese were besotted with Rajinikanth and the female lead, Meena.[14]

It was while he was shooting this film that director Mani Ratnam was attacked. Earlier that year, Ratnam had released *Bombay*. The film was about a romance between a Hindu man and Muslim woman against the backdrop of the 1992 communal violence that shook the country. The movie was controversial even before it was released. The Central Board of Film Certification demanded that portions of it be cut. Some states banned the movie altogether.

---

[13]Ibid.
[14]Digital Native, 'Digitally enhanced version of Rajinikanth's *Muthu* to be re-released in Japan', *News Minute*, 21 Nov 2018.

'I was at the shoot of the film *Muthu*, at Adyar,' wrote Rajinikanth in an article for *Thuglak*, 'when we got the news that bombs were thrown at Mani Ratnam's house and that he was hurt.' Rajini rushed to Devaki hospital where Ratnam had been admitted. The director and a domestic worker in the house had sustained injuries. 'He looked dazed and was in a state of shock.' The bomb had landed close to him. But luckily it had not gone off. Rajinikanth went on to say in the article that he felt that no one could feel safe if a man of Ratnam's stature could be attacked like this. Ratnam had received a threatening call saying that they would get him the next time. The Inspector General had then assigned protection to Ratnam's home. But the chief minister—who had not called on or enquired after the director—was reportedly annoyed that she had not been consulted and ordered the protection to be withdrawn. Rajini was appalled. 'When I heard this my blood boiled,' he wrote.

The day of the attack on Ratnam, Rajini and Latha had a dinner engagement at Taj Coromandel. He was shocked to see that hooligans had smashed the glass panes of the hotel's façade and ransacked its interiors. This was because T. N. Seshan, the Chief Election Commissioner, who had reformed the electoral process, and had imposed the model code of conduct on politicians, was staying there. He had earned the wrath of the chief minister. Rajinikanth was very upset. He could not sleep that day.[15]

Because of a spate of such events, Rajini was convinced that Jayalalithaa's reign was one of terror. By his own admission, Rajinikanth did not have a deep understanding of the politics of Tamil Nadu. His reaction was knee-jerk and his anger was that of a layman. He felt compelled to speak because he believed that his words had the power to impact large sections of the people of the state.

---

[15]*Thuglak*, issue dated 17 Apr 1996. Translation by author.

In April 1995, a huge crowd had thronged the venue to hear him speak. The function was to celebrate the silver jubilee of Sathya Movies that had produced *Baashha*. It was also to celebrate the success of the movie that had run for over 100 days. R. M. Veerappan, popularly known as RMV, producer and owner of Sathya Movies, was a minister in Jayalalithaa's cabinet. A staunch MGR supporter, RMV had never had a good rapport with Jayalalithaa. In fact, when MGR was alive, RMV did his best to keep Jayalalithaa away from him and tried to throttle all her efforts to gain status in the AIADMK. But when Jayalalithaa came to power, she invited him to join her cabinet. RMV knew that she would not approve of him participating in a function that celebrated a Rajini movie. RMV did not want to sit on the dais but Rajinikanth insisted that he do so and also asked him say a few words. Rajinikanth spoke right at the end. He had been agitated by all that he saw as atrocities committed by the ruling party: the blatant corruption; the acid attack on IAS officer Chandralekha[16]; the grievous attacks on advocates K. M. Vijayan and R. Shanmugasundaram[17]; the humiliation of Subramaniam Swamy[18]; assaults on media houses that were critical of the government—the list was long.

When he travelled to other states, he was asked why the people of Tamil Nadu were putting up with these atrocities. Haven't the Tamils, from time immemorial, fought for justice?[19]

All this had been building over the months and so he spoke about it at this function. He spoke of the bomb attack culture that had spread in the state. 'I request the chief minister to put

[16]Indulekha Aravind, 'Eulogised in death, Jayalalithaa leaves a checkered legacy', *Economic Times*, 11 Dec 2016.

[17]G. C. Shekhar, 'CBI report implicates Tamil Nadu minister in assault on Madras High Court lawyer', *India Today*, 15 Oct 1995.

[18]Dhanya Rajendran, 'Frenemies forever: Tracing the 25-year history between Jayalalithaa and Subramanian Swamy', *News Minute*, 12 Oct 2016.

[19]*Thuglak*, 1 May 1996. Translation by author.

an end to this trend immediately. I say, nip it in the bud. Give full freedom to the police. Only then will this problem be solved. I am very serious. I am speaking as a citizen of this country.'[20]

Perhaps it had slipped his mind that RMV, a minister of the government, was sitting on the dais with him. He did not realize the adverse impact his speech would have on the minister. Rajinikanth's speech was the last of the day, so RMV could not respond. He knew that Jayalalithaa would not forgive him for his silence. As expected, he was summoned to Poes Garden. When he arrived at her residence, she did not meet him, speaking to him over the intercom instead. She admonished him for not speaking up. RMV's explanation of the situation fell on deaf ears. 'It is a fact that the function was held to insult me,' she said and hung up the phone. RMV left for the US as planned.[21]

When RMV returned from this trip, he was relieved that Jayalalithaa behaved like nothing had happened. But she moved him from the Food Ministry to an insignificant portfolio and finally removed him from the party altogether. Following this, rumours began doing the rounds that RMV and Rajinikanth were going to form a new party.

The direct fallout of this outburst was that visitors to Rajinikanth's house, which was next to the CM's residence, were put through security checks like never before. Fans were stopped, vehicles were stopped and checked, and the road was blocked for hours together when Jayalalithaa's cavalcade had to leave for the secretariat.

Rajinikanth had now made it a habit to travel soon after completing a film. These were spiritual trips that he took either to the Himalayas or to Yoga Ville in Virginia, USA. He had become an admirer of Swami Satchidananda, a disciple of Sivananda Saraswathi, founder of Integral Yoga, who had his ashram at Yoga Ville. It was

---

[20]He said this at the function celebrating Sathya Movies Silver Jubilee, also referred to in 'Those Five Functions', *Thuglak*.
[21]RMV, interview with the author, 2004.

therapy that he had assigned himself to ease the stress he had undergone during filming schedules. Added to that, there was now the pressure from the government and its arrogant chief minister.

So, he was relaxing and rejuvenating at the ashram at Yoga Ville, unaware that the Tamil Nadu Congress unit was desperate to meet him.

Eleven

....

Karate R. Thiagarajan, president of the All India Karate
Association, a former member of the Indian National Congress
(he was suspended in June 2019 for anti-party activities[1]) is an
ardent supporter and close friend of Rajinikanth. We met in
his palatial house. It's surprisingly ornate with heavy furniture
like a set from the film *Baashha*. The garden is well manicured.
Perhaps because he is a karate master, Thiagarajan speaks like he's
throwing out a challenge. He anticipated questions and answered
them before I get a chance to ask them. He seemed to think
that Rajinikanth's announcement (on 30 December 2017) about
entering politics was always expected. He quoted that famous
line from *Annaamalai*: 'I do not know when I will come or
how I will come, but when the time comes, I will be there',
to illustrate his point. 'He has always shown interest in politics,
making political statements through his films even if he did not
directly join any party.'[2]

Sitting regally on the velvet-cushioned sofa in the midst of
scores of karate trophies, he spoke with fervour about the political
manoeuvring during the period before the parliamentary and
Tamil Nadu assembly elections held in May 1996. He said that
Rajinikanth lending his 'voice' to the Opposition was the deciding
factor in the results that shook the centre and decimated the
AIADMK in the state.

It was a turbulent political phase in the state. Jayalalithaa's

---

[1]D. Govardan, 'Chennai: Congress suspends Karate R. Thiagarajan for comments',
Times of India, 28 Jun 2019.
[2]Interview with the author, 28 Mar 2018.

popularity had sunk to a dismal low, and the writing was on the wall, but she seemed unaware of it. The DMK, led by the shrewd M. Karunanidhi, was gearing up with a vengeance for the elections. For nearly four years, the Tamil Nadu unit of the Congress party had opposed the AIADMK on grounds of corruption, maladministration, violence, and fascist tendencies. Congress senior leader G. K. Moopanar (he had been president of the Tamil Nadu Congress Committee—TNCC—between 1976 and 1980 and then again in 1988–89) had been alerting the high command of the party in Delhi about the humiliating slights that TNCC members had faced from Jayalalithaa and her party members in spite of being an electoral ally in the 1991 elections. And, more importantly, that she was losing popularity and that for the upcoming parliamentary and assembly elections it would be politically expedient to align with the DMK, which was sure to win because of the anti-incumbency factor. He felt that the high command had not clearly understood the ground reality in Tamil Nadu and therefore went to Delhi to impress this on Prime Minister P. V. Narasimha Rao. However, Moopanar was not aware that the Congress high command had already decided to align with Jayalalithaa. The Congress only had a 20 per cent vote share in the state and had to align either with the AIADMK or the DMK. Aligning with the DMK was a problem after the assassination of Rajiv Gandhi at the hands of a suicide bomber from the Liberation Tigers of Tamil Eelam (LTTE) as the DMK was suspected of helping the LTTE indirectly, and for creating conditions that allowed the assassins to succeed, as observed by the Jain Commission.[3] The Congress leaders were hesitant to hurt the feelings of Sonia Gandhi, Rajiv's widow, though P. Chidambaram, who was then a minister at the centre tried to convince them that the DMK had distanced itself from the LTTE and pointed

---

[3]Prabhu Chawla, 'Rajiv Gandhi killing: Jain Commission report indicts DMK for colluding with LTTE', *India Today*, 17 Nov 1997.

out that the Jain Commission had not indicted the party. The
Congress, he said, should now be concerned with the issues of
1996 and not those of 1992. There were rumours that Narasimha
Rao's sons had some financial obligation to Jayalalithaa which is
why they had persuaded Rao to ally with her.[4]

Rao, of course, could not have foreseen that his decision would
spark off a conflagration in Chennai. At Sathyamurthy Bhavan, the
headquarters of the TNCC, party workers burnt effigies of the
prime minister. They abused him and garlanded his effigies with
strings of slippers. As the flames reached the skies, forming a hot
canopy above Royapettah High Road, one of the busiest roads of
Chennai, Moopanar watched the scene and let the anger run its
course. A staunch Indira Gandhi loyalist, Moopanar was saddened
by these developments but had already made a decision that would
change the political equation in the state. The atmosphere was
charged that day on 27 March 1996 when S. Peter Alphonse, a
senior Congress member warned Moopanar: 'If you let go of this
moment, history will not forgive you.'[5] Moopanar declared that
he was splitting from the Congress.

It was said that Cho Ramaswamy, editor of *Thuglak*,
Rajinikanth's friend, and once a good friend of Jayalalithaa's, had
persuaded a reluctant Moopanar to meet Karunanidhi and discuss
an alliance. It was widely speculated in the newsrooms that Cho
urged Moopanar to form a new party. Thiagarajan discounts Cho's
role, saying that he and a few other Congressmen were in touch
with Rajinikanth who was away in America and briefed him
about the developments. Rajinikanth must have felt vindicated.
Thiagarajan and his friends were delighted when Rajini said he
would support the breakaway Congress faction and its alliance with
the DMK. It was then that he gave a statement, 'You can purchase

---

[4]Ibid.
[5]Ibid.

Delhi but you cannot purchase the people of Tamil Nadu,'[6] implying that Jayalalithaa had bought off Narasimha Rao. The statement was splashed across all the dailies of Tamil Nadu.

On 30 March, Moopanar met Karunanidhi, and the newly formed Tamil Maanila Congress (TMC) and the DMK formed an alliance. Rao's Congress went ahead with its alliance with Jayalalithaa. The parliamentary elections were also held simultaneously and so the alliance gained more importance.

It was then that many of the Rajini fan clubs started urging Rajinikanth to enter politics. It was even said in TMC circles that Moopanar, convinced that Rajinikanth's charisma and popularity would get the Congress a majority, was willing to make the Superstar the chief minister if he joined the party. But Karate Thiagarajan said Rajinikanth was not interested and had declared, 'I have absolutely no desire to enter politics.' Surya talked of a fan club member in Madurai saying Thalaivar became very angry when he heard some fan club members suggesting that if they were given a chance to contest, they might have a future in politics. He is believed to have asked such persons to leave the club.[7]

Once he returned from the US, Rajini spoke to the press. It was at this time that he made his explosive statement: 'Even God cannot save Tamil Nadu if Jayalalithaa comes back to power.'[8]

He also appeared on Sun TV (a channel launched in 1993 by Kalanidhi Maran, the son of Murasoli Maran, a nephew of Karunanidhi) and asked the viewers to vote for the DMK–TMC alliance. 'Karunanidhi and Moopanar are great statesmen and Tamil Nadu would be safe in their hands,' he said in a SUN TV interview at that time.

The alliance won handsomely with the DMK winning

---

[6]Karate Thiagarajan, interview with the author, 28 Mar 2018. Surya, Rajinikanth's fan, was also present.

[7]Surya, interview with the author, 28 Mar 2018.

[8]Anna Isaac, 'Rajinikanth once swung an election with one sentence: Does Thalaivar still have that clout?', *News Minute*, 31 Dec 2017.

167 seats and the TMC 39. The DMK came to power with an absolute majority. The AIADMK won just 4 seats and, shockingly, Jayalalithaa was defeated in her own constituency, Bargur, and the Congress was routed. The DMK–TMC combine won all 39 parliamentary seats as well. The United Front government was formed at the centre under I. K. Gujral. The DMK was part of the government. The Congress gave support to the government from outside at the centre. It was a minority government and Congress's support was crucial. Though Thiagarajan insists that the stupendous victory was due to Rajinikanth's intervention, the reality was that the anti-incumbency sentiment in the state was so strong that the AIADMK would have lost in any case. Rajini was sure that Jayalalithaa's defeat was divine retribution for the atrocities committed by her government.

K. S. Radhakrishnan (now a member of the DMK), who was a member of Marumalarchi Dravida Munnetra Kazhagam (MDMK) that was in an alliance with AIADMK, says all the MDMK candidates, including himself, were defeated because of Rajinikanth's televised request to viewers. Rajinikanth's fans who were in the MDMK listened to him and voted en masse for the DMK–TMC alliance. Such was the power of his 'voice'.[9]

That power exists even today, Thiagarajan believed. He brushed aside the speculation that Rajini may have decided to enter politics only at the age of sixty-eight because of the Bharatiya Janata Party's (BJP) prodding. Rajinikanth was always considered to be closer to the BJP than any other party.[10]

'Rajini sir has his own mind. All the decisions are his. There is no need for anyone to push him.'

'Why now?'

---

[9]K. S. Radhakrishnan, interview with the author, 21 Mar 2018.

[10]See R. Rangaraj, 'BJP hopeful of an alliance with Rajini, tie-up with AIADMK not final', *Federal*, 7 Dec 2020 and A. R. Meyyammai, 'Rajinikanth takes the political plunge in Tamil Nadu, only to play spoilsport?', *India Today*, 3 Dec 2020 and Uma Sudhir, 'How Rajinikanth Will Impact Tamil Nadu Politics', NDTV, 3 Dec 2020.

'There is a political vacuum that he sees now.'[11]

He repeatedly said: 'Rajini sir will sweep the assembly election in 2021 and will be the next chief minister' with a certainty that is almost comical. At that point, the elections were nearly three years away. And that is a long period in politics.

Thiagarajan claimed that Rajini was not interested in entering politics and becoming the chief minister in the 90s. At a function at MGR University on 5 March 2018, Rajini clarified that he was entering politics not for position or fame. If he had such notions he would have gone after it twenty years ago and become the chief minister in 1996. 'It was offered to me on a platter,' he said. According to Thiagarajan, Narasimha Rao offered to make him the chief minister if he stood with the Congress. It is mere conjecture to think so, really. At that time, it would not have been a sensible decision to make. Rajinikanth was at the peak of his film career, making crores of rupees for each film he made. He was ambitious and hungry to work and make money. Producers and distributors considered him their golden goose.

The voice that he lent to the political situation largely came from his personal clash with Jayalalithaa and because he felt that his fans were being mistreated. It would have been unthinkable to enter a world dominated by political giants like Karunanidhi and Jayalalithaa, who would most likely come back to power at some point. Rajinikanth did not utter a word when Jayalalithaa was arrested six months later. In the DMK election manifesto, Karunanidhi had vowed to attach the wealth of Jayalalithaa and her associates, hold enquiries into various allegations, and mete out punishment to the guilty. He had the judicial sanction to do so. The courts, while rejecting the anticipatory bail pleas submitted by Jayalalithaa, also admonished the Karunanidhi government for delay in taking action. Besides, the public mood had transformed from silent acceptance during Amma's rule to anger against blatant

---

[11]Karate Thiagarajan, interview with the author, 28 Mar 2018.

corruption. Karunanidhi knew that her arrest had the potential to turn into a bitter battle between the two kazhagams. If his government was seen to be victimizing Jayalalithaa, the strategy could boomerang. Karunanidhi himself would have preferred not to send Jayalalithaa to jail since that could set off a sympathy wave in a state where such events are known to provoke mass hysteria. Instead, he wanted to ensure that the string of cases (a total of twenty-seven) would keep her running from one court to another, leaving her little time to attend to party matters or even try to return to power. But the arrest of Jayalalithaa had become a political necessity. His own party cadres were crying for blood and were growing impatient. When the state cabinet met on 5 December, Chief Minister Karunanidhi discussed at length with his colleagues the political fallout of sending the AIADMK chief to jail. Halfway through the meeting, they made their decision. On the afternoon of 6 December, Justice C. Shivappa of the Madras High Court rejected Jayalalitha's seven anticipatory bail applications, including the one in the ₹8.53 crore colour television scam for which she was ultimately arrested. The next morning, as the police waited at Poes Garden, Jayalalitha bathed, draped herself in a maroon sari, completed her puja, packed a suitcase, and had breakfast. And the Thalaivi (leader) finally appeared at the portico of her house and said to her followers who had assembled outside in pained silence, 'Nalai Namathe!' (Tomorrow is ours).[12] Aided by two grim policewomen she stepped into the police van that was to take her to a city magistrate before going to Madras Central Jail and being reduced to remand prisoner No. 2529. Within minutes, SUN TV beamed news of the arrest.[13] She spent twenty-eight days in jail and after her return on bail went into self-imposed exile for nearly a year. At that time, Rajini must have thought that he had achieved what he had set out to do and went back

[12]'The Lone Empress', *Open*, 1 Oct 2014.
[13]Vaasanthi, *Jayalalithaa*, p. 104.

to the business of filmmaking. He then went on a philanthropic spree as it were, almost like he was fulfilling a vow, according to his fans. He performed the wedding of twenty couples, giving each three sovereigns of gold jewellery, all household essentials, and ₹10,000 in cash.

It was at this time that Kalaipuli Dhanu, who had been behind the publicity drive for *Bairavi* that first named him Superstar, met Rajinikanth and made a request. He knew that Rajinikanth had produced *Valli* to help his friends who were not very financially successful. Dhanu suggested to Rajini that he once again do something similar to help those who had helped him at the beginning of his career and had not seen much success in their own careers. Rajini agreed and chose seven such people to work with him in his next film, *Arunachalam* (1997). Five of them were producers of his first few films and two were actors—V. K. Ramasamy and Pandari Bai who had acted with him in several films. The film was produced under Rajinikanth's in-house banner Annamalai Cine Combines. The story is not all that different from other Rajini films of the time. It had all the essential elements—spectacular introduction sequences, punch lines, a rich versus the poor story. The fans whistled and cheered every sentence of his. When he uttered his punch line in Tamil: 'God speaks and Arunachalam acts', the fans roared in approval. And when he heard the temple bells, turned to the camera, and said with a charming smile, 'God has spoken' even old women swooned!

But things were happening elsewhere as all this was going on. Jayalalithaa was not about to stay silent for long. In 1997, the Jain Commission Report was published. The 5,280-page report investigated the conspiracy behind the assassination of Rajiv Gandhi. The report singled out the DMK, holding Karunanidhi and his party responsible for abetting Rajiv Gandhi's murderers. It also concluded that the LTTE was getting its supplies, including arms, ammunition, explosives, fuel, and other essential items for its war against the IPKF from Tamil Nadu with the support of the Tamil

Nadu government and the connivance of the law enforcement authorities. When the report was made public, the Congress, which had supported the I. K. Gujral United Front government, felt 'it was totally unethical to support the DMK's participation in the government if the interim report held it responsible for their leader's death'.[14] The Congress Working Committee demanded that the united front exclude the DMK from the ministry or face withdrawal of Congress support. Karunanidhi refused to bow out voluntarily, fearing that it would legitimize the report's findings. Once the Congress Working Committee sent the prime minister its ultimatum, Gujral waited for four days, and when the DMK did not resign, he sent his resignation letter to the president.

The country was now headed for a snap general election that the majority of the Lok Sabha did not want. Jayalalithaa calculated that the Congress had not regained its strength, while the BJP seemed to be rising as never before. She engineered a quiet alliance with the BJP leader L. K. Advani, creating history in Dravidian politics. The AIADMK had now joined hands with what Dravidian parties considered a North Indian, Hindu fundamentalist party.

Rajinikanth now realized that once he had stepped into the quagmire of politics, it was not really possible for him to stay away. In January 1998, a poem criticizing Rajinikanth was read out on stage at an AIADMK meeting. His fans were furious and went on the rampage. They painted the town red by putting up posters that abused Jayalalithaa and held meetings to condemn the AIADMK. A bomb was thrown at the AIADMK office in Coimbatore. The police suspected it to be the work of the fans. The head of the Rajini fan clubs, Satyanarayana, had to work hard to appease them and get them under control. Parliamentary elections were due in February and the fans were waiting for word from Rajinikanth.

---

[14]Prabhu Chawla, 'Rajiv Gandhi killing: Jain Commission report indicts DMK for colluding with LTTE'. Also see Chawla, 'Jain Commission Revelations: Damning the DMK', *India Today*, Mar 1996.

Rajinikanth was close to Advani, and it was expected that he would support the BJP, but because of his enmity with Jayalalithaa, he gave a delayed nod to the DMK. He didn't seem to have taken on board the Jain Commission's indictment of the DMK. On Pongal day, 14 January, he announced his support for the DMK–TMC alliance, met Karunanidhi the following week, then left for Hong Kong as planned. He did not make any statement. Though Karunanidhi was happy, Rajini's fans did not care to campaign for the DMK. They had little interest in helping third parties—they wanted Rajini himself to stand for elections.

Rajinikanth was also upset that posters were being put up in the name of the fan clubs that were abusive and instigated violence. A poster of Rajini was put up right opposite the AIADMK office that had words of warning to Jayalalithaa. The police could not find out who was behind it. Jayalalithaa asked her party workers to ignore it. The AIADMK did not want to give any importance to Rajinikanth.

Meanwhile Rajinikanth tried to forget the political turmoil in Tamil Nadu as he walked the streets of Hong Kong. He revelled in the anonymity he was experiencing. He marvelled at Victoria Peak and visited Disneyland. Though not much of a shopper, he was fascinated by the colours and vibrancy of the illuminated night markets. He would take in all the shimmering colours from his hotel room as he sat with a drink in his hand. When he returned to India, the situation had become more complicated.

Some years earlier, in the aftermath of the demolition of the Babri Masjid in Ayodhya in December 1992, a fundamentalist organization called Al Ummah had started gaining ground in Coimbatore. It was based in Kottaimedu, a Muslim neighbourhood, under the leadership of its general secretary, Mohamad Ansari. A number of unemployed uneducated Muslim youth were attracted to Al Ummah. When the police briefed the then chief minister, Jayalalithaa, about their activities, she ordered the setting up of police checkposts in Kottaimedu, a step that the Al Ummah members resisted. During the election campaign of 1996, Karunanidhi had promised the Muslims of Kottaimedu that the checkposts would be removed once the DMK was voted to power. The DMK had always been 'considered to be the party that would accommodate the concerns of the minority community, as well as of the various marginalized castes that were its primary constituency'[15].True to his word, once the DMK did come to power, the pickets were removed. Kottaimedu soon became a hotbed of unlawful activity. Arms and ammunitions were stored in many houses, some of which also sheltered militants.

On 14 February 1998, the day BJP leader L. K. Advani was to address a meeting in Coimbatore, a series of bomb blasts at thirteen places left at least fifty people dead. Advani was not hurt in the attacks as his meeting had been rescheduled. The bomb blasts shook the DMK and rattled Karunanidhi because his government was blamed for having ignored the warnings.

Rajini's fans were eagerly waiting to hear what their Thalaivar would say. Two years earlier, when Mani Ratnam was attacked with a bomb, he had accused Jayalalithaa's government of being responsible for the growing bomb culture in the state. Surely, he would condemn such mindless violence that had killed innocent people. But as soon as he landed in Chennai, Rajini only said to the reporters and news cameras that the 'Coimbatore blasts cannot be the work of Muslims'.[16] His fans, who were agitated about the incident and aware that it was the handiwork of a Muslim fundamentalist group, were surprised and unhappy at his words. Even worse, he went on to say, 'There will not be another bomb blast. If it happens, Karunanidhi will himself resign.' The DMK was shocked and embarrassed. And journalists and politicians concluded that his knowledge of politics was zero.

---

[15]P. G. Rajamohan, 'Tamil Nadu: The Rise of Islamist Fundamentalism', SATP, available here: https://www.satp.org/satporgtp/publication/faultlines/volume16/Article5.htm

[16]'Rajnikanth claims blasts attempt to unseat DMK-TMC', Rediff.com, 16 Feb 1998.

Twelve

The DMK paid the price for its lax approach to the terrorist threat in the state. Its candidates fared poorly in the Lok Sabha elections that took place shortly thereafter. Jayalalithaa took the opportunity to blame Karunanidhi's government for turning Tamil Nadu which, during her regime, had been a 'garden of peace' into a safe meadow for terrorists[1]. She also made a contemptuous reference to Rajinikanth and said 'there have been so many bomb blasts in one day. Why doesn't that actor open his mouth now?'[2] She thundered that the DMK had no right to govern the state and demanded Karunanidhi's resignation.[3] The public, in a state of rude shock, agreed with her—forgetting that they had voted her out a couple of years ago—security, after all, was more important than corruption. More importantly, she looked the epitome of the 'woman wronged'—she had been jailed; had had several cases filed against her; her bank accounts had been frozen; and property and jewellery sealed. Whenever she lashed out at the villainy of Karunanidhi on the campaign trail and narrated the ordeal of her stay in the prison, and rhetorically asked the crowd what sin she had committed, the 10,000-odd people who assembled on average at her public meetings would respond, 'No sin at all!' They did not care what her opponents said. Women, especially, did not believe Karunanidhi when he launched his counterattack. They had seen Jayalalithaa resplendent in fine clothes and jewellery and could not bear to see her shorn of them. The public mood

---

[1]Vaasanthi, *The Lone Empress*, p. 186.
[2]*Kalki*, 27 Feb 1998.
[3]Vaasanthi, *The Lone Empress*, p. 186.

shifted. In the February 1998 Lok Sabha elections, of the total 39 parliamentary seats in Tamil Nadu that were contested, the DMK combine got just 9 seats while the Jayalalithaa-led alliance bagged 30 seats, the AIADMK alone securing 18 of them.[4]

Rajinikanth realized then that he should not make any political comments. This time, the Rajini magic didn't work and his support for the DMK did not help. His comments after the bomb blast were widely criticized. He tried to mend matters saying that his words had been misconstrued. What he had meant was that you could not blame a community for the wrong done by some fringe groups. But he couldn't convince anyone. Many AIADMK men, who were also members of his fan clubs, were unhappy. In many places, his effigies were burnt and slipper garlands adorned his posters and cut-outs. There were reports that many of his fan clubs were disbanded.

He decided to dive into his safe space— films. He announced that his next film, *Padayappa,* would be released in 1999. And while he greatly respected his mentor, Rajini did not want to consult Balachander on political matters. He felt his bond with the director did not mean that Balachander should have a say in his personal choices. Pushpa Kandaswamy says that her father never interfered with Rajini's personal habits like smoking or drinking and, more importantly, his views on politics. He respected the individual's space in such matters. She believes that is why the relationship worked as well as it did. But once in a public forum Rajinikanth asked him what would make the director happy (about Rajinikanth's life choices). Balachander answered, 'I will be happy if you did not enter politics.' Perhaps that was another reason Rajinikanth did not want to enter politics at that point. Pushpa says her father felt Rajinikanth's temperament would not allow him to cope with the politics of the day. Superstar he may

---

[4]PTI, 'LS poll tie-up with BJP mirrors Amma's strategy, says AIADMK', *Times of India*, 23 Feb 2019.

be, but he was always tense, impatient, and short tempered. From the moment shooting began for a film until it was released he would be a bundle of nerves; how could such a man face the constant criticism and abuse that a politician had to bear?[5]

In the meanwhile, Jayalalithaa did something that the nation did not foresee. With its 18 seats in the Lok Sabha, the AIADMK was a valuable partner in the BJP-led NDA government of Atal Bihari Vajpayee at the centre. In other words, the BJP depended on the support of her 18 MPs to stay in power. This, then, was the best time to strike a good bargain to facilitate her one-point agenda—the dismissal of the DMK government in Tamil Nadu. The reason for dismissal—the breakdown of law and order in the state. She also wanted to be able to influence the appointment of the prosecution counsel who would argue the cases against her. Under pressure from her, the AIADMK's M. Thambidurai was given the portfolio of law in the NDA government.[6] It was imperative that she use her political clout to nullify all the pending cases against her. She could not wait for the people to vindicate her. The next assembly election was three years away and she feared that the BJP would not dare dismiss Karunanidhi and impose President's Rule in the state. Of the nine cases pending against her, eight were being handled by the state government. Many cases were due for trial and the hearings would begin soon. She was vulnerable.

When she had given her 'unconditional support' to the NDA government, she had been expecting the prime minister to instantly dismiss the DMK government, to protect and perpetuate her special status of being an important ally. To some extent, Jayalalithaa misread the situation in Delhi. She believed that the BJP and Vajpayee were so desperate for power that they would give in to all her demands. But her behaviour baffled the gentleman statesman,

---

[5]Interview with the author, 22 Jan 2019.
[6]K. M. Thomas and K. Govindan Kutty, 'AIADMK chief Jayalalitha's pressure tactics paralyse BJP-led Government', *India Today*, 30 Nov 1999.

Prime Minister Vajpayee. For twelve months he humoured her, even allowing her to influence the choice of ministers in the central government and the appointment and dismissal of senior civil servants. However, he stopped short of dismissing Karunanidhi's elected government, and that irked Jayalalithaa tremendously as she was in a tearing hurry to put her legal troubles behind her. The BJP-led coalition government began to feel the strain of having to depend on her. She went to Delhi and dropped hints that she was not averse to shaking hands with the Congress, thereby toppling the BJP-led government. When repeated hints did not work to her satisfaction, the inevitable happened. Jayalalithaa withdrew her support in 1999, and the NDA government fell, defeated by one vote in the dramatic no-confidence motion that followed.

In the Lok Sabha elections that followed, the DMK took a conscious decision to align with the BJP. As a natural consequence, Moopanar's TMC alliance with the DMK broke down. Rajinikanth was friends with both Karunanidhi and Moopanar but chose to keep his mouth shut and got busy with *Padayappa*. The shoot began in October 1998 with K. S. Ravikumar directing. When it released, it became the highest grossing film of that time. Rajinikanth once again stole the hearts of his millions of fans, making them forget his political failings. The film was carefully scripted to make his character, Padayappa, appear the dashing hero who is just, brave, fearless, and romantic. It tells the story of Padayappa's clash with a haughty woman, Neelambari, played commendably by Ramya Krishnan. The US-returned Neelambari falls in love with Padayappa's rustic charm but when he spurns her advances, she is humiliated. He shows his dislike for her conceited, pompous behaviour. When Padayappa marries her maid instead, Neelambari is unable to take the slight and goes into self-inflicted exile. She holds on to her anger for twenty years and finally returns to the scene of her humiliation with a view to getting revenge. She asks him to meet her. When Padayappa enters her house, the huge hall is empty, bereft of any furniture, and Neelambari dramatically walks down the stairs. Only one chair is brought for her, forcing Padayappa to remain standing. Padayappa looks around, pulls down the swing that has been suspended from a hook in the ceiling and jumps on to it, seating himself regally, dramatic swishing sounds accompanying this move. Rajini's friend, Ashok, recalls that Rajkumar, the Kannada matinee idol, clapped in appreciation when he saw this scene and exclaimed, 'Who else but Rajinikanth can do this?'[7] Neelambari looks at him admiringly and says, 'You know why people like you so much? It is because even as you have aged, your beauty and style have remained the same.' Padayappa answers, with a rush of 'Thank you, thank you, thank you' and drawls, 'I was born with it. It will never leave me.' The fans broke into a thunderous applause and gushed, 'That is true of Thalaivar. His charisma will never die.'

Ashok remembers that Rajini spoke to him before the shoot. 'He told me about the script and that at the end Neelambari would fall at his feet and ask for forgiveness. I said, "This is the obsession with stars like you, Rajkumar, MGR, and Sivaji Ganesan. You want your machismo intact and women to fall at your feet. In this story, Neelambari is a vengeful, strong character. Would you expect Jayalalithaa to ever fall at anybody's feet? Neelambari should not, even on her deathbed, apologize. She should die saying that she will avenge her humiliation in births to come." Rajini was very happy with what I said. He told Vasu the director that is how the end should be. And that is how it was.

'As a matter of fact, it was Neelambari's role that was much talked about when the film was released and Ramya Krishnan bagged the best actress award. Shivaji was always generous with his co-actors. He would argue with directors to allot space to his co-stars. He never felt threatened by the presence of others.'[8]

Ramya Krishnan was quoted as saying that she did not want

---

[7]Ashok, interview with the author, Bangalore, 10 Jun 2018.
[8]Ibid.

to play a negative role against Rajinikanth. But she could not turn it down when she was told it would be a very strong role. She did not hesitate after that. During the first week after the release, she heard that Rajini's fans threw slippers at the screen when she appeared.[9] But, gradually, her acting skills were appreciated and she won the state award for Best Actress and the Filmfare Award for Best Actress in Tamil. Rajinikanth got the State Best Actor Award.

There was, of course, a punch line in the film that was much quoted: 'In all of recorded history there is no man who was avaricious or a woman who did not control her anger who has prospered.' There was no doubt which woman the film was referring to. Even the politically naïve Tamil viewer could tell that Ramya's character, Neelambari, was meant to portray Rajinikanth's real-life adversary. K. S. Radhakrishnan, who was a member of the Censor Board when the film came up for perusal, says that Jaya Arunachalam (social worker and founder of Working Women's Forum), who was on the board, strongly objected to giving it clearance saying that Neelambari's character was a critique of Jayalalithaa, the former chief minister of Tamil Nadu. Radhakrishnan countered by saying that the objection was meaningless since it was a creative fictional work. The film got its certificate of clearance because of his argument.[10] The film was released on 11 April, to correspond with the Tamil New Year on the 14th. *Padayappa* proved to be a greater hit than *Arunachalam*.

Karate Thiagarajan believes that the film had a great impact on the parliamentary elections that took place in September–October. He says it was evident in the results—the DMK-BJP (NDA) alliance won 26 seats and Jayalalithaa's AIADMK-Congress front got only 13. The BJP came to power again at the centre and the DMK was able to get plum posts in the cabinet.

Rajinikanth's last words to Neelambari in the film, 'You won

---

[9]TNM Staff, 'I was scared to play negative role opposite Rajini: Ramya Krishnan on *Padayappa*', *News Minute*, 16 Sep 2017.
[10]Interview with the author, 21 Mar 2018.

once, it opened my eyes!' were prophetic, says Abu Ahmed, a member of a fan club in Coimbatore. After Rajini's controversial remarks about the Coimbatore blasts and rumours of the disbanding of many fan clubs, Rajini supporters, and Rajini himself, was worried about what the response would be for *Padayappa*. But when it broke even the high record of *Arunachalam*, Rajinikanth was greatly relieved and said so during the victory celebrations of the film, says Ahmed, 'Thalaivar's words were loud and clear. "When there were blasts in Coimbatore, the whole nation was burning. I was worried how to douse the fire without creating communal tension. I do not know if others understood my intention, but I now know that my fans understood me perfectly. They will never forsake me. It shows clearly in the success of *Padayappa*." Ahmed says with emotion, 'We will never forsake Thalaivar, ever.'[11] At sixty-five, Ahmed, who works as a car mechanic, has been Rajinikanth's fan for fifty years.

Rajinikanth invited Karunanidhi to see the film and the writer-politician was extremely pleased with it. 'Padayappa, you are an achiever, appa!' he said to the Superstar.[12] He must have seen that the film was a direct critique of his arch-rival and could foresee that it would help the DMK in the elections. Rajini fans in the DMK who were unhappy with his earlier remarks were now appeased and went to see the film repeatedly.

⏑

Despite his brief forays into politics and the huge success of his films, the big change in Rajini's life during this period was his growing interest in spirituality. As has been noted, he became close to Swami Satchidananda, who hailed from Coimbatore, and was a disciple of Swami Shivananda Saraswathi. For some time now, Rajini had been visiting the swami's ashram in Virginia every year after

---

[11]Interview with the author over phone, 15 Apr 2018.
[12]Priyan, interview with the author, 20 Mar 2018. (Priyan wrote for the Tamil weekly *Kalki*.)

completing a film. This interest in spiritual matters was unsurprising as for some time now, there had been a mix of two opposing forces in Rajini. While he was concerned about the success of his films and the financial aspects that went along with it (as Mani Ratnam said, he was not naïve in matters of business), he was also spiritually inclined and would periodically travel to the Himalayas, and spend time with ascetics. There are several unverified reports that describe how he would enter tunnels that were so narrow that no one would dare enter them and lose himself for hours in meditation. He has spoken about his experience to his close friends. In the soothing silence of the caves, he would meditate and discover intimations of divine grace. Away from the distractions of the world, these intimations would transcend time and space and he would be engulfed by a great calm that smoothed away all anxiety and fear. He wondered if he were imagining it all. Was it just his mind yearning for an escape from the stresses of life, from the frightening image trap that he had got into? He realized that travelling to the solitude and remoteness of mountains helped him escape the stresses and pressures of his superstardom. Dressed in just a simple kurta-pyjama, without any of the trappings of a superstar, he became a completely different person, and he enjoyed the transformation. On these spiritual quests, he did not want even his close friends with him, says Raghunandan. He would say to them, 'The mountains speak to me.'[13]

Swami Satchidananda once told him about a holy man who was many hundred years old. Ever since Rajini heard this, he had not been able to shake the thought of this magical, powerful Baba. He often dreamt about him and even had hallucinations that featured the holy man. He was convinced that the Baba had a message for him. He had felt his touch, his push, and his call to him during all hours, anywhere. Once he felt the call when he was alone in his Bangalore flat. He was half asleep when he

---

[13]Raghunandan, interview with the author, Bangalore, 23 Jun 2018.

heard a commanding voice asking him to rise. He rose and saw a beam of light enter the room and permeate his being. It was an exhilarating feeling. He felt a vibration all over his body and the feeling was sublime. He saw this as a message from Baba. That evening the complete script of the film *Baba* came to him. He cancelled the rest of his appointments and left for Chennai and immediately started working on the script. He spoke about his experience to Swami Satchidananda. The swami told him that what he had experienced was the call of Baba, Mahavir Baba, about whom all that is known is that he is ageless.[14] After this spiritual experience, Rajini became obsessed with the idea of making a film on Baba. He felt that Baba wanted him to spread his message to the public through the medium he was familiar with. The idea consumed him.

The story of *Baba* was also in a sense his own story. He seems to have used it to understand himself and his motivations. It was a hotchpotch of sentiments and seemed like he was trying to look at his own past objectively. It appeared that he wanted to seek redemption for the years of debauchery in his youth. The story is about a divine child who is born to a simple couple. Feeling blessed, they name the child Baba after the saint they revere. Holy men tell the couple that the child has to overcome his past karma and therefore should not be stopped from doing things that they might not approve of. He has to satiate his base desires before he attains spiritual wisdom. The child grows up to be a ruffian but everyone who knows him sees that he has a heart of gold.

He goes on to master siddha and the rogue becomes a yogi after realizing the impermanence of mortal pleasures. He refuses political power that is offered to him and turns away from the material world. But the call of the yogis and siddhas has to be

---

[14]'Superstar Rajinikanth speaks about Baba Movie', *Thanthi TV-YouTube*, 4 Feb 2017, available here: https://www.youtube.com/watch?v=QBovXqM3p4I

put off for a while because chaos breaks out the minute he leaves. 'Baba turns back and strides towards the mayhem as a song plays out: I won't forget the Tamil land, I won't crave political power or position. The picture freezes on the image and the caption "To be continued" appears on the screen.'[15]

Suresh Krissna who directed the blockbuster hit *Baashha* was engaged to direct *Baba*. Krissna had never worked on such a subject before and was initially hesitant to take it on. But when he saw how keen Rajinikanth was on the film, he agreed. He thought it could be like a fantasy film and different from Rajini's usual fare. It did have the usual Rajini elements in the first half. It was during the shooting of the later portions of the film that Krissna felt that Rajinikanth indeed was a very spiritually blessed person. But despite all their efforts, the film flopped. According to Krissna, it was because people compared it to the previous film that they had worked on together—*Baashha*—which had been a stupendous success. Expectations were too high. Besides, they expected a film like *Baashha* and had no clue about the spiritual stuff that this film had in it. Rajinikanth had played it close to the vest and didn't reveal the theme of the film in advance. Distributors bought the rights at a very high price, expecting the kind of returns that Rajini films usually earned. The ticket prices were raised to an unaffordable level. Four tickets at ₹75 were given to fans, and they went on to sell for ₹400 each. Not even the most ardent fans wanted to watch the film after the first show. They didn't go to the movies for spiritual succour.

Rajinikanth also suffered a personal loss at this time. He had wanted his guru Swami Satchidananda who had told him about Mahavir Baba, who had been the film's inspiration, to be present at the inaugural release function on 14 August 2002. But the swami fell ill during the function. He began choking for breath, suffocated by the bewildering crowd he was not accustomed

---

[15]Ramachandran, *Rajinikanth*, p.189.

to. He passed away soon after at the hospital he was rushed to. Traumatized, Rajinikanth took his body to his ashram in Virginia and had him buried there, as the swamiji had desired.

When the distributors of the film lamented that they had suffered huge losses, Rajinikanth repaid every paisa they had lost. This was unheard of in the industry, says Krissna. His friend Ashok recalls, 'When *Baba* flopped, he called me to say that he had compensated the distributors for the loss incurred.' Ashok told him that the film was a mistake. 'Your fans watch your films to see your action and style, not to hear some spiritual lectures. Cinema is entertainment not a moral lesson class.' The Superstar agreed.[16] While Tamil moviegoers didn't care for the film, it found an audience far across the Pacific. As we've seen, Rajinikanth's 1995 film *Muthu* had fascinated Japanese audiences. Kandaswamy, Balachander's son-in-law, who had produced the film, marketed it to Japan after a chance encounter with a Japanese businessman. Rajinikanth and his co-star Meena became very popular among Japanese filmgoers. *Baba* also became quite successful in Japan. Two Japanese actors played small roles in the film—a female Bharatanatyam student who was a fan of Rajinikanth's, and a male Japanese student. According to some reports *Baba* did well in Japan.[17]

The film was deeply spiritual but also had an underlying political theme. It ends with Baba walking towards a large group of supporters and the title card reads 'To be continued'. This ending invites the viewer to speculate on the possibility of Baba/Rajinikanth's entry into active politics. In hindsight it is intriguing how Rajinikanth kept his fans' hopes of his entry into politics alive through his films. Perhaps it was a business gimmick by the producers. Now he very likely thinks it was folly to have played along.

---

[16]Ashok, interview with the author, Bangalore, 27 Jun 2018.
[17]Arun Ram, 'Brand Rajinikanth is hot in Japan', *DNA*, 30 Aug 2005.

S. V. Srinivas, professor of Arts and Sciences at Azim Premji University, writes: 'The brazenness of the equivalence between the stardom and divinely ordained destiny is not to be discounted as the actor's megalomania. It is a pointer to a serious problem with the reification of star-image over time, leading to the difficulty of finding story level explanations for the star's extra ordinariness, as well as also identifying crises for a hero we all know is too big to fail.'[18] This might go some way towards explaining Rajini's misjudgements when it came to *Baba*. Srinivas also talks about how *Baba* made legal history of sorts when Rajinikanth's lawyers attempted to restrict his gestures and dialogues in the film from being copied by others or even mimicked, claiming that such a use would constitute a trademark violation. Legal scholars dismissed this as untenable. The Mimicry Arts Association greeted the announcement with a statement of 'hurt'. 'What was Rajinikanth trying to achieve by this ill-advised attempt?' the Association asked.[19]

In addition to the financial losses of the film, it also ran into trouble with a political party—the Pattali Makkal Katchi (PMK). The party president, Dr S. Ramadoss, had been attacking Rajinikanth for some time, ostensibly about his portrayal of drinking and smoking on screen. But the animosity also had to do with Rajinikanth's view of Veerappan, the forest brigand, sandalwood smuggler, and poacher. On 30 July 2000, Veerappan had abducted the Kannada film industry's legendary star, Rajkumar, for ransom. Rajkumar was a captive and stayed in the forest for 108 days. Senior Kannada journalist Bhaskar Rao says that Rajinikanth, who was a great admirer of Rajkumar's, worked with S. M. Krishna, the then chief minister of Karnataka, to get Rajkumar released. It is an open secret, says Bhaskar Rao, that Rajinikanth contributed to the huge amount of money paid to

[18]S. V. Srinivas, 'Rajinikanth and the "Regional Blockbuster"', Chicago Tamil Forum Working Papers, May 2016.
[19]Ibid.

Veerappan to release the actor. Rajkumar was helicoptered out to Bangalore unharmed. He became emotional as he alighted from the chopper, kissed the earth and cried out, 'O, nanna Kannada mathe!' (O, Kannada, my mother!)[20] a metaphor that had the potential to rouse language passions on either side as he had been abducted by Veerappan, a Tamil. As things developed, this became a regional, language, caste issue. Rajinikanth was invited to participate in the celebration of the release of Rajkumar son's film in Bangalore on 10 August 2002. During the function, Rajinikanth said in chaste Kannada, 'Veerappan is a raakshasa. He has to be finished.'[21]

Dr Ramadoss took serious objection to his statement. Veerappan and his gang had a close caste affinity with Ramadoss— they both belonged to the Vanniyar caste. In the areas where Veerappan held sway—Gopinatham, Sathyamangalam, Mettur, Govindapaadi—Ramadoss was popular; these places were party strongholds because of the support of Veerappan. Ramadoss, who had been campaigning against smoking and drinking, started attacking Rajinikanth for spoiling the youth of Tamil Nadu by glorifying these habits. 'The fools here spend their hard-earned money to see his films and learn all the vices that this man personifies on the screen. He, an outsider, is poisoning the young minds of Tamil Nadu. Youth of Tamil Nadu, wake up! Don't spoil your health and life. Stop watching his movies. Do not allow his movies to run,' Ramadoss said in his public speeches that were covered by the local Tamil papers and journals. He did not stop with that. 'Rajkumar says he was looked after well for the hundred odd days he was in the forest. But, according to Rajinikanth, Veerappan is a raakshasa, he should be finished. Veerappan is a Tamilian, a Vannian. I am a Tamilian and a Vannian. Will Rajini say I should also be finished? He has earned more than 1,000

---

[20]Witnessed by author as journalist for *India Today*.
[21]K. S. Velayudan, 'Rajni Politics', Chapter 20, *The Hindu* (Tamil), 6 Feb 2018. (Translation by author.)

crores, they say. Of what good is it to Tamil Nadu? What has he done for Tamil Nadu?' [22]

Rajinikanth did not react. When some fans complained that PMK men were harassing them, their leader, Satyanarayana, asked them to be patient; the Superstar would give a fitting reply later.

There were open clashes between PMK men and Rajini fans. It was reported that at a theatre in Jayankondam, the box that contained *Baba* film prints was stolen and that at some places the screen was torn and at another, the screen was set ablaze.[23] The film's cut-outs and banners were torn to pieces. It was said that all this was the handiwork of PMK men. Priyan, a senior journalist who reported for *Kalki,* said that Rajinikanth paid compensation to the theatre owners for the loss of their screen and made arrangements to install a new one. A fresh box of the film prints was sent to Jayankondam poste-haste. In many areas, the film was screened with police protection. Despite all this, in the northern districts where the PMK had strong support, the screening was stopped to avoid law and order problem.[24] All this invariably added to the loss that the film incurred.

Rajinikanth retreated to Bangalore. He roamed the streets of Hanumanthanagar, Basavanagudi, and Gandhi Bazar with his friend Raj Bahadur. He would tie a towel around his head to disguise himself and enjoy the roadside eateries, sit on the floor in his room and drink the local arrack that he was fond of. He would open a sachet of liquor, pour it into a glass, add a pinch of salt, squeeze some lime into it, dip his fingertips in the drink, shake the liquor from his fingers on to the floor as an offering to the gods and say, 'Mari, Mahamari'—he would then gulp the shot down at one go. It was a sublime feeling.[25]

---

[22]*Kalki*, 14 Dec 2003. Translation by author.

[23]'Anbumani takes on Dhanush for on-screen smoking, remember the Ramdoss-Rajini face off?', *News Minute*, 20 Jul 2015.

[24]Priyan, interview with the author, 15 Mar 2018.

[25]Ragunandan and Bhaskar Rao in separate interviews with author, Bangalore, Mar 2018.

Thirteen

When he returned to Chennai after his Bangalore sojourn, Rajinikanth had to face some harsh realities. When he had left his place of birth many years ago, in search of new shores to carve out a decent life, he was not really aware of some of the affilations that would become weightier as his fame grew. When he was starting out, he was young, with a burning passion in his heart and a raging hunger to succeed. He had just one agenda—to prove his acting skills and make a name for himself. Language and borders had no meaning for him then. The world of art did not care where you were from. There was one language you had to master—the language of the artist that was universal. The audience did not see the difference either. They embraced him as he was. And what an embrace it was. It was overwhelming and overpowering. In all this, his origins and the affiliations that came with it were forgotten. When he became a superstar, these affiliations and labels made themselves felt. When he began to rule the film world, his admirers, and detractors were always curious to hear from him about the issues of the day. Many also began to question his loyalties—was his allegiance to the state that had given him opportunities, status, and wealth? Did he feel a debt to the salt of Tamil Nadu or was he still loyal to the land of his birth? Some of these questions were raised when he had criticized Veerappan but they really came to the fore when a long-running dispute between Tamil Nadu and Karnataka once again began to dominate the headlines.

The Cauvery water-sharing dispute between the two states was a century old.[1] With years of political mishandling and because of the intense emotion that it raised on both sides, the dispute had not been resolved. The Cauvery was Tamil Nadu's lifeline but the source of the river was in Karnataka. This meant Tamil Nadu's water supply depended on Karnataka releasing the water. The genesis of this conflict rests in two agreements—one signed in 1892 and the other in 1924—between the then Madras Presidency and the kingdom of Mysore. The 765-kilometre-long Cauvery has a basin area of 44,000 square kilometres in Tamil Nadu and 32,000 square kilometres in Karnataka. As per the agreements, water sharing was to be determined as per the basin area of each state. But Karnataka claims that the agreements were unfair to Karnataka and that new agreements were needed to ensure equitable sharing. Tamil Nadu argues that an equal share is not possible since the state has already cultivated 12,000 square kilometres of land around the river and is heavily dependent on the current usage pattern. Any change would affect the livelihood of millions of farmers in Tamil Nadu. Following repeated demands by Tamil Nadu to constitute the Cauvery Water Dispute Tribunal, it was created in 1990 at the direction of the Supreme Court. The tribunal passed an interim award which required Karnataka to release 205 tmcft water to Tamil Nadu every year. But Karnataka refused to comply, stating that the state did not have enough water for its own consumption.

Agitations and demands by both states continued over the decades and things came to a head in 2002. The monsoon failed in both states. Reservoirs fell to record low levels and tempers predictably rose on both sides. The crucial question was: how could this distress year be handled amicably by both the states? The tribunal had overlooked this point when it gave the interim award.

---

[1]Geetika Mantri, 'Explained: What the Cauvery water dispute between Karnataka and TN is all about', *News Minute*, 15 Feb 2018.

Karnataka ruled out releasing any water in the circumstances that prevailed. A meeting of the Cauvery River Authority (formed in 1998)—which was a modified version of the tribunal but expected to have more powers—was called on 27 August 2002. But Tamil Nadu chief minister Jayalalithaa walked out of the meeting saying that the Cauvery River Authority was a toothless tiger, pointing out that Karnataka had refused to abide by the interim order of the authority to release 1.25 tmcft to Tamil Nadu every day.[2] Tamil Nadu went to the Supreme Court with an appeal. In response to the appeal the Supreme Court ordered Karnataka to release 1.25 tmcft to Tamil Nadu every day as per the order of the tribunal and river authority. Karnataka was forced to release water but insisted on another meeting with the Cauvery River Authority to present its case. Following the meeting, the authority revised the court order and asked Karnataka to release a reduced volume—0.8 tmc per day.

This angered the farmers of Tamil Nadu who were faced with parched farmlands and also fanned passions in Karnataka. The Karnataka government, succumbing to the large-scale protests that began in the Cauvery districts of the state, refused to release any water at all, echoing the sentiments of the protestors—'not a drop of water can go to Tamil Nadu'. Jayalalithaa (who, ironically, originally hailed from Karnataka) was furious and once again knocked at the doors of the Supreme Court. Karnataka resumed releasing the water for a few days, but stopped on 18 September as the protests began to turn ugly and threatened to spread to other parts of the state. A farmer jumped into the Kabini reservoir in protest and died.[3] Vatal Nagaraj, leader of the Karnataka Rakshana Vedike, a Kannada chauvinist unit thundered, 'Not a drop shall go

---

[2]TNN, 'Jaya walks out of Cauvery Water Meet', *Times of India*, 27 Aug 2002.
[3]Sadananda R., 'Farmer jumps into Kabini reservoir to protest Cauvery water release', *Rediff.com*, 19 Sept 2002.

to Tamil Nadu.'[4] The protests and dispute spilled into the streets of Mandya in Karnataka and Tanjavur in Tamil Nadu. Soon more people joined—artists, writers, and film stars on both sides raised their voice. Tamil TV channels and the screening of Tamil films were blocked in Karnataka. All buses and vehicles from Tamil Nadu were barred from entering Karnataka.

With passions running high, many were curious to see how Rajinikanth, the Tamil superstar from Karnataka, was going to react. Members of the Tamil film industry, led by well-known director Bharathiraja (the director of one of Rajini's early films, *16 Vayathinile*) called for a protest rally at Neyveli on 12 October, demanding the stoppage of power supply to Karnataka from the Neyveli Lignite Corporation.[5] Rajinikanth refused to join the agitation as it would 'aggravate tensions'. He suggested a non-confrontational mode of agitation, perhaps in Chennai.[6] He felt that linking the supply of power to Karnataka with the release of water from the Cauvery was preposterous.

Chief Minister Jayalalithaa extended indirect support to the protesters and agreed to provide them police protection. DMK president Karunanidhi, mainly to counter her stance, questioned the validity of the demand since electricity production and sharing came under the centre's jurisdiction. Jayalalithaa was fully aware of this, of course, but the Cauvery water dispute was an emotive issue, and she wanted to show that she was a leader who would go to any lengths to protect the rights of the Tamils. Despite hailing from the 'enemy' state, Karnataka, she wanted to show her Tamil followers that she could be more ferocious in protecting Tamil interests than her chief native-born rival, Karunanidhi, the

---

[4]'We Won't Give Even A Drop Of Water To Tamilnadu From Cauvery--Vatal Nagaraj', *Thanti TV*, 19 Sep 2015, available here: https://www.youtube.com/watch?v=NwYM70PONJ4. (Translation by the author.)

[5]N. Sathiya Moorthy, 'Rajnikanth steps in to cool tempers on Cauvery', *Rediff.com*, 5 Oct 2002.

[6]PTI, 'Rajnikanth to participate in Oct 12 rally', *Rediff.com*, 6 Oct 2002.

'Thamizina thalaivar'—leader of the Tamil community.

An estimated 5,000 members of the film industry—even those who were known to be DMK supporters—staged an anti-Karnataka demonstration in Neyveli attired in black and carrying black flags and placards. Bharathiraja launched a vitriolic attack on Rajinikanth. He accused Rajinikanth of showing his true colours by keeping away from the Neyveli stir. Giving a clarion call to Tamils to save their land, he said, 'We can tolerate enemies, but not traitors.' In a thinly veiled reference to Rajinikanth's possible entry into politics, Bharathiraja said, the 'Tamils are hospitable to outsiders, but should not be gullible and gift away their land.'[7]

In response, Rajinikanth announced he was fasting on 13 October to protest Karnataka's refusal to release Cauvery water. 'He is trying to divide the Tamil film industry', Bharatiraja cried. But the next day, other big stars from the film world including Kamal Haasan, Vijayakanth, and Sathyaraj joined Rajinikanth in the fast. Even Karunanidhi offered to join, but was requested not to, considering his age. Rajinikanth did not respond to Bharathiraja's taunts. Perhaps he thought it would only make matters worse.

Many years later, he narrated a fable: Three frogs were on a difficult journey up a mountain. People kept warning them of the dangers inherent in such a journey. They kept climbing anyway, while the warnings continued. Two of the frogs succumbed along the way to fatigue or fear or a fall. The third frog advanced doggedly and reached the top. People wondered how the frog had managed it. It turned out that the third frog was stone deaf and did not hear any of the warnings or doubts that the other frogs did. So, he had climbed unhindered by fear. 'I am like that frog,' said Rajinikanth. 'I don't hear what people say. Therefore, my mind is not confused.'[8]

Rajinikanth believed that this issue could not be resolved by

---

[7]Velayudan, 'Rajni Politics', Chapter 35.
[8]Available here: https://www.youtube.com/watch?v=TYmrkP51jDc

protests. He wanted to find a practical solution for a real problem. He envisaged a grand interlinking of the southern rivers, which he thought would be the only way to satiate the thirst of both the states. He agreed to contribute one crore rupees towards the cost of such an undertaking if the centre initiated such a project.[9] Raghunandan says that Rajinikanth gave serious thought to the plan of linking of the rivers. He believed that India could approach other nations and international organizations for funds for the project. But before anything concrete could be done by the governments, nature solved the problem. The monsoon rains started, the Kabini River overflowed and the reservoir filled up. Karnataka had to open the floodgates and release water to Tamil Nadu.

Rajinikanth returned to filmmaking. The first thing that Rajini had to do was a find a way to resurrect his image after the disastrous flop of *Baba*. During a trip to Bangalore, he and Raj Bahadur watched the 2004 Kannada film *Apthamitra* directed by P. Vasu, a remake of the 1993 Malayalam film *Manichitrathazhu*. Rajini was intrigued by the story and decided it would be the perfect engine for his comeback. He contacted Shivaji Productions, founded by the renowned thespian Sivaji Ganesan and now run by his sons, Prabhu and Ramkumar, and asked if they would produce the film. He told them it had to be a 'big film'. Prabhu was excited at the prospect of making a film with Rajini. The production house liked the storyline of the original Malayalam film, but agreed that the story needed to be altered and packed with all the commercial elements that the Superstar was associated with. They decided the film's title would be *Chandramukhi* (2005), and engaged P. Vasu who had directed Rajinikanth in the film *Mannan* (1992) under the same production banner, as well as the Kannada version of the film.

---

[9]Pratibha Parameswaran, 'Cauvery water-sharing dispute: Is the Tamil film industry a soft target or a political tool?', *Scroll.in*, 26 Sep 2016.

In this film, Rajinikanth, now fifty years old and balding, would be playing the role of a young psychiatrist. There was speculation among the film fraternity—would he fit the role? Vasu was confident that it was possible to give Rajinikanth the required makeover. Rajinikanth was still agile, and his sense of timing was as perfect as ever. He had kept himself slim with regular exercise and a strict diet. All he needed was the right wig. 'He looks very handsome in the film,' Vasu gushed, obviously relieved. That aspect handled, the team discussed the story threadbare. Vasu was particular that the film appeal to the entire family. Unlike the star's fans, the general audience would want a good story, and would not be satisfied with just the Superstar's trademark mannerisms and one-liners. *Chandramukhi* had an intriguing plot that would appeal to women as well. The songs, too, were composed and choreographed differently. The songs in his other films would highlight the hero and his heroism. In this movie, Rajinikanth didn't play a formulaic hero, and the songs tried to 'lift the fans' says Vasu, 'who have selflessly played a great role in his phenomenal growth'.[10] For instance, in the song 'Devuda Devuda', Rajini's character asks the Almighty to bless those who are employed in different menial trades—janitors, sewer cleaners, farmhands, and washermen—referring to his fans.

Vasu might have gushed about Rajinikanth's look in the film, but the women in the audience were more fascinated by the character played by Jyothika. Her role was challenging—she played the innocent and childlike Ganga as well as the vicious, long-dead dancer, Chandramukhi. In the story, Ganga and her husband, Senthil, live in a mansion that is believed to be haunted. Ganga hears the story behind this belief: about 150 years ago, Chandramukhi, a dancer, was abducted by the king of the land and kept captive in this mansion. The king was obsessed with her, but Chandramukhi spurned his advances because she was in love

[10]Ramachandran, *Rajinikanth*, p. 205.

with Gunasekaran, another dancer. Overcome with jealousy and rage at not getting what he wanted, the king killed Chandramukhi and her lover, Gunasekaran. People believe that Chandramukhi's ghost is still locked up in the palace, raging with fury and waiting to take revenge on the king. When Ganga hears this story, she is deeply affected by it. Soon after, the legend seems to come to life and Ganga starts to behave strangely. Saravanan, the psychiatrist played by Rajini, must determine if Ganga is possessed or if she's suffering from a psychiatric condition.

The film found the right balance between mystery, horror, and comedy and when it released on 15 April 2005, it became a superhit. It was just the heart-warming comeback that Rajinikanth had hoped for. Rajinikanth, according to Vasu, was nervous during the first few days of the shoot and confessed that he felt like a novice. He had taken a break of three years after *Baba*.

In the midst of making the film, Rajinikanth had an opportunity to hit back at the PMK for what they had done at the release of *Baba*. The 2004 Lok Sabha elections were approaching and they presented him with the opportunity he had been waiting for. *India Today*'s senior correspondent Arun Ram wrote: 'There was a time when [Rajinikanth] flicked his cigarette in [the] air [and] cinema halls in Tamil Nadu were set on fire. Now, superstar Rajinikanth threatens to reduce the S. Ramadoss-led Pattali Makkal Katchi (PMK) to ashes in the coming elections.'[11] The memory of the deep hurt he felt when *Baba*, a film made with great devotion and dedication to his patron saint, bombed could not be erased. He was certain that the film ran into losses because of the problems Dr Ramadoss and his party men created. He had not retaliated then even though his fans had complained. He had asked them to remain calm and assured them that he would tackle the problem legally. He was biding

---

[11]Arun Ram, 'Rajnikant threatens S. Ramadoss-led Pattali Makkal Katchi', *India Today*, 19 Apr 2004.

his time, crouching like a patient leopard, waiting to strike at the
opportune moment. During the run-up to the elections, he asked
his fans to boycott PMK and work to support the candidates
who stood against the PMK. He didn't care that the PMK was
in alliance with the DMK, the party he had supported so that
Jayalalithaa could be defeated. He now asked his fans to support
Jayalalithaa's alliance partner, the BJP. His fans were confused and
unhappy. Many of them belonged to the Vanniyar caste group
that the PMK represented.

In any case, the results of the election came as a shock to
Rajinikanth. The BJP–Jayalalithaa front that he had supported
drew a blank, winning not a single seat. The PMK that he had
vigorously opposed won all the 5 seats it contested. The DMK–
Congress–PMK–MDMK–Left parties combine won all 39 Lok
Sabha seats from Tamil Nadu. Rajini's detractors, the PMK in
particular, gleefully declared that Rajinikanth was a zero as far
as Tamil Nadu politics was concerned. The belief that his words
had the power to alter political waves was clearly a myth. In
1996, the atmosphere had been charged with an anti-incumbency
mood which made Jayalalithaa's fall imminent. It was not the
power of his words.

Rajinikanth retreated to films. This political loss spurred him
to take on an even bigger film project next. He had one ready
to shoot *Sivaji: The Boss* (2007). The producer, A. V. M. Saravanan,
approached the big-budget director S. Shankar. Shankar had a
reputation for often exceeding the set budget of a film. The film
was meant to commemorate the centenary year of AVM founder
Avichi Meiyappa Chettiar (also known as A.V. Meiyappan). Shankar
was given free rein to make the film the way he wanted—the
final production budget went over 60 crore rupees, which the
banks financed.[12] Saravanan knew he was taking a big risk, but
having given his word, he had no choice but to go through with

---

[12]Ramachandran, *Rajinikanth*, p. 209

the production. Rajinikanth was reportedly paid 'a whopping ₹55 crore for his role in *Sivaji*. At that time, he was the highest paid actor in Asia after Jackie Chan.'[13]

According to Saravanan, Rajinikanth offered to take his payment 'after the film does business'. During the film shoot in Pune, Saravanan explained, he had booked a luxury suite for Rajinikanth, but the latter refused it, saying all he needed was a single room. He 'wanted a room to sleep, bathe, do yoga, meditate and eat food. A hot case with food had to be placed at his door. He would take the case inside, eat alone, wash the case and keep it back outside. He came out only at the time to go for shoot.'[14]

During the shoot, the rest of the unit was amazed by his sheer presence and his discipline—his lifestyle was ascetic, except for his evening drinking. Rajinikanth didn't think there was any contradiction there, though. He once explained to a friend 'Don't you know that the rishis of the Vedic period had no qualms about drinking somarasa, that was alcohol.' He gave examples from *Autobiography of a Yogi* (Paramahamsa Yogananda) and *Walking with a Himalayan Master: Swami Rama* (Justin O'Brien) that clearly showed that the spiritually-inclined smoked and drank alcohol. Nobody dared dispute his logic.

[13]Janani K., 'Rajinikanth, Kamal Haasan, Simbu: How much do the biggest Tamil actors earn?', *India Today*, 26 Apr 2018.
[14]Ramachandran, *Rajinikanth*, p. 209.

Fourteen

Bollywood films that had international reach and market had not seen the kind of production budget that *Sivaji: The Boss* boasted. Different reports carried different figures: ₹60 crore, ₹80 crore.[1] The director Shankar was from the newer crop of filmmakers that made technologically advanced films. So high was the excitement around this film that the news even made it to national TV channels, that were usually not interested in films made in the South. The buzz was not only because of the film's budget but also due to rumours about Rajinikanth's remuneration being higher than that of Amitabh Bachchan and close to what Jackie Chan made for his Hollywood films. As has been noted earlier, Rajinikanth was believed to have been paid ₹55 crore, nearly the same amount as the film's production budget. The North Indian media and film aficionados did not understand the mass appeal and reverence that Rajinikanth commanded. He was, after all, not traditionally good-looking. And the investment in the film and expectations that the turnover would be triple that baffled the Indian film industry at large. It pointed to the huge surge in popularity that Tamil films had—even big star-studded Bollywood films that had a certain market in the Middle East, UK, and US had not had such a large turnover. The English news channels were fascinated by this phenomenon.

Rajini's fans performed the usual pre-release rituals and propitiated the gods, asking for the film to become successful. They were anxious to see his look in his hundredth film. The film,

---

[1]Krishna Gopalan, 'The boss, no doubt', *Business Today*, 29 Jul 2009 and '"Sivaji The Boss" to call the shots world over today', *Financial Express*, 14 Jun 2007.

when it released in June 2007, 'broke records for collections [in the first 100 days] by a Tamil film not only in India but also in countries like Malaysia, Singapore and Britain'.[2] Shankar seemed to have the Midas touch. Combined with the Superstar's appeal, the film was a hit. It was first released all over Tamil Nadu, then the Tamil version was released in Singapore, Malaysia, and South Africa, in Delhi, Mumbai, and Calcutta simultaneously. The film didn't have subtitles and yet the response was incredible.[3] In Tamil Nadu it attracted new segments of viewers who had not been avid Rajini film watchers. 'The release of the film *Sivaji: The Boss* was an important cultural event in 2007', said a critic.[4]

Rajini plays the film's eponymous hero, Sivaji. The title is an obvious reference to his own name—Shivaji Rao Gaekwad—and the star is in nearly every frame. After the deplorable failure of *Baba* in which Rajini looked old and shrivelled up, viewers wanted to see the Thalaivar of the golden past. They got that and more. Shankar made brilliant use of special effects, make-up, and computer-generated images. There were so many ingredients in the mix—romance, action, humour, music, dance, and special effects—that the film appealed to a range of tastes and regular viewers didn't get bored of seeing so much of the Superstar. Die-hard fans got exactly what they wanted.

Apart from the commercial and entertainment elements, the story pandered to the fans' desire to see Rajinikanth anointed the next ruler of Tamil Nadu. Sivaji in the film is a 'vigilante extraordinaire'[5]. He takes on greedy villains, corrupt politicians, bureaucrats, and the government. He extorts hoarded black money and turns it into white through a hawala network. He runs

---

[2]E. T. B. Sivapriyan, '"Sivaji—The Boss" continues reign at box office', *Outlook*, 21 Sep 2007.
[3]Ramachandran, *Rajinikanth*, p. 216.
[4]Andrew Wyatt and M. Vijayabaskar, 'The Many Messages of Sivaji', *Economic and Political Weekly*, Vol. 42, No. 44, 3 Nov 2007.
[5]Ibid.

a parallel government and goes on a development spree—the projects just materializing one after the other. He magically creates educational institutions and hospitals, signing deals with both hands simultaneously. He teaches people the benefits of card payments and wipes out corruption by establishing a cashless economy.

The hero is Shankar's idea of a vigilante who offers simplistic solutions to serious problems. 'There is an alarming lack of logic', wrote film critic Baradwaj Rangan. He also says that the parts of Shankar's films that are usually strong 'are horribly written and the execution is worse.... ...the impression you get is that the film was used merely to build up an image—a political image. ...the next time Rajini picks a script, he thinks also about the legacy he's going to leave behind as an actor'.[6] One wonders if Rajini really believed one could solve societal problems with the simplistic solutions that the film offered. But the fans saw a message in this film—Thalaivar's future role as the chief minister of Tamil Nadu. They believed nothing was impossible for him, he was god-like. He was a good man and would bring prosperity to all if he did become chief minister. Banners saying: 'Thalaiva, come take command of the army that waits for you. Tamil Nadu awaits you, the future Chief Minister of the State' showed up all over Chennai.

The film, when it released, became the subject of a number of interpretations and economic analyses by critics and researchers. 'It is easy to dismiss *Sivaji* as an over-sugared cinematic confectionary,' said Professors M. Vijayabaskar and Andrew Wyatt. 'Rajinikanth is a highly-skilled popular entertainer, a fact that is ignored when critics infantilize his audiences. *Sivaji* is an entertaining film. However, it would be a mistake to overlook the various political themes that the film brings to our attention. Firstly, it serves as an important footnote to Rajinikanth's extremely uneven political career. The

---

[6]Baradwaj Rangan, 'Review: Sivaji', available here: https://baradwajrangan.wordpress.com/2007/06/17/review-sivaji/

film raises interesting questions about his future in politics. The film could be seen as a statement of Rajinikanth's disillusionment with the current political dispensation in Tamil Nadu. *Sivaji* is a film on politics and it is a film that confirms Rajinikanth's immense popularity.'[7]

Special separate screenings were arranged for Chief Minister Karunanidhi, who had come back to power in 2006, and the leader of the Opposition, Jayalalithaa, in Chennai. The chief minister of Andhra Pradesh, Rajasekhara Reddy, also had his own special screening. There was a special irony to all this as the film shows complete disdain for the state bureaucracy; the political class is portrayed as illiterate and hence unfit to govern, and corrupt. Redemption comes through the activism of an educated and wealthy businessman who wants to do good. 'There is a good deal of product placement as global brand names are less than discreetly displayed. The film speaks to a new Indian economy based on connectedness, technology and conspicuous consumption.'[8]

M. Madhava Prasad (Professor of Film and Cultural Studies, English and Foreign Language University, Hyderabad) wrote: '…the director of this film is Shankar, who is most strongly associated with the post-modern style of recent Tamil cinema addressed to youth. The coming together of the absolutist power of Rajinikanth and the global-capitalist digital-age style of Shankar is an event in itself, comparable to the meeting of the *Titanic* and the iceberg. The result is a film in which Rajini's sovereignty has been turned into capital, losing the political surplus, the virtual community, built upon its scarcity value…. With *Sivaji*, it appears that Rajini, too, has been converted into a commodity. The political surplus, which was the property of the fans, the foundation of their sovereignty, has been converted into an investible economic surplus. Will the fans go along with this dissolution of their

---

[7]Wyatt and Vijayabaskar, 'The Many Messages of *Sivaji*.'
[8]Ibid.

cherished virtual monarchy? It is hard to predict. But we can certainly now explain the triumphalism of the media in reporting "Rajinimania". It was a celebration of the triumph of profit over rent, the trumping of politics by economics, which is the Indian media's favourite news item.[9]

Rajinikanth may not have been aware of the academic analyses of the movie and his role, but he was aware that as an actor he would remain relevant only as long as he was commercially viable. Cinema was not a vehicle of art. It was business. He owed answers and profits to the producers and distributors. He was very aware that his films had to have a wide reach, catering to the expectations of his fans. A god's relevance depended on the collective faith of the masses, after all. In a quest to keep him relevant, directors were beginning to wean him away from his old gimmicks. Chewing gum had replaced the cigarette. He was mouthing political rhetoric written by scriptwriters, portraying characters based on the director's philosophy and political agenda. There was a danger that it could go overboard and he could become a caricature. According to some critics, this had already happened. From his larger-than-life commercial hero image, he was getting trapped in a different sort of image—that of a politician-activist. It was a pity that he started believing it and in his invincibility.

While the fans again clamoured for Rajini to enter politics and began calling him Tamil Nadu's future chief minister, Rajinikanth showed that he had a long way to go along the political path. This was evident when the Cauvery water dispute came up again. After many rounds of discussions, the UPA government at the centre and the two state governments agreed to set up a project—the Hogenakkal Integrated Drinking Water Project—to provide drinking water from the Cauvery to the deprived districts

---

[9]M. Madhava Prasad, 'Fan bhakti and subaltern sovereignty', Elleke Boehmer and Rosinka Chaudhuri (ed.) *The Indian Postcolonial: A Critical Reader*, London and New York: Routledge, 2011, p. 98.

of Krishnagiri and Dharmapuri in Tamil Nadu. But the project never took off because protests broke out in Karnataka against it. Rajinikanth reacted aggressively: 'I condemn what is happening in Karnataka in the strongest possible terms and I am pained. Where is our country going? What is happening? Is there a government there? Is there a Supreme Court? Who are the people listening to?' he said in a public speech in Chennai.[10] He did not stop there. He thundered that those who refused to share the water should be beaten up. He accused Karnataka's politicians of precipitating the problem because state elections were coming up. It was a rabble-rousing speech filled with bravado. He joined other Tamil stars who were on a fast, protesting Karnataka's irresponsible behaviour. Protestors in Karnataka went on a rampage and burnt effigies of the actor. They demanded an unconditional apology from him. Vatal Nagaraj, who was head of the Karnataka Border Protection Commission at that time, said the organization would prevent Rajinikanth from entering the state and would not allow his films to be screened in Karnataka.[11]

That was a blow that he had foolishly failed to anticipate. *Kuselan* (2008) was about to be released and Karnataka was a big market for his films. Not being able to screen the film in Karnataka would entail a considerable loss of revenue. He came to his senses and appeared on Kannada TV channels and sheepishly apologized.[12] Speaking in Kannada he explained that he had not meant all Kannadigas should be beaten up (he had said protesters should be kicked). He was only referring to those who indulged in anti-social activities. 'I made a mistake, I know, but it is important that the mistake is not repeated. I am not a politician, please keep politics and cinema separate,' he pleaded.[13]

[10]Ramachandran, *Rajinikanth*, p. 220–21.
[11]Ibid., p. 221.
[12]PTI, 'Rajini apologises, pro-Kannada groups allow Kuselan release', *Times of India*, 31 Jul 2008.
[13]Ramachandran, *Rajinikanth*, p. 221.

The Karnataka Rakshana Vedike withdrew their opposition and agreed to let the movie release in Karnataka.

But his fellow actors in Tamil Nadu were not convinced by Rajinikanth's twists and turns. Neither were the Kannadigas. They knew that Rajinikant's sole aim was to protect his film's interest. They were right, of course. Unfortunately, '*Kuselan* didn't work, not in Karnataka, nor anywhere else'.[14] Serves him right, said the Kannada activists. His detractors claimed that Rajini was done. To make matters worse, a Coimbatore-based Rajini fan club floated a political party in his name without his knowledge. They put up posters all over the city proclaiming Rajinikanth the future chief minister of Tamil Nadu. The actor was furious. He issued a statement saying that anyone who used his name without his permission would be removed from the clubs. He also warned them that they would face legal action if they continued with such activities. He further explained that he was fully involved in the making of his next film and not interested in politics. In the words of film critic and Rajini biographer Naman Ramachandran, 'Rajinikanth also continued sitting on the political fence and left himself a lifeline, in case he changed his mind.'[15]

Soon after, he became fully immersed in his next film—the mega-budget *Enthiran* (2010). He was still a big player in the field of cinema. *Enthiran* was directed by Shankar of the Midas touch. For a long time, Shankar had been toying with the idea of making a science fiction film based on a story written by popular writer Sujatha (nee Rangarajan). The project never took off due to problems he had encountered negotiating with stars and producers. He had now got Eros Entertainment on board as producer and approached Rajinikanth to play the lead. Rajinikanth found the story novel—he had not done a movie like this before. But he was concerned if at his age he would be suitable for the double

---

[14]Ibid., p. 222.
[15]Ibid., p. 223.

role the lead actor in the movie would need to play—that of a scientist and a robot. But Shankar assured him that they would make it work—make-up, prosthetics, as well as special effects could work miracles. But they ran into problems with the producer and Rajinikanth decided to approach Kalanithi Maran of Sun Pictures, part of the Sun Group media empire, to finance the movie. Maran, a shrewd businessman, knew he would be betting on a winning horse. *Enthiran* (called *Robot* in the Telugu and Hindi versions) is estimated to have cost ₹130 crore to make and is reported to have recovered more than three times its investment, making it the highest grossing Tamil movie of its time.[16]

Enthiran was released in 2010 in India and in 2012 in Japan. Japanese entertainment company Nikkatsu Corporation found the film 'unique, funny, interesting and marketable'. It was a 'new experience for a Japanese audience to see such a high-tech but at the same time a very local kind of Indian film.'[17] *Enthiran* was a new genre for the Superstar—there were no snappy dialogues, no Rajini mannerisms that had been the hallmark of every movie of his up until now. But Shankar was a taskmaster who made Rajini act the way *he* wanted. He had a vision for the movie and what part the actor would need to play to make his vision a reality. All he needed was an actor who would cooperate and work hard and Rajini was just the actor for it.

Enthiran was a story of the struggle between man and machine. Vaseegaran, the scientist played by Rajini, succeeds in creating the perfect android, Chitti (also played by him), who is also highly intelligent. But Chitti lacks human emotions. On being challenged to address this lack, Vaseegaran manages to imbue the robot with emotion. But the robot then starts developing his own ambitions and desires and falls in love with the scientist's girlfriend, played by Aishwarya Rai. Now the scientist has to control his creation

---

[16]Ibid., p. 227.
[17]Ibid., p. 234.

which is determined to live its own life. Rajinikanth had always enjoyed playing the villain and was in his element as the evil Chitti.

One of the many awards *Enthiran* bagged at the Vijay Awards (presented by Tamil television channel STAR Vijay) was Best Villain for Rajinikanth. In his acceptance speech that his son-in-law, Dhanush, read out on his behalf, he said, 'I have always preferred to play Ravana to Rama, Duryodhana to Krishna. I am therefore happy to receive this Best Villain Award.'[18]

Was he working through his own demons via these negative roles? Were they manifestations of his mind when he was troubled? Were these the demons that he was trying to root out during his trips to the Himalayas and spending time with saints and yogis? Drawing a connection between his spiritual quests and his villainous characters is a stretch. 'Playing a negative role is a challenge to the actor,' says S. V. Srinivas. 'There is more scope to bring out his true histrionic talents.'[19]

In the finale of *Enthiran*, Rajinikanth turns into a gigantic metal snake composed of a thousand clones of the robot. 'Perhaps it is the vicarious fantasy of this larger-than-life existence that appeals to fans,' says Sadanand Menon. '*Enthiran* could have been his swan song. Even then, his image was so big that his character had to multiply himself a thousand times to satisfy consumer demand.'[20] His fans were euphoric—this imagery was reminiscent of the divine, mythical Adisesha with a thousand heads. They imagined that when Rajinikanth became the leader of the state, the streets would run with milk and honey.

During the production of *Enthiran*, another highly charged political issue was being discussed. The civil war in Sri Lanka between the Liberation Tigers of Tamil Eelam (LTTE) and the government in power across the sea in India was an emotive issue in Tamil Nadu politics. Although never a factor in the

---

[18]Ibid., p. 232.
[19]Interview with the author, 18 Jun 2018.
[20]Interview with the author, 16 Mar 2018.

elections, since it was not a local issue, it managed to stir up emotions among Tamil nationalists and some political groups. They insinuated that the Indian central government was aiding the Sri Lankan army against their Tamil brethren and brought up the issue to embarrass the Congress. The civil war in Sri Lanka worsened in 2008–09 after the government withdrew from the cease fire agreement on the pretext that 'the LTTE was not willing to enter the peace path'.[21] As the war wore on, the LTTE suffered heavy losses in the Eastern sector and retreated north. The Sri Lankan army pursued the LTTE fighters, determined to end the country's twenty-five-year-old brutal civil war. It broke through the LTTE defence lines, destroyed its bunkers, and conducted air strikes on civilians. The army then launched artillery strikes against a hospital in Mullaitivu that killed more than a hundred innocent people and wounded hundreds.[22] This brutal violation of human rights shook the world and angered the Tamils in Tamil Nadu. There were wide protests by various groups in the state condemning the atrocity. The Tamil film industry held a solidarity meeting in November 2008 to highlight the plight of the Tamils in Sri Lanka caught in the civil war. Almost all the big names in the film industry assembled to express their grief and condemn the attack on civilians. Rajinikanth made a statement as well. He might not have been aware of the entire history of the struggle. We know from his speech that he did not even know for how long the war had been going on. But there was no doubt that the army had been ruthless and that he had to condemn its actions. He made a speech using the strongest terms: 'I have met many Sri Lankan Tamils here and abroad.... But to see how they have to live in other nations, away from their home country, makes me sad. They fought for equal rights. They took up weapons for this. Everybody says that our central and state governments should

---

[21]PTI, 'Sri Lanka on alert as government scraps ceasefire agreement', *Rediff.com*, 3 Jan 2008.

[22]'Sri Lanka insists rebels disarm before further peace talks', *New York Times*, 3 Jan 2008.

take steps to stop the war. What we are saying here will reach the ears of the President of Sri Lanka.... I wish to tell [him that] Tamil people only asked for equal rights. You didn't grant those. That's why they are fighting for it. And you announced the war. ...for thirty to thirty-five years [the war had been going on for twenty-five years], you have been unable to break them. What kind of "heroes" are you? The people who have been dying for years...even if you kill all of them...these seeds will grow again tomorrow and make your life miserable. Set aside I, me, mine and arrogance. If you don't understand this, bigger countries will make you understand.'[23]

It was a rather pompous, cinematic speech. Rajinikanth seemed to think that his words had the power to alter the fate of the Tamils living on the island across the Indian Ocean. The fans were deeply touched and moved to tears. Not all of them were well-versed with the issue. But they must have felt a sense of relief that Thalaivar had said the right thing and redeemed himself after the humiliation he had suffered during the release of *Kuselan*.

---

[23]Ramachandran, *Rajinikanth*, p. 224.

Fifteen

....

'Rajinikanth is back as if born again,' said an emotional Raj Bahadur, Rajini's closest friend of over forty years. He looked out at the crowd that had assembled at the Raghavendra Kalyana Mandapam and said, 'You know how? It is because of you, your collective love and prayers wishing him a quick recovery; your selfless penances; fasts and vigils; how will god not heed your entreaties?'

Raj Bahadur wiped away his tears and went on. 'I know of two young men who prayed for him in a unique way. They climbed the 1,308 steps of the holy hills of Palani, not on their feet but on their knees. 1,308 steps! It must have melted the heart of the Lord. It moved Rajini's heart so deeply that he wept. You know why he always addresses you saying, "Ennai vaazavaikkum deivangalaana rasiga perumakkale—my dear fans who are the gods who have kept me alive"? It is his way of acknowledging the fact that he lives because of you. You call him god, but you are his god!' Rajini's fans broke into thunderous applause, overcome with emotion.

Raj Bahadur went on. 'When I heard that he was unwell and was taken from Chennai's Ramachandra Hospital to Singapore for treatment I could not contain myself and left for Singapore. Rajinikanth, Shivaji to me, and I are not separate beings—we are merged together in such a bond. The hospital would not allow me to see my friend in the ICU. After a great deal of persuasion, the doctors finally let me in. When I saw Shivaji lying crumpled in his bed, shrunk to half his size, I was too shocked and grieved for words. It is a miracle that he has returned cured of his sickness. I am certain that it was your prayers and love that brought about the miracle.'[1]

It started as a rumour. 'Rajinikanth unwell during a film shoot'. When the news that he had been rushed to hospital was confirmed in the media it spread like wildfire all over Tamil Nadu. The fans panicked. They rushed to the nearest temple, church, mosque, to offer prayers for their idol's swift recovery. Rajinikanth's illness came as a shock to the film industry, especially to Eros International, which had just announced the making of a blockbuster *Rana* (unreleased) with Rajinikanth playing a triple role in it. K. S. Ravikumar, the man who had directed hits like *Muthu* and *Padayappa,* was to direct. It was poised to be Rajinikanth's most ambitious film to date.

The first day's shoot (on 30 April 2011, following the puja and photo shoot on the 29th) was a song sequence with Rajinikanth and Deepika Padukone. Rajini started throwing up on the set. Initially it was believed this was due to food poisoning. He was taken to St Isabel's Hospital in Mylapore, Chennai, and admitted to the ICU. He was, however, discharged the same day and was advised rest. That was something of a relief to Rajini fans who had lost their minds with worry. On 4 May, he was again admitted to the hospital, complaining of breathlessness. This time, he remained there for a week and the problem was believed to be bronchitis and a viral infection. But soon misinformation was being shared and wild rumours began making the rounds. There was talk of the Superstar's failing health. Latha Rajinikanth had to call a press conference to quell the rumours and assure the fans that the star was doing well and resting at home.

The main preoccupation of the media—television and newspapers—at this time was the 2011 assembly elections. It was shaping up to be a tough fight between the old adversaries—Karunanidhi and Jayalalithaa. Determined to get back in power,

---

[1]'Super Rajini's Best Friend Raj Bahadur Speech', available here: https://www.youtube.com/watch?v=3wwzsCXkoiw

Jayalalithaa was fighting a no-holds-barred campaign. The DMK was struggling with allegations of corruption regarding the 2G spectrum allocations by A. Raja when he had been union minister for Information and Technology. Jayalalithaa made the most of this scandal. In every town that she campaigned in, lakhs of people thronged her meetings despite the police's efforts to stall them at the borders. The writing was on the wall for the DMK and on 13 May 2011, she won with a thumping majority. So, when on 14 May 2011, Rajinikanth was admitted at Sri Ramachandra Medical Centre for 'recurring respiratory infections and gastro-intestinal issues'[2], it wasn't headline news for a while. But soon the TV channels started flashing the news in every bulletin. Panic spread among the fans, making them hysterical. The grief- and panic-stricken fans surrounded the hospital.

The rumour mill went into overdrive—the Superstar was suffering from alcohol withdrawal symptoms; others held that the ailment was liver sclerosis. Rajinikanth's brother, Satyanarayana, who had rushed to Chennai, told the media that his brother was suffering from a lung infection and liver-related problems. 'As you know, Rajini was a chain smoker and a heavy drinker. The doctors have identified some problems in his lungs and liver.' He said that they might take Rajini to the US for treatment. The hospital only announced that all his tests were normal and he had been advised rest.[3]

Even though his relationship with Jayalalithaa had turned rocky many years ago, Rajinikanth sent his daughters to convey his congratulations to her on her stupendous victory.[4] 'I wish the star a speedy recovery', Jayalalithaa responded. 'I would like to visit him in the hospital.'[5] Other major politicians were already doing so—then Gujarat chief minister, Narendra Modi, and Chandra

---

[2]Ramachandran, *Rajinikanth*, p. 237.
[3]'Brother slams Rajini's cancer rumours', *Hindustan Times*, 17 May 2011.
[4]Ramachandran, *Rajinikanth*, p. 239.
[5]Karate Thiagarajan, interview with the author, 15 Mar 2018.

Babu Naidu, former chief minister of Andhra Pradesh, who were in Chennai for Jayalalithaa's swearing-in ceremony, visited Rajini in hospital and wished him a speedy recovery.

However, it was finally decided on the advice of the doctors and friends that Singapore would be a better destination for treatment for his ailment—though so far no one had clearly said what that was. In any case, he was admitted in Mount Elizabeth Medical Centre, Singapore. The treatment appeared to have worked well. It was reported that he was discharged from hospital on 15 June but he stayed on in Singapore for a month to recoup and have medical check-ups. Once back on his feet, Rajini made it a point to call Jayalalithaa and congratulate her on her massive victory. He said that Tamil Nadu had been 'saved' by her coming back to power. Jayalalithaa must have surely had a hearty laugh— this was the same man who had campaigned against her saying that nothing would save the state if she came to power.

His fans were puzzled when the news appeared in the Tamil papers the next day. Rajinikanth called Karunanidhi and said to him soothingly, 'You have seen many battles and many ups and downs. You should not worry about this defeat. You must take care of your health.'[6]

The veteran statesman was probably not amused. But he was also aware that it would not be wise to antagonize the Superstar.

When he returned to Chennai, Rajinikanth was in a reflective mood. His body had protested the many years of recklessness that he had subjected it to as a young man. Swami Satchidananda used to say that the body was like a temple. In its sanctum sanctorum resided the mind. Both body and mind had to be nurtured and respected in order to travel the spiritual path. Abusing either would only lead to self-destruction. Rajinikanth's body had given him many warnings over the years. He could no longer ignore them. But taking care of his body would mean denying himself

---

[6]Ibid.

many things. No alcohol, no cigarettes—would he be able to cope with the withdrawal? And what sort of a life would it be without these comforts? But the doctors had painted a realistic picture of what could happen if he did not change his ways.

After his health scare, Rajinikanth began to worry about his mortality. Were his days numbered? No, said his loved ones, but he would need to be much more disciplined about the way he led his life. Latha, in particular, reminded him that this was what she had been telling him all these years: be more disciplined, take things easy. He had no choice but to rest now. With his family around him—his wife and daughters, grandchildren—he allowed himself to relax and his body began to heal.

Sixteen

S oon Rajinikanth was back at work. On 24 November 2011 came the announcement of his next film *Kochadaiiyaan* (2014). It would be India's first 'performance-capture photorealistic film' along the lines of *Avatar* and *The Adventures of Tintin*.[1] The fans were not sure what this meant but they were happy that another blockbuster with the Thalaivar in the lead was being produced. But the film was delayed, embroiled in technical and financial problems, and was released only in 2014. According to rumours, the Superstar had made this film to help Soundarya, his younger daughter, establish herself as a director. Soundarya was a graphic designer who had worked on many of his films.

Kochadaiiyaan was conceived as an animation film written by K. S. Ravikumar and directed by Soundarya. The characters bore the likenesses of the actors. Rajinikanth enacted and voiced the two lead roles he played. Deepika Padukone and Shobana were the female leads. The narrative follows the quest of an eighth-century warrior who seeks revenge after witnessing the unlawful punishment administered to his father, a kind-hearted king. The film was a new experience for the Superstar. He conceded that this film was a technician's show, not an actor's, but this didn't bother him, he was proud of his daughter's directorial debut.

Kochadaiiyaan was promoted as 'a tribute to the Centennial of the Indian Cinema' and released worldwide in 3D and 2D on 23 May 2014 in Tamil and five other languages.[2] The film bombed at the box office, leaving distributors and producers with huge

---

[1] Ramachandran, *Rajinikanth*, p. 242.

[2] Available here: https://en.wikipedia.org/wiki/Kochadaiiyaan

losses. By the time the film was released, it had lost the novelty of being a computer-animated film, according to critics. More pertinently, it didn't focus on telling a compelling story, but on celebrating the legend with larger-than-life incarnations. 'A disaster from start to finish', said critic Mihir Fadnavis.[3]

Most importantly, the fans could not relate to the animated version of their Thalaivar. There was no fire in his delivery. His mesmerizing eyes that usually sparkled with life looked like glass beads. They just could not identify with the Superstar in this movie. The film was not only a flop, the controversy surrounding it haunted the Rajinikanth family for more than four years after its release.

There had been reports of a tussle between Ad Bureau Advertising, and Media One Global Entertainment, and Latha Rajinikanth.[4] Latha, one of the directors of Media One Global Entertainment Limited, had reportedly taken a loan of ₹14.9 crores from Ad Bureau Advertising, for completing the post-production of the movie. Ad Media claimed that of the ₹14.9 that was borrowed, ₹6.2 crores were left to be repaid by Media One. Legal action ensued and the case reached the Supreme Court. On February 2018, the apex court rejected Latha's claim that she was not related to Media One and ordered her, as one of the directors of Media One, to assume responsibility and fully settle the remaining amount within twelve weeks.[5] Strangely, Rajinikanth has not spoken a word about this. Surely, the whole controvesy was an embarrassment to the Superstar at a time when he had made public (on 31 December 2017) his intention to enter Tamil

---

[3]Mihir Fadnavis, 'Kochadaiiyaan review: A disaster of a film with terrible animation', *FirstPost*, 24 May 2014.

[4]ANI, 'SC questions Rajinikanth's wife over payment to Ad Firm', *Business Standard*, 3 Jul 2018.

[5]'Kochadaiiyaan row: SC pulls up Latha Rajinikanth over non-payment of dues', *India Today*, 3 Jul 2018.

Nadu politics in a big way.[6]

Y. G. Mahendran has said that Rajinikanth does not interfere with his wife's work. But this was a movie that he had acted in, and it was directed by his daughter. Surely, silence was not an option. Considering his financial worth, ₹6.2 crores would be a pittance, remarked a former fellow artist who does not want to be named. No one knows the reason behind his silence. Nor is there any clear information if the dues were paid off.

On the political front, there were big developments in 2014. The nation was getting ready for the Lok Sabha elections. The incumbent Congress-led UPA government was reeling under attacks by the BJP in the Opposition with allegations of various corruption scams, with the 2G spectrum allocation being one of the worst.

There were a lot of unexpected twists and turns that Tamil Nadu saw in the political arena at that time. Jayalalithaa, who had come back to power in the state in 2011, by winning a massive majority of 203 out of 234 seats in the assembly and had reduced the DMK to a mere 31 seats,[7] now began to campaign for the parliamentary elections with renewed energy and confidence. She seemed to be gunning for the prime ministerial post. Hoardings all over Tamil Nadu declared Jayalalithaa the prime minister in waiting. She even behaved like she was already the prime minster, making audacious decisions, though fully aware that they would not go unchallenged. She had always been a severe critic of the LTTE but now suddenly announced the release of the seven prisoners who were serving life terms in jail for the assassination of former prime minister and Congress leader Rajiv Gandhi, plotted by the LTTE. It was a highly emotive issue and she was projecting this action as a humanitarian gesture. It was a move

---

[6]'In Rajinikanth's big plan for Tamil Nadu politics, he won't be the CM face', *Hindustan Times*, 12 Mar 2020.

[7]'2011 Tamil Nadu Legislative Assembly election', Wikipedia, available here: https://en.wikipedia.org/wiki/2011_Tamil_Nadu_Legislative_Assembly_election

to embarrass the incumbent Congress led–UPA government that had been in power for ten years. It also served to score one over Karunanidhi, who had all along projected himself as the sole leader of the Tamils. Her admirers said it was a political masterstroke.[8] Her opponents were confused. (Before this, she had not taken a stand on the matter. Besides, the state had no legal right to interfere in a matter that was being handled by the CBI.) As were members of her own party—but they were caught up in her enthusiasm. The centre moved the Supreme Court against Tamil Nadu's decision on 20 February and predictably the apex court stayed Jayalalithaa's move to release the convicts.[9] She was unnerved by the development but felt the gamble had been worth it. If she were hoping to win all 40 (39 in Tamil Nadu and 1 in Puducherry) parliamentary seats in Tamil Nadu, her moves would need to be bold. And if she did sweep the polls, even if she didn't become prime minster, she could play kingmaker with the number of seats she controlled.

As the election drew closer, talk of a third front came up, an alternative to the Congress-led coalition and the BJP grouping. West Bengal chief minister Mamata Banerjee offered her support to Jayalalithaa if there was to be a third front. And if that did not materialize, and the BJP-led NDA alliance did not get the required number of seats, it would have to come to Jayalalithaa for support. Either way, she presumed, victory was hers. She said to her party workers, 'The AIADMK can make it to the Centre and redeem this nation to a new freedom. Yes, we can,'[10] she said borrowing the slogan President Barack Obama had made famous. Her supporters believed her. Rajinikanth made no comment at this time, preferring to wait and watch.

In the event, the Narendra Modi wave that swept the BJP to power swallowed Jayalalithaa's dreams, even though the AIADMK

---

[8]Vaasanthi, *The Lone Empress*, p. 311.
[9]'Supreme Court halts release of Rajiv Gandhi's killers', *Hindustan Times*, 21 Feb 2014.
[10]Vaasanthi, *The Lone Empress*, p. 324.

won 37 of the 39 seats. Rajinikanth, who is known to be a friend of Modi and the BJP, sent his congratulations to the new prime minister. Jayalalithaa's ambitious plan to play a crucial role in the formation of the government at the centre fell flat. But she was not one to regret what might have been. She was happy with her position—after all, her party was the third largest in the Lok Sabha and she was convinced that she was invincible in Tamil Nadu.

Perhaps she had forgotten the sword hanging over her head—the disproportionate assets case—that was pending in the sessions court of Karnataka. Jayalalithaa had been accused of misusing her office during her first tenure as chief minister 1991–96 to amass properties worth ₹66.65 crore and depositing the amount in proxy accounts. The case had been transferred from Tamil Nadu to Karnataka in 2003. The hearings from both the prosecution and defence had taken place. The verdict was awaited. In the past, she had been acquitted in almost all the cases filed against her, and she must have expected that she would be acquitted in this case as well. On the day the verdict was to be announced, 27 September 2014, hundreds of her party men thronged the precincts of the sessions court at Parappana Agrahara in Bangalore, ready to burst crackers to celebrate her victory. The verdict came at her like a thunderbolt. She stood convicted, and was sentenced to four years in prison, and asked to pay a fine of ₹100 crores.

Rajinikanth was perhaps shocked at the harsh judgment but he did not comment on it. Karunanidhi must have been relieved—the party felt vindicated but he cautioned his cadres not to go overboard in exhibiting their emotions, aware of how sensitive the matter was. When a reporter asked for his reaction, it was just a crisp one-liner: 'the judiciary has done its duty'.[11]

Jayalalithaa spent about twenty-one days in jail in Bangalore. During this period her entire cabinet and the senior party brass

---

[11]Ibid., p. 323.

went on religious pilgrimages or observed penance or offered special prayers to almost all the deities they could think of. The Supreme Court granted her bail on 18 October 2014 on her appeal against the conviction before the Karnataka High Court. There was jubilation in the streets and at the AIADMK party office in Chennai. Cadres burst crackers in celebration—Amma would be with them to celebrate Deepavali. They failed to understand that she had only been released on bail and was still a convict, not yet absolved of the charges against her. Once home, she did not step out of her Poes Garden residence even to wave from her balcony at her followers waiting outside the gates. It was said that she did not wish to see even senior members of the party who had assembled to welcome her. There were rumours that she was seriously ill. The twenty-one-day stay in jail must have certainly affected her health that was already said to be delicate.[12]

Rajinikanth, her neighbour, no longer had the sort of anger towards her that had repeatedly landed him in trouble. Perhaps he even felt sorry for her—a loner like him. He knew how lonely it was at the top and how much harder to suffer humiliation. At this time, Rajinikanth was busy with the shoot of his next film, *Lingaa* (2014), but he was among the first to send his greetings to her when she came out on bail. He sent her a bouquet of flowers. Once the shoot was complete, he sent her a letter. Addressing her as 'Respected Jayalalithaaji', he said he was very glad to see her, his neighbour, back home in Poes Garden. 'Always wishing you well for good health and peace', he signed off with a 'Happy Deepavali'.[13]

The Tamil Nadu unit of the BJP was confused by the gesture—they had been trying to rope him in to provide the party a popular charismatic face to make an entry into Tamil Nadu, a

---

[12]Ibid.

[13]The AIADMK head office issued it as Press Release dated 19 Oct 2014, 'with the approval of Puratchi Thalaivi Selvi J. Jayalalithaa', Karate Thiagarajan, interview with the author, 15 Mar 2018.

state where it was still struggling to make a mark. AIADMK
leaders said it was a gracious, humane gesture on his part. But
the DMK thought he had reached out so that he would face no
obstacle in the release of *Lingaa* during the Deepavali holidays. The
AIADMK was in power after all. 'Mr Rajinikanth is always keen
to protect the business interest of his films and never gets caught
in political quagmire ahead of the release of any of his films,' said
a producer (requesting anonymity), with an understanding nod.
A senior BJP leader of the state said to me that Rajinikanth's
letter was a signal to the party that he was not willing to jump
into the political fray anytime soon.

Lingaa, directed by K. S. Ravikumar and produced by Rockline
Entertainment, was made on an ambitious budget 'in excess of
₹100 crore'[14]. After *Enthiran's* stupendous run,[15] producers came
to believe that investing in Rajinikanth was sure to give them
huge returns. *Lingaa* was released on Rajinikanth's birthday, 12
December 2014. On that day, he was nowhere to be seen.

It was believed that he would usually leave for Bangalore the
night before his birthday so that he could be in the sanctum
sanctorum of the Gangadheeshvara temple at Gavipuram in the
early hours of the morning to receive the Lord's blessings.[16] This
year as well, Rajnikanth went to visit the temple on his birthday.
Early in the morning, it was still dark and the wind a little chilly.
The priest, Somasundara Dikshit, his childhood friend, waited for
Shivaji to arrive incognito. Rajinikanth beamed at Somasundara
but refrained from hugging the priest, who had undergone the
necessary ablutions. Wearing the special 'pure' dhoti and a silk
angavastram over his bare shoulders, the priest alone was authorized
to enter the sanctum sanctorum to perform the pujas. When they

---

[14]K. R. Balasubramanyam, 'Why Rajnikanth handpicked Rockline to produce
"Lingaa"', *Economic Times*, 24 Nov 2014.
[15]Raja Sekar, '2.0: Revisiting Shankar's Enthiran and how Rajinikanth became India's
most loved superhero Chitti', *FirstPost*, 29 Nov 2019.
[16]Rohini (journalist), interview with the author, Bangalore, 20 Jun 2018.

were very young, Soma's father had been the priest and Soma would give Rajini a generous portion of the pongal or sajjige prasadam. Now Somasundara chanted the prayers and beseeched the Lord to bless his friend Shivaji. Somasundara believes that Shivaji is blessed. How else could a child who was always hungry, always asking for food, have risen to such heights? When Shivaji was a young boy waiting for the prasadam to be distributed, Soma's heart would fill with pity and love. Now as he watched Shivaji with his head bent and eyes closed before the deity, he was overcome with emotion. He was not sure if it was pride or happiness that filled his heart. Shivaji then walked to the priest's house, climbed the narrow flight of stairs and entered the hall that had an old sofa. Shivaji did not seem to be in a hurry and chatted with Somasundara, drinking the coffee that Soma's wife gave him in a steel tumbler. Shivaji felt at home in this modest house that smelt of flowers, camphor, and sacred ash. He was at ease, as if he had forgotten that it was a big day—the day of his film's release.

Somasundara is a much sought-after priest, often visited by political leaders from the BJP who came to the temple. There are framed pictures on the wall of leaders like Ananth Kumar and Subramanian Swamy standing before Somasundara as if seeking his blessings. There are none of his friend Shivaji. Soma respects his friend's request not to put up one.[17] Shivaji left as quietly and unnoticed as he came. He did not think about his film, *Lingaa*. He would worry about it once he reached Chennai.

Unfortunately, *Lingaa* failed. Its storyline was confused, built around an anecdote of the building of a dam during the British Raj. Perhaps if the movie had stuck to historical details and had not been a vehicle for the antics of its Superstar, it might have been reasonably watchable. The film did not even break even. Distributors who claimed they had lost a lot of money threatened

---

[17]Author's recreation based on interview with Somasundara Dikshit, 20 Jun 2018.

to go on a hunger strike at Rajinikanth's door. Rajinikanth paid them a third of their demands, says Ashok, which came to ₹10 crore and more to each of them.[18]

---

[18]Ashok, interview with the author, 27 Jun 2018.

Seventeen

It was August 2015. Rajinikanth was excited about his next venture. *Kabali* was to be directed by the young director Pa. Ranjith, who had won critical acclaim for his debut film *Attakathi* (2012) and a political film *Madras* (2014). Rajinikanth was impressed with the young man's passion both for the form and content of the film he had in mind. At times he sounded more like an activist than a film director. But in his films, he camouflaged any political message by the clever use of his craft. Pa. Ranjith reminded Rajinikanth of his friend Ashok who was an activist. Whenever they met in Bangalore, Ashok would frequently bring up the issue of corruption in the political system. Although a very talented actor, Ashok didn't get a good break in films. But at heart he was an activist more than he had ever been an actor. He ran an organization—Karnataka Film Artists, Workers and Technicians Union—to represent film technicians; he had organized protest marches of farmers' rights organizations (Raitha Sangha). He spoke eloquently of the issues he was involved with. From the late 90s onwards, his plea had always been: 'Let us build an honest society based on self-respect, self-reliance, humility, simplicity, truth and non-violence'. would repeatedly say in Kannada 'system kettogithe'—the system is spoilt[1]—a phrase Rajinikanth would repeat in Tamil later when he announced his intention to enter Tamil Nadu politics.

Ashok bemoaned the fact that he did not have the money needed to enter politics and fight an election. But he knew that his friend did: 'Shivaji, you have earned enough; you must give

---

[1]Ashok, interview with the author, 27 Jun 2018.

something back to the people who have helped you reach this height. You can achieve something only if you have political power!'[2]

In any case, getting involved in politics in Tamil Nadu, which is filled with veteran leaders in various parties, would be a fool's errand. These lifelong politicians have a thorough knowledge of the state and its history and culture. His Tamil friends like Cho Ramaswamy urged him to take the plunge. But he hesitated. He thought the idea was preposterous. He had heard that when Karunanidhi was asked why he would not enter national politics, he retorted saying, 'I know my height.' Rajini cannot compete with him.

Ashok advised him to wait for the opportune moment. 'You are getting old too.' Rajinikanth knew that, of course. He trusts his friend's instincts more than that of anyone in Tamil Nadu. Ashok was his political guru.

'But in the meanwhile, try to act in films that will bring a new dimension to your persona,' Ashok suggested. He believed that would attract new segments of the Tamil society.[3]

When Rajinikanth heard the story of *Kabali* from Pa. Ranjith, he knew that this movie will help him expand his image, and connect him with more sections of society. It is unfortunate that Pa. Ranjith is referred to as a Dalit director, as if that were his only qualification. Ashok, who is an Ambedkarite, was doubly happy that Rajinikanth's next project was with Pa. Ranjith.

'All this is important for your future,' he assured his friend. Rajini wondered if Ashok overestimated his ability.[4]

Frankly, Rajinikanth wanted to work with Ranjith because of his talent and sharp intellect. There was a spark in his eyes, a hunger that was captivating. The shoot was to take place mostly in Malaysia, Bangkok, and Hong Kong.

---

[2]Ibid.
[3]Ibid.
[4]Ibid.

In the midst of all the hectic preparations for the overseas shooting schedule, Rajinikanth heard about a dramatic swing in Jayalalithaa's fortunes. On 11 May 2015, the Karnataka High Court acquitted her and others in the disproportionate wealth case. He was happy that he had sent his greetings when she came home on bail. She surely appeared blessed. But he also heard that there was a strange silence next door, at Jayalalithaa's residence in Poes Garden. There should have been great jubilation and celebration, but she puzzled everyone, including her cabinet ministers by refusing to give them an audience. All she did was make a statement to the press: 'The verdict gives me immense satisfaction. It has been established that I am innocent. Let my political foes stop their vicious schemes against me. I thank all the party men and women and the cadres who prayed for me.'

She stayed in her room. The ministers waited with huge flower bouquets, and when there was no response from the Thalaivi, went back silently not saying a word. The bouquets remained piled up in the living room. She perhaps feared that the Opposition might bring a stay order to the verdict, which was considered by the media and the public as most controversial. It had the potential to be challenged in the Supreme Court. But she would, in the next few months, stand for election from her R. K. Nagar constituency and win handsomely to be sworn in again as the chief minister of Tamil Nadu. *The Hindu* editorial termed it, 'A sensational comeback' and said that 'the resurrection of Jayalalithaa is extraordinary—no politician has been reinstated after losing power twice.'[5]

Rajinikanth thought her silence was strange. He was aware that thousands of her followers had gathered in front of her gates on hearing the incredible verdict. Their prayers were answered and not merely she—*they* were blessed. They danced, they sang, and shouted slogans praising her and proclaiming their loyalty to her.

---

[5]Vaasanthi, *The Lone Empress*, p. 328.

They would be loyal to her even if the verdict were against her. They never believed their Amma was guilty. They waited for their leader to come out, acknowledge their love, and wave from her balcony but there was no sign of her. However, Rajinikanth did not have the time to ponder over the matter and left for Malaysia to shoot for his movie.

The story of *Kabali* revolves around a gang war between Kabali and Tony Lee. Kabali (Rajinikanth), a Kuala Lumpur-based don, has just been released from prison where he has spent twenty-five years on the false charge of starting a massacre at a local temple that killed many including his own wife. Kabali was the protégé of Tamilnesan, a don who fought for the rights of the Tamil Malaysians. The old don was also a stickler for certain rules and banned the gang from getting involved in activities such as drugs and prostitution. A gang member, Veera, who does not care for these strictures, kills Tamilnesan. Kabali takes charge of the gang after his mentor's death but Veera creates trouble between the old don's son and Kabali, leading to Kabali getting attacked and his wife being killed. Once Kabali is released from jail, he takes charge of his gang, determined to get revenge on Veera. He hears that his wife and daughter may be alive and so tries to find them, indulging in more gang wars along the way. The other storyline deals with the issue of the rights of the Malaysian Tamils (who are portrayed as Dalits).

The film took around eight months to shoot. In the meanwhile, the political arena in Tamil Nadu underwent many changes. Jayalalithaa had finally stopped being a recluse and bounced back to activity. Having won the by-election in June 2015, she was back as chief minister. The assembly elections were less than a year away in May 2016. All the schemes and projects that had stalled during her absence in jail were launched. She was still operating from her residence, but the government was taking action. She was ignoring the fact that her acquittal was being appealed in the Supreme Court. That was a long process in any case and governance and fighting elections needed to continue. Equally, she was ignoring the charges of rampant corruption in her government. The verdict that acquitted her seemed to have whitewashed her alleged sins completely. Moreover, she knew that if there were in fact instances of corruption in the bureaucracy and in the government, the people would not blame her. The welfare schemes that she had launched—all bearing her name, Amma—had improved the quality of life of the common people. Amma was their well-wisher, redeemer, and saviour.

However, despite putting on a brave face, the chief minister was dealing with health problems. There was no public information about this, but it became clear that all was not well with her. In November–December 2015, the Coromandel coast was devastated by floods. In Tamil Nadu, several low-lying areas were flooded, hundreds died, and many lakhs of people were displaced. The flooding in Chennai was severe. At this time, the government needed to take swift and decisive action. But it seemed Jayalalithaa was too ill to direct her ministers. She was not able to react promptly. Her ministers, who were used to taking their orders from her, were paralysed. She finally managed to act and prevent further damage. But the DMK, under the leadership of Karunanidhi's son, Stalin, grabbed the chance to blame the government's inefficiency.

The assembly elections were approaching, and the main opposition party, the DMK, was confident that Jayalalithaa would be defeated due to the anti-incumbency factor. But Jayalalithaa, sure of her popularity, decided to contest all 234 seats in the 2016 elections without an alliance. She no longer feared the Opposition or the DMK leader, Karunanidhi. They had been at war for many years, but he was now over ninety years old and no longer had the strength for a drawn-out fight.

Karunanidhi tried his best to ally with as many parties as possible to form a united opposition. A new group came together at this time, called the Makkal Nala Koottani (MNK)—there were rumours that Jayalalithaa was behind this front. MNK consisted of the Dalit party Viduthalai Chiruthaigal Katchi, the Marumalarchi Dravida Munnetra Kazhagam, and the Left parties under the leadership of actor Vijayakanth's Desiya Murpokku Dravida Kazhagam (DMDK). The MNK drew a blank in the elections that followed but split the votes of the DMK, preventing it from getting a majority. Jayalalithaa's AIADMK managed to get a majority (134 seats) and formed the government once again. The DMK-Congress combine lost by less than 2 per cent of the votes and sat in the Opposition with a commendable strength of 97 seats. The AIADMK coming back to power was a stupendous achievement—the only time a party had overcome the anti-incumbency factor was during the time of MGR.

When Rajinikanth returned from the shoot of *Kabali* to the news of the election result, he was astonished. He could not help but admire Jayalalithaa's iron will and determination and her firm grip over the party. This time around, however, she seemed to have mellowed. She was sixty-eight years old after all. She made a dignified speech thanking the voters as well as her party cadres who made the victory possible. She said with utter humility: 'Makkalaal naan, makkalukkaagave naan—I am because of the people. I am only for the people.'

Rajinikanth had once said to her that she came to power because of poor people and because of circumstances, not because of her effort. He must have seen how wrong he had been. It was not luck that raised her to that level. It was her effort, her intelligence, her strategy. Even if Rajinikanth had been in the country at the time of the elections, it's doubtful if he would have lent his support to the DMK.

Kabali released on 22 July 2016. The movie, produced by Kalaipuli Dhanu who gave him the moniker 'Superstar', was hyped to a great degree and the fans' expectations reached fever pitch. Sadanand Menon writes: 'In the past few years, film after film starring Rajinikanth has flopped, despite the huge euphoria and media build-up preceding it. *Baba, Sivaji, Kuselan,* and *Enthiran* formed a chain of flops. Which is why *Kabali* was anticipated with such excitement. This was to be a do or die moment for both Tamil cinema and its global audience. Director Pa. Ranjith has played a deft trick in the film by subduing Rajini's personal stylistics and on-screen antics to pave the way for an explicit theme of social justice and for restoring dignity to Dalits'.[6] While *Kabali* is an emotional roller coaster with enough Rajini-style masala, it's not clear if the social message embedded in it was received. The song 'Neruppuda!' (Fire!) ignited Rajini fans, and his dialogue delivery gave them the chills, but it's doubtful whether they fully endorsed his role as a spokesperson of the Dalits.

Menon speculates on how the film could impact Rajini's fan base. 'It opens out two options for Rajini—either of being redeemed or of self-destructing.' He goes on to say that his fan base is 'not rooted in the social justice ideas of Ambedkar or Periyar Ramaswamy Naicker. On the contrary, this is a population that believes in maintaining caste distinctions.... The Tamil film audience, which depends on an iconized Rajini to valorize the "rakshasa" aspect of their pathology—endorsing all their cultural negatives—will resist this "politicized" Rajini who ends up critiquing his own fan base in the film.... However, he might actually end up becoming a Dalit icon and a new emblem on the side of Dalit assertion.'[7]

That is perhaps stretching it too far, but if that did happen and if he had contested the elections—especially since Rajini went on to act in *Kaala* (2018) directed by Pa. Ranjith which is more pronouncedly about Dalit rights—it could have created an interesting twist in the electoral politics of Tamil Nadu. Film critic Bharadwaj Rangan says, 'The meat of *Kabali* is a gangster story that attempts to tease out some history about Malaysian Tamils. ...Ranjith is an intriguing filmmaker. On the one hand

[6]Sadanand Menon, 'How Rajinikanth might become the new emblem of Dalit assertion', *Hindustan Times*, 1 Aug 2016.
[7]Ibid.

he seems to load his films with Dalit subtext. On the other hand, he makes sure that it is all just subtext.'[8]

Rajinikanth had no fear that his fans would switch gears. They were not interested in his political ideology about which he was not clear himself. In any case, the film was released and the producers claimed that it was a commercial hit, although figures have been difficult to verify.

But he was happy with the new image he had created for himself. He was pleased that his friends, especially Ashok, whose opinion he valued on these matters, also liked the film.

On the political front, Jayalalithaa was back in power but according to rumours, she hardly attended office. The files were mounting and important decisions pending. *Ananda Vikatan*, the popular Tamil weekly, carried an exhaustive article that held that her stay in prison must have taken a toll on her health. There was no rejoinder from her Poes Garden house to this. She participated in the flag-hoisting ceremony to celebrate Independence Day on 15 August. People observed that she appeared to be walking slowly, with measured steps. She showed no obvious signs of exhaustion or illness. A month later, on 22 September, Rajinikanth heard that Jayalalithaa had been admitted to the ICU of Apollo hospital. His household staff often gossiped about the goings-on in the chief minster's house. But he decided to ignore that. He heard that Jayalalithaa, a diabetic, never took insulin shots and was not careful with her diet. He saw something of himself in her. He too, had once been careless with himself, full of such conceit. He had come to his senses only when death knocked at his door. He thought it would give her a knock and cause her to change her ways. She was a strong woman.

Special prayers were offered in temples all over the state. Rajinikanth marvelled at the irony. Jayalalithaa was a believer

---

[8]Baradwaj Rangan, 'An unsatisfying clash between impulses of a director and a star', *The Hindu*, 24 Jul 2016.

and she made no secret of it though she led a party that was an offshoot of the Dravidian movement that had been formed on atheistic ideals. But mystery surrounded the health bulletins that were issued. VIPs who tried to visit her in the hospital were turned away. Journalists grumbled that Jayalalithaa's aide and friend Sasikala was controlling even the police and the doctors and preventing the truth from leaking out. What was happening? Rajinikanth too was intrigued but stayed away from this. The strong woman, who had once been feared, now appeared pathetic and vulnerable.

Rajinikanth left for Bangalore. During the trips into the jungles with his friends Ashok, Raj Bahadur, and Raghunandan, he spoke about the sad state of affairs in Tamil Nadu. Governance had come to a screeching halt; there were reports of blatant corruption; rumours of secret plots and schemes in the corridors of power; and ministers were circumambulating the sanctums of the gods, doing penance to save the life of their Amma. Rajinikanth was upset by the state of affairs. His friends fell silent. After a long pause, Ashok said, 'Shivaji now is the time for you to think. If something happens to her, there is going to be a vacuum in Tamil Nadu politics.'[9]

9Ashok, interview with the author, Bangalore, 10 Jun 2018.

Eighteen

When *Kabali* was released in July 2016, Rajinikanth expected that it would get the same sort of reception that his other blockbusters had. He thought it would run in theatres for months and that his fan base would go back to watch it show after show. It was not to be. On 23 April, it was reported that the film had completed 275 days at a theatre in Madurai,[1] but the film was not successful anywhere else. Although there were reports that it grossed ₹262 crores in its total collection, the figures were disputed. Figures given in December 2016 by the *Financial Express* indicated an estimated domestic gross of ₹215 crore and an international gross of ₹262 crores for a worldwide total of ₹477 crore.[2] Critics were not impressed, saying that this film was neither a regular Rajini film nor what one might expect from Pa. Ranjith. It looked like they were both testing the waters and experimenting with something that was new to them. The movie didn't catch the interest of even die-hard fans. After the first couple of showings, they didn't go back.

In September that year, Jayalalithaa had been admitted to the ICU at Apollo Hospital. And now the drama was on the streets. Beyond the police barricades around the hospital, could be heard the cries, chants, and prayers of her loyal followers. But the police frequently shooed them away. Rumour was that they were taking their orders from Sasikala, Jayalalithaa's friend

---

[1]Aravind Sundaram, 'An Astonishing Feat by Kabali!', *Behind Woods*, 23 Apr 2017.
[2]See FP Staff, 'Rajinikanth's Kabali has earned ₹600 crore at the global box office. Or has it?' *FirstPost*, 3 Aug 2016 and FE Online, 'Rajinikanth starrer Kabali box office collections rise to over ₹650 crore, turns No. 1 movie in India', *Financial Express*, 2 Aug 2016.

and aide. The chief minister had referred to her as 'udanpirava sagothari' (sister though not born of the same womb). The men and women of AIADMK were unhappy with this development. They kept vigil day and night all around the hospital, making it difficult for other patients and their caregivers to move around. Jayalalithaa had been in the ICU for more than a month, but no one knew what her condition was. The hospital bulletins were confusing and no doctor would speak to a journalist. The cabinet ministers and senior members of the party made routine visits to the hospital in their starched snow-white veshtis and shirts. With their heads bent, they would visit Sasikala and then go away, refusing to speak with members of the press. It was well known that Jayalalithaa had an iron grip over members of her party. It was rather amazing that this power had shifted easily and completely to Sasikala. Journalists who had contacts within the party said that the ministers were just as terrified of Chinnamma (as Sasikala was known) as they had been of Amma. Apparently, they felt beholden to her because it was she who had chosen their names as candidates during the assembly elections since Jayalalithaa had already been in poor health at the time.

Rajinikanth heard all these reports and rumours and was baffled. He marvelled at the power that Jayalalithaa's aide had acquired. Moreover, he was upset that regular patients who had to access the hospital were made to face difficulties. There was no information on what ailed the chief minister. What was the illness that had her stay in hospital for more than a month? If it was that serious, why wasn't she being shifted to a hospital in the US or Singapore as it happened with other VIPs? Rajinikanth reached out to those he knew in the government and asked what was really happening, but got no answer.

It was a strange time. Cho Ramaswamy, Rajinikanth's friend, who had been a close friend of Jayalalithaa's as well, was himself grievously ill and had been admitted in the same hospital. (He died on 7 December in the hospital, a day after Jayalalithaa's death.)

Karunanidhi was also unwell and was being treated in Kauvery Hospital. The shadow of gloom and death seemed to be hovering over Tamil Nadu. The people were waiting with concern to see how things would turn out. With both the powerful leaders of the state in bad health, perhaps dying, the political situation became fraught. Over the past few years, the schism within the DMK had been growing. Karunanidhi's sons, Stalin and Alagiri, as well as his daughter, Kanimozhi, were all well-established leaders with their own political careers. But there had been many hiccups.

In 2011, Kanimozhi, who was a member of Rajya Sabha, was arrested as co-accused in the controversial 2G scam and sent to Tihar Jail in Delhi. She spent six months in prison before she got bail.

In 2014, as Karunanidhi, the patriarch of the DMK party, was ageing, his sons Alagiri and Stalin, started to flex their muscles. Each thought they deserved to be the next leader of the party. Alagiri was short-tempered, brash, and jealous of his younger brother. Stalin, who began his political career as the leader of the youth wing of the DMK, was being nurtured as the successor to his father. Aware of the brewing trouble between the brothers, Karunanidhi tried to balance the power tussle by giving Alagiri charge of the southern regions, keeping him away from Chennai, which was Stalin's base. He even got Alagiri a ministerial berth in the centre when the DMK was in coalition with the ruling Congress. But nothing seemed to appease Alagiri. He abused Stalin in public and defied the warnings of the high command. He was suspended from the party in January 2014 for 'anti-party activities and speaking against his younger brother who was considered by many as the forerunner to take over the party from his father'. Karunanidhi revealed that Alagiri had barged into his room and hurled abuse at Stalin and said his brother would die soon. 'No father can tolerate such behaviour,' he said to the press.[3]

---

[3]Sangeetha Kandavel, 'MK Alagiri expelled from DMK', *Economic Times*, 26 Mar 2014.

Alagiri who was considered a political heavyweight in the southern parts of Tamil Nadu, especially in Madurai, denied all this, but did little to mend his ways. On the other hand, he was seen openly talking to rivals and meeting national leaders.[4] He dared to speak against the party's stand and aired divergent views on the issue of forging an alliance with actor Vijayakanth's DMDK. The *Economic Times* reported: 'The move [to expel Alagiri] comes after leaders from Congress (Bharath Natchiyappan), BJP (H. Raja) and MDMK (Vaiko) knocked on Alagiri's doors seeking support. Alagiri has also openly supported BJP's Narendra Modi becoming the prime minister.'[5] The veteran leader wanted to show that he would not spare his own son if he violated the party's norms of kadamai, kanniyam, kattuppadu—duty, decency, and restraint.

Rajini felt sorry for the old man. So, when Alagiri asked to meet Rajinikanth, on 14 March, the Superstar must have felt uncomfortable. The 2014 Lok Sabha elections were scheduled to be held from 7 April to 12 May. Rajini was worried that he would be asked for advice about matters that concerned the Karunanidhi family. Or, perhaps, Alagiri was planning to float a new party for which he wanted Rajinikanth's support. Or he might ask him to lend his support to Narendra Modi. Rajinikanth was known to be a friend of Modi and close to the BJP. But he wanted to distance himself from these matters. He had great respect for Karunanidhi and felt bad about the difficult times that the family was going through. In any case, he could not refuse to meet Alagiri who, film journalists say, is close to the Superstar. Alagiri was shrewd enough to be careful. He came to Rajinikanth's house with his son, Durai Dhayanidhi, who had been in film production and distribution since 2008 and was considered successful.

Their meeting lasted for half an hour. Though the details of what they discussed will never be known, it can be assumed

---

[4]Ibid.
[5]Ibid.

that Alagiri put forward his case with great emotion and fervour. Alagiri was like Duryodhana from the Mahabharata—a character who personified anger and jealousy. It was a role that Rajinikanth had played with great passion a long while back.

After the meeting, Alagiri addressed the media waiting outside Rajinikanth's house and said he came to meet Rajinikanth for 'peace of mind'. 'No, I did not discuss politics with him,' he clarified. 'Rajini is my old friend. I came here to inquire about his health.'[6]

But according to reporters who were following this story, Alagiri's followers made statements that Alagiri went to persuade Rajinikanth to enter politics. If Vijayakanth could manage to get 8 per cent of the vote share in his very first political entry, Rajinikanth, with his massive fan base that cuts across caste and religion, could easily muster much more. Alagiri's supporters claimed that 40 per cent of the DMK party was behind him. With his support Rajinikanth could sweep the polls. There was no comment from Rajinikanth. There was no further move from Alagiri—his influence in the South had diminished considerably after his expulsion, but DMK sources said he asked his men to work for the defeat of the party during the 2016 Tamil Nadu assembly elections. The DMK lost to the AIADMK by less than 2 per cent in these elections.

Two years had passed since Alagiri met Rajinikanth for a confidential talk. Now that the leaders of both the Dravidian parties were bedridden, speculations were rife. Leaders in waiting were making plans for succession. Tamil Nadu appeared to be on the verge of a great crisis. But the elected government had just come to power five months earlier. Rajini did not make any statement on the political situation. He became busy with his next film, *2.0* (2018), a sequel to the 2010 *Enthiran*. The plan was to release it in mid-May 2018 but it was eventually released on 29

---

[6]Ramasubramanian, 'Alagiri meets Rajinikanth, denies discussing politics', *India Today*, 14 Mar 2014.

November 2018. It was another mega-budget film directed by Shankar—with unbelievable figures being quoted for the budget. According to *Outlook*, it was produced on an estimated budget of ₹600 crore—'the most expensive Indian film to date'.[7] Whatever the cost of the film, Shankar was a magician. Not only could he create magic on-screen, but the collection was reported to be three times that of the sum invested. The film made nearly ₹520 crore in its opening weekend to become the second highest grossing film in India.[8] Exactly a month after its release, *India Today* reported on 28 December 2018: 'According to trade analysts, the film has raked in about 700 crore.'[9]

Around this time, Rajinikanth was getting ready for the production of *Kaala* (2018), directed by Pa. Ranjith. Reviewers and analysts were intrigued—they thought it was a daring choice for the director and the star to team up again. Pa. Ranjith, who has a very clear political ideology, appeared to be using Rajinikanth's immense popularity to get the message out. Having taken Ashok's advice on board, Rajinikanth was looking to explore new aspects of his public persona. Critics wondered who was using whom.[10] Rajini knew his existing fans would never desert him. What he needed to do was win over a new segment of people. In Tamil Nadu, the Dalits are split into three prominent groups and are not unified under a single leader. Rajini, an outsider and a popular icon, was above caste. No doubt many Dalits were also members of his fan clubs. But to get their votes in an election, a new strategy had to be devised. Ashok seemed to be watching Tamil Nadu politics with keen anticipation. He also seemed certain that this was the time for Rajinikanth to take the plunge.

Rajinikanth threw himself into the two projects at hand—

---

[7]'2.0 Made On A Lavish Budget Of ₹600 Crore: Rajinikanth', *Outlook*, 3 Nov 2018.

[8]'Top All Time India Grossers All Formats—2.0 Second', *Box Office India*, 20 Dec 2018.

[9]'2.0 box office collection day 19: Rajinikanth-Akshay Kumar film on its way to ₹1000 crore', *India Today*, 18 Dec 2018.

[10]Prof. Srinivas, interview with the author, 18 Jun 2018.

the movies were nearly polar opposites. Shankar's *2.0* was a fun, light, science fiction story. Pa. Ranjith's *Kaala* was full of passion and fury. Film critic Baradwaj Rangan wrote: 'This is a story about land.... A "social issue" is so often reduced to an easy target, so the hero can deliver clap-worthy punch dialogues about exploitation.' But Ranjith's *Kaala* is different, he goes on. 'If Mani Ratnam looked at the *Mahabharata*, Ranjith takes his inspiration from the *Ramayana*—though not the traditional versions.' Ranjith's hero is Ravana. 'In a stretch towards the end...we are told that each time a head of Ravana's fell, a new one would take its place. The subtext is absolutely revolutionary for a film with a megastar like Rajinikanth. It's not about a single hero. It's about a people's movement, where if the hero falls, someone else will rush to take his place and continue his work.'[11]

Dharavi, Mumbai, had been recreated on the film sets, and peopled with actors. But as he donned the role of Kaala, the protector, the patriarch of the people of the slums of Dharavi, Rajinikanth became one of them—he felt their pain, admired their sense of dignity, their warmth, and simple pleasures, their awareness of their rights, their anger at its denial. All through his film career he had lived in make-believe worlds of phantoms and fantasies, but such was the magic that Ranjith created that the Superstar experienced a whole new world.

Once the shoot for the films was over, Rajinikanth began paying attention to current events and developments. On 5 December 2016, Apollo Hospital officially announced that Jayalalithaa had had a cardiac arrest and died in the night. There appeared to be a lot of secrecy not only around her illness but also the time of her death. From this point on, things in Tamil Nadu got more bizarre. Is this what prompted Rajinikanth to decide to enter politics? Was it his conscience or the words of his friend, Ashok, that pushed him to make the decision?

---

[11]Baradwaj Rangan, 'Kaala Movie Review', *Film Companion*, 7 Jun 2018.

Nineteen

In December 2016, following the death of Jayalalithaa, the chief minister, the shenanigans in the AIADMK, the ruling party, descended into a shameless farce, openly staged by one whose voice had never been heard before; one who had remained backstage in the party that was run by Jayalalithaa with an iron hand. With the hand gone, buried under the earth, the party looked brittle, ready to crumble at any moment. Jayalalithaa's legacy was being contested by Sasikala whom Jayalalithaa had endearingly called 'her sister though not born of the same womb'.

The ascendance of O. Panneerselvam (OPS), a Jayalalithaa loyalist, as chief minister after the death of the leader should have been smooth and legitimate—the humble OPS had been the caretaker chief minister chosen by Jayalalithaa when she had been jailed twice. After taking charge, he had indeed performed his duties with diligence. He had made trips to Delhi to get permission for an ordinance to bypass the judicial ban on jallikattu, the traditional sport involving bulls, winning the affection and admiration of the Tamil people, including opposition parties. He had gone to Hyderabad for a congenial meeting on water sharing. But now, most unexpectedly, he had to contend with a new challenger—Sasikala, who had so far been Jayalalithaa's aide and companion, but had not been given any official post in the party by the Thalaivi. Now she seemed to be aiming to occupy the chair that the leader had occupied! When a shocked OPS realized that Sasikala was making her move and questioned her decisions, he was called a rebel. The people of Tamil Nadu were appalled by the open power struggle that unfolded and grew murkier by the day, feeding the hungry press. Rajinikanth was bewildered and disgusted by Sasikala's theatrics. So far, she had stayed in Jayalalithaa's shadow and he had barely even noticed her.

OPS had been surveying the ravages of an oil spill along the coast of Ennore when he was called to Poes Garden, which Sasikala had taken over, and told that Chinnamma was going to be elected chief minister in his place by the legislators of the AIADMK. The signatures of MLAs had already been collected, he was told, and he had to abdicate once again. But then he was used to that. He was not one to rebel against orders from the party leadership but this was a humiliating blow. Dedicated and humble he might be, but OPS was also a shrewd politician who knew how to use optics. He went to Marina Beach and sat in meditation at Amma's memorial. He emerged after an hour and addressed the press. 'I came to Amma's memorial as my conscience hurt me. I wish to put forth some truths before the people and cadre, because Amma's soul asked me to do so.'[1] That was a powerful metaphor to the Tamils, who had strong beliefs about the wishes of the dead, about commitment and loyalty. But Amma's spirit could not help OPS against Sasikala's Machiavellian ploys. She had adroitly stepped into Jayalalithaa's shoes as AIADMK general secretary, started wearing her benefactor's Iyengar naamam, her hair in a bun, travelled in her cars, and operated from 36, Poes Garden. She was calling the shots with the authority that she claimed the late chief minister had passed on to her. But she could not get everyone to do her bidding. The Governor of Tamil Nadu, C. Vidyasagar Rao, went missing when he was to swear her in on 7 December 2016,[2] two days after the AIADMK party elected her as its leader, a post traditionally held by the party general secretary. Sasikala had made all the preparations for the swearing-in ceremony at the nineteenth-century campus of the Madras University facing the Marina Beach. It was an audacious decision considering what

---

[1]'O Panneerselvam breaks silence: Full text of speech', *New Indian Express*, 8 Feb 2017.
[2]Anna Isaac, 'Missing in action: Is Governor Vidyasagar Rao's absence contributing to TN's political turmoil?', *News Minute*, 16 Jun 2017.

she was up against. The judgment in the disproportionate assets case was pending—she would go to jail if she were convicted. People had also been whispering about her role in Jayalalithaa's death. Further, there was widespread discontentment in the state regarding her shockingly swift rise in politics.

But more audacious things were going to happen. OPS was trying to prove that he had the numbers in the assembly. Sasikala, frustrated that the governor was refusing to let her take the chief minister's post, transported the MLAs to the Golden Bay Resort at Koovathur just outside Chennai to prevent them from moving over into OPS's camp. Although they were prisoners of a sort, the MLAs had a gala time, eating good food, watching movies, and listening to Sasikala's passionate speeches.[3]

But everything changed when on 14 February 2017, the long-awaited verdict of the Supreme Court convicted Sasikala in the disproportionate assets case, upholding the Special Court's verdict, in which Jayalalithaa was also convicted as prime accused.[4] She had to leave almost at once for Bangalore and surrender. But she got in a parting shot by appointing Edappadi Palaniswami, who was her supporter, as chief minister in place of OPS. Rajinikanth's words that 'the system has become rotten'[5] were more apt than ever before.

So, would this not be the perfect moment to announce his arrival on the political arena? But he was not the only one with political ambitions. There were a few others too surging into the fray with a sharp sense of timing—no, not to fish in troubled waters, to cleanse the system, trust them. The people of Tamil Nadu never had it so good. There was not a dull moment for

---

[3]Deepu Sebastian Edmond, 'Not forced to stay at resort: AIADMK MLAs', *The Hindu*, 11 Feb 2017.
[4]Krishnadas Rajagopal, 'Sasikala convicted in DA case; can't contest elections for 10 years', *The Hindu*, 14 Feb 2017.
[5]Udhav Naig, 'Tamil Nadu has good leaders but the system is rotten, says Rajinikanth', *The Hindu,* 19 May 2017.

the man in the street. Jayalalithaa, the powerful and most feared leader of the AIADMK, was dead; Karunanidhi, the indisputable leader and president of the DMK was ninety-three, ailing, and had lost his ability to speak—his most lethal weapon.

The epic battle between the indefatigable film scriptwriter Karunanidhi and the former actor and relentless fighter Jayalalithaa—leaders of the two Dravidian parties that engaged the history of the state for more than two decades—had come to an end. Political analysts had predicted that with the death of Jayalalithaa, the imperious queen who had an astonishing hold on the Tamil masses, and her party, Tamil Nadu would lose its colour and verve; they too, were in for a surprise. The theatre was back. The symbiotic relationship between cinema and Tamil politics is still alive. The second and third generation cinema heroes who had had a great innings in the silver screen are the entertainers in the street, some bold, confident, some egoistic but hesitant, some adventurous, testing the waters. They look in the mirror, their constant companion in their profession, and hear, as King Janaka did, the grey hair growing out of their ears whispering: 'Hey, you are getting old.'

Kamal Haasan, for instance. Rajinikanth's long-time rival, who is just four years younger than the Superstar, decided that this was time to take the plunge into politics. Kamal had stayed apolitical for the most part, but months after the death of Jayalalithaa, took to social media to criticize the ruling AIADMK and to bring up the issue of corruption in the government. When challenged by the party, who questioned his knowledge of governance and politics, he dropped hints that he might enter the arena himself. Rajini fans were worried. Kamal looked set to enter the race—he might topple their hopes for the Superstar. Kamal Haasan is known as a cerebral filmmaker. And in his nascent political outings, he used high-brow language, quoted English scholars, and foreign filmmakers that the earthy Tamil people were not familiar with. He met the chief ministers of other states and caught the attention of the nation. He was tech-savvy and launched a phone app to facilitate anti-corruption activism. The media thronged to him; the national English channels loved interviewing him in English. 'The entry of Kamal Haasan in Tamil Nadu politics is exciting', the NDTV news anchor gushed. But it was far from clear what he intended to do.

Thalaivar could sense the urgency in the cries of his fans— Ezunthu vaa, Thalaiva (Get up, leader). March ahead. They were behind him all the way. They were also worried that there were more movie stars waiting in the wings to establish their political credentials as well, like the boyish looking Vijay, who has a massive following among the youth. They had started speaking—through their films or on public platforms and were more articulate. But Rajini fans knew that anyone else was but a dewdrop that would vanish when the sun came up. To them, he was the sun, the one who could bring sense to the prevailing madness.

As is well known, there has been a great social churning in Tamil Nadu due to the Dravidian movement and the result has been the resurgence of various marginalized sections, each of them vociferous, and all of them looking for a single charismatic leader—one whom they can trust. This is especially true after the passing of dominant leaders like Kamaraj, Rajaji, Annadurai, MGR, Karunanidhi, and Jayalalithaa. Rajinikanth, his fans think, represents the marginalized. They have seen him donning this role in so many of his films—*Muthu, Annamalai, Padayappa, Arunachalam, Thalapathi, Kabali*—the innocent young man, cheated and exploited, who is loyal to his friends and community, and who fights for their rights. Above all, he is an honourable man. The people were surely disillusioned with the corruption that they had seen their leaders indulge in. They wanted someone with a clean slate. Rajini's fans saw that he had the same kind of appeal that MGR did. MGR had been voted to power thrice because his fans believed that he would be able to bring them the justice they saw in his movies.

Rajinikanth was aware that this is what his fans wanted, even needed from him. When he spoke in his movies, the words sounded confident and sincere. He was able to speak with authority, gesture with panache—snap his fingers, clap his hands. His fans applauded at the reference to the then current political atmosphere in the state. But the words he spoke on screen had been written for him. He was no orator like Karunanidhi or a fiery speaker like Jayalalithaa had been. He could not even compete with Kamal Haasan in this. But then, the one time he had spoken from the heart and said that even the gods will not forgive Tamil Nadu if Jayalalithaa was voted back to power, the AIADMK had met a humiliating defeat. That was the 'Rajini effect', his admirers said. Was it really? That was more than twenty years ago. Don't hesitate, urged the fans. Your popularity will carry you through. They said this even twenty years ago. But he took his time. There is no way he could have thought of it when Karunanidhi and Jayalalithaa were the ruling stars. But now the deck appeared to be clear.

Rajinikanth, at sixty-seven, decided to dip his toe in political waters. At a large gathering of his fan clubs, at Raghavendra Mandapam in Chennai on 19 May 2017, he announced that he might enter politics. 'Tamil Nadu politics needs a change,' he declared. 'Be ready for war. The system is corrupt, we all need to work together to change it.'[6] The fans were jubilant.

From the very early years of his stardom, Rajini fans have wanted to see him as chief minister. They wanted him—and by extension themselves—to become part of the political life of Tamil Nadu that saw the birth of the Dravidian movement and chanted 'udal mannukku, uyir Thamizhukku—this body unto the soil, this life unto Thamizh (Tamil)'. No matter that Rajini's mother tongue was Marathi and that he was born in Karnataka and spoke Kannada. Even after all these years in Tamil Nadu, he has not shaken off the Kannada accent. He cannot speak the

---

[6]'Rajinikanth says system is corrupt, hints at entry into Tamil Nadu politics', *Scroll. in*, 19 May 2017.

chaste Tamil the Dravidian leaders spoke, did not have the skill of oratory that came so naturally to them. MGR, after all, was a Malayalee who was born in Kandy, Sri Lanka, but he grew up in Tamil Nadu having come there as a child and had become fluent in Tamil and a spell-binding orator. He had become a darling of the masses, a superstar of his times. He had also been the most popular chief minister of Tamil Nadu. Where was the comparison?

Also, there was some scepticism among his fans about whether he would actually enter politics. Especially, since he added after his call to arms, 'It is not easy. It is not enough to show valour in words. We have to strategize....' So, the question remained—was he going to enter politics or was he going to keep strategizing? He had spoken of war, but not all his fans were sure if *he* was ready for war. He asked with passion, 'What is wrong in serving the people who have raised me to the top? Why should I not expect their lives to prosper?' There was also some belligerence. 'Don't be swayed by the negative abusive comments that keep circulating online. It is an opportunity to grow, mind you. A plant can grow only if you press the seed under the earth. They are applying pressure on us to help us grow. They do not know that.'[7] In this speech there was a seriousness that had not been there earlier. In consecutive meetings with fans, he repeated his plans for entering politics. But he ended the speeches by saying everything depended on the call of the gods. He was waiting for a message from above.

Sceptics among his fans have seen how he dangled this dream before them before the release of his films only for it to disappear like a mirage. At the time of this latest speech, he was about to release *2.0*. They wondered if this latest announcement of his political plans was to help the film.

In recent years, many Rajini films have flopped. Even his

---

[7]'I am a "Pachai Tamizhan"--Superstar Rajinikanth's Speech at Last Day Fans meeting, Thanthi TV, 18 May 2017, availabe here: https://youtu.be/m3VdLLbGp4Q

fans accept that Rajini is no longer the young hero that he used
to be. Off-screen, he makes no effort to hide his baldness. On
screen, he is often digitally altered and doesn't look like himself.
In addition to his name, the film needs a strong script. Producers
and directors have been trying all they can to make their films a
commercial success. Yet the hundreds of Rajini clubs are funded
and run in his name because of the hope of a commercial windfall
as well as the hope that he will be chief minister some day, in
the process of which they will be empowered politically. He has
to be an icon. It is the fan clubs that build up the hype before
the release of every film of his and bear the disappointment of
having wasted their efforts when the film flops. They also face
the wrath of the distributors who mortgage their assets to get
the distribution rights thinking they would earn gold, believing
the hype built by the clubs. Asking him to enter politics seems
like their desperate effort to gain the ground lost in these losses.

Rajini must have felt nervous about Kamal's possible entry.
His announcement at a time when he was toying with the idea
himself must have taken the wind out of his sails. The BJP had
been knocking at his door and, although he felt closer to their
ideology, he didn't want to antagonize the minorities among his
fans. He had praised at the same meeting the DMK's deputy
chief Stalin as 'a good administrator'[8], said Anbumani Ramadoss
of the PMK as an educated man who had some good schemes
and avoided mentioning Modi's name. In fact, he even applauded
the controversial dialogue criticizing the BJP government's
demonetization in the film *Mersal* (2017) that starred another
political aspirant, Vijay. The fans were utterly confused.

But after all these hints and quasi-announcements, he seemed
to develop cold feet. He went silent; not another word about
entering politics. The gods must have failed to call him. Perhaps
he realized how hard this would be. He and his fellow actors

---

[8]'Rajinikanth says system is corrupt, hints at entry into Tamil Nadu politics', *Scroll.in*.

with political aspirations are mere ideas. Ideas that just have larger than life billboards as their base; completely disconnected from the problems on the ground. Like the robots in *Enthiran* and *2.0*. To become real is a dream. To think that the deck is free is a delusion.

Theodore Baskaran, film critic, and author of the award-winning book on Tamil cinema, *The Eye of the Serpent*, says that stars that aspire to enter politics in Tamil Nadu today think they can repeat MGR's success story. 'MGR was the ultimate political star. His fans were homogeneous, as they were all from the Dravidian movement. The fan clubs worked as political units after MGR split from the DMK and formed his own party, the AIADMK. That is what made him so politically powerful. But Sivaji Ganesan, a better actor and also popular, failed miserably when he entered politics because his fans were not homogeneous nor did they have a political ideology. They were a motley collection of cinemagoers. Rajinikanth's fans are no different. Rajinikanth entering politics banking on the fan clubs, which are just numbers, will not be politically significant.'[9]

When Karunanidhi had been ailing, Prime Minister Modi visited him at his Gopalapuram residence on 6 November 2017. The Congress high command got jittery at what this could mean. But Modi insisted that it was a courtesy call. To make sure that rumours didn't get out of hand, Stalin led an anti-BJP and anti-demonetization protest rally with members of his party. The Congress, the Left, and other secular parties joined in the protest. According to senior journalist Priyan, the courtesy visit from the prime minister caused a lot of damage to the DMK's prospects.[10] In the by-election that was held in December 2017 at R. K. Nagar (Jayalalithaa's constituency), the DMK met with a humiliating defeat. Its candidate lost to T. T. V. Dhinakaran, Sasikala's nephew,

---

[9]Interview with the author, 10 Jun 2018.
[10]Interview with the author, 21 Mar 2018.

who stood from there as an independent candidate. The Muslims of the area, who usually voted for the DMK, rejected it en bloc this time, much to the shock of the party. The DMK's candidate lost his deposit. The ruling AIADMK lost, despite retaining the two leaves party symbol. The convulsions in state politics seemed to galvanize Rajinikanth into action. It appeared to be time for him to take the plunge.

Twenty

There was resounding applause. Superstar Rajinikanth—their icon, their god—had just said the words his fans had been waiting to hear for over twenty years. Years ago, they had put up posters entreating him: 'Thalaiva, vaa, dharani aala vaa—come, leader, come and rule the earth'. But he had taken his time. Finally, on 31 December 2017, he made the announcement. His words were crystal clear though he began by reciting a verse from the Bhagavad Gita in Sanskrit that they could not understand. Then he went on to say in a clear loud voice: 'Naa arasiyalukku varuvathu uruthi! (It is certain that I am entering politics.)' The audience broke into a thunderous applause as if they were taken unawares. He paused for it to subside. 'I shall announce the formation of our party before the next assembly election and we shall contest all the 234 constituencies.' This announcement sent shock waves, going beyond the walls of the Raghavendra Kalyana Mandapam through the streets of Chennai and reaching the offices of the time-tested Dravidian parties—the DMK and the AIADMK. 'I am entering politics not for money or status or fame,' he thundered. 'If I wanted that, I could have joined in 1996 itself. When I was forty-five, I did not want it, would I want it now at sixty-eight?... As a spiritual person I say politics has become rotten…. Recent events have shamed us, the people of other states are laughing at us. If I didn't do something to redress it, my conscience will prick me for not doing my duty to Tamil people who have made me achieve such heights.'[1]

---

[1]'Super Star Rajinikanth Confirmed His Political Entry During Meeting With Fans In Chennai', Puthiyathalaimurai TV, 30 Dec 2017, available here: https://www.youtube.com/watch?v=B1D6Clmiwsw

It sounded like he believed, as his fans always had, that he would be the redeemer. He promised that his government (once elected to power) would follow a spiritual path above caste and creed. The word 'spiritual' was not something that had been heard during the last fifty years of Dravidian rule, based as it was on an atheistic philosophy. Not even the spiritually-inclined, temple-visiting Jayalalithaa had brought that aspect into governance. What then was he referring to? A clean regime based on dharma—was it Ramarajya? Or Gandhian philosophy? He did not explain.

Those listening were not aware that Rajinikanth had just returned from Bangalore after a visit to Mantralayam, the shrine of Saint Raghavendra, with his friends Raj Bahadur, Raghunandan, and Ashok. As he had done over the decades, he turned to these true friends. When Tamil Nadu politics seemed to have touched new lows, he spoke to them of his feelings of anger and disgust at the state of affairs. The pressure from his fan clubs had been building and many others seemed ready to take the plunge. But he was more careful, thoughtful. There was a lot riding on this and he could not afford to fail. His friends suggested that he test the waters. That is what he was doing when he convened several fan club meetings in different towns, dropping hints about his political plans. He was overwhelmed by their response and enthusiasm. They pounded their chests and shouted, 'We will make sure you are successful.' He was flattered when a Tamil scholar and Gandhian activist Tamilaruvi Manian, said that a good and noble man like him should be the one to rule the state that had been destroyed by corrupt Dravidian rule in the last fifty years. Dravidianism and Dravidian ideology are myths, he said. Tamil nationalism is mere rhetoric he assured the actor. 'People have been hearing slogans of hypocrisy all along and are tired. They are tired of both the Dravidian parties; they are looking for an alternative. You are a good man, they know it. Come, take the plunge. I shall travel all over Tamil Nadu and speak for you.'[2]

Rajinikanth was touched. The man's words comforted him at a time when he was still unsure. Were his encouraging words hiding an agenda? There was no way to know. More than being sounding boards for his worries and plans, Ashok was also the one who drew up the first steps. He reminded Shivaji that he had to compete with the very well-structured cadre-based Dravidian parties. He would need to constitute a group of experts to guide him about the problems that the state faced that had not been addressed. The fan clubs would have to be turned into poll support units. Ashok, left-leaning, was wary about 'spiritual politics'.[3] Ashok had advised Shivaji to broaden his reach so that all sections of society—including the minorities and Dalits—would feel heard. He had also suggested that Shivaji choose appropriate topics in forthcoming films that would help him stay in people's minds. He could not abandon films, that was clear. After all, he needed to act to make money; politics was an expensive business. Shivaji agreed that he would need to keep making films. 'I'm not entering politics to make money!' Since the elections were a few years away, in 2021, Ashok suggested that he build his base in the meantime.

There were also rumours that a big corporate that was allegedly close to the ruling BJP leaders at the centre had assured him that they would back him financially if he entered politics favouring the right-wing party. His friends don't talk about it; after all, it was just a rumour. They knew, of course, that he had some financial issues. The pressures from his family were a worry, and they felt free to tell him about it. Ashok felt that Shivaji appeared still a little hesitant, perhaps nervous to make a public statement yet about his entry into active politics. He understood that Shivaji wanted to seek the blessings of his guru Raghavendra before he made the announcement. So, a trip to Mantralayam, the holy

---

[2]Interview with the author, 17 Mar 2018.
[3]Interview with the author, 27 Jun 2018.

shrine of the saint with his friends was planned. It was also to celebrate his birthday on 12 December. As always, the trip was full of fun, light banter, and laughter that also helped release the tension he was feeling. Once at the shrine, he sat in deep meditation before the image of Raghavendra and prayed for clarity of mind. 'Bless me, tell me if the road I have chosen is the right one.' He rose from his meditation feeling blessed. 'I shall make an announcement,' he said.

And so, he did—as has been noted at the beginning of this chapter, he made an unambiguous statement on 31 December 2017 that he would enter politics by starting his own party ahead of the next assembly elections in 2021 to provide an 'honest, transparent, secular and spiritual' alternative to combat the undemocratic and corrupt styles of governance the state has seen for the past five decades. He promised he would dismantle his government if his party's performance fell short of its promises within a span of three years. 'Over the last one year, the happenings in Tamil Nadu have made the state a laughing stock of people from other states. If I do not act, I would feel guilty for the rest of my life,' Rajini said to the cheering fans at the Raghavendra Mandapam, the wedding hall, he owns in the city. He hit out at parties that 'plunder their own people'. The fans noticed that on the stage there was the symbol called the Baba yoga mudra—the snake surrounding the hand depicting divinity—that was first seen in the Superstar's 2002 film *Baba*. But what was important to them now was the message that Thalaivar has come to a decision at last.

Then he said his fans had to do their duty too. 'I was hesitant because I know the hazards that are in politics. If we decide to go for war, we should win it. Veeram—valour—alone is not enough. We need a good strategy.' His strategy was to increase the fan clubs and register the unregistered groups that favoured him which were spread all over Tamil Nadu. For the next three years that would be the work of his 50,000 fan clubs. 'What I want are watch dogs not mere party workers. I want watch dogs who hold leaders responsible.'[4] The fans felt empowered by his words and applauded cheerfully.

The sceptics among the journalists and political analysts and Tamil Nadu politicians, however, wondered what to make of this announcement. What was his ideology? He is not able to say. As he was leaving in his car after the meeting, a journalist asked him, 'What is your ideology, sir?'

'Anmiga arasiyal (spiritual politics),' he answered and sped away. He said in his meeting with the fans that his head reels when he hears such questions about policies and ideologies.[5] On 2 January 2018, just two days after the announcement, he met the media informally outside the gates of his Poes Garden home. He said at the outset he did not want to entertain any questions related to his ongoing political journey. There had been criticism from the film fraternity, Dravidian parties, and Tamil nationalists who questioned his knowledge of Tamil Nadu politics. His admirers like Karate Thiagarajan and Tamilaruvi Manian retorted saying he had been in politics for more than two decades. Hadn't his words been potent enough to decide a political turn in the nineties? He admitted that he was not very comfortable interacting with the media. 'But you are important, I know,' he smiled. He told them he wanted to bring about a revolution in Tamil Nadu. 'Tamil Nadu has historically been a place of major political happenings. It was here that Mahatma Gandhi started wearing the loincloth. I too want to create a political revolution. If there is a change now future generations will live better.' He added that in order to fulfil his aim of creating a revolution, he required the media's cooperation.[6]

Soon after, a website 'Rajinimandram' was launched along with an app for fans to register with their voter ID cards. According to

---

[4]'Super Star Rajinikanth Confirmed His Political Entry During Meeting With Fans In Chennai', Puthiyathalaimurai TV.

[5]'Spiritual Superstar, political war cry: Full text of Rajinikanth's speech', *News Minute*.

[6]'"Want to create a political revolution," says Rajinikanth in his first interaction with the media', *News Minute*, 2 Jan 2018.

Rajini fan Surya, the site server remained busy for a while with people frantically trying to log in. Over 3 lakh people registered in the first few hours. The website was expected to bring all the unregistered clubs under one roof. The site underwent some updates and the name was changed to a more inclusive one—Rajini Makkal Mandram (Rajini's People Mandram)—hinting that he intended to reach beyond his fans and turn the website into a public platform. The fans worked overtime to reorganize their groups in new, unfamiliar ways. They were excited, unaware that all their toil done with great faith and love for the Thalaivar would ultimately come to nothing.

There was criticism that his 'spiritual politics' had a saffron tinge, hinting at a possible alliance with the BJP. To assure people that this was not the case, he made the right moves. He had already announced that his party would contest all the 234 assembly seats which meant that he would not have an alliance with another party. He visited the ailing DMK chief Karunanidhi at his Gopalapuram residence. The media picked up this piece of news and flashed it on all TV news channels. It was clear from Stalin's expression that he was not pleased with the visit. Immediately after meeting Karunanidhi, Rajinikanth met R. M. Veerappan, a close aide of MGR. Perhaps he wanted to quell any speculations regarding his closeness to the BJP. He needed to keep his fans happy and most of them were either members or supporters of the Dravidian parties.

According to Surya, Thalaivar then went on a fan club expanding spree: 'There are many unregistered fans now. We will register them all and the movement will become very big.' Surya also confided that the Thalaivar had been holding talks with experts from various sectors, seeking their advice on drawing up a strategy.[7] Raju Mahalingam, the creative head of Lyca Productions that produced *2.0* joined the political team of Rajinikanth. There

---

[7]Interview with the author, 28 Mar 2018.

was not all that much support for his political plans from the film fraternity—many called him an opportunist. Director Bharathiraja criticized his move and said Tamil Nadu could only be ruled by a son of the soil and not by an outsider.[8] Seeman, producer, actor and leader of Naam Thamizhar Katchi, expressed the same view on 31 December 2017.[9]

The fans though applauded his every word without pausing to scrutinize his utterances for any false notes or unspoken messages. They were his vassals, after all. But he said that he did not want vassals, but soldiers. And he would be their commander. But many wondered how this would work. He was known to be short-tempered. Would he tolerate dissent? He had no patience with reporters asking him questions. But to be a politician meant facing criticism and answering even awkward questions. Would he tolerate it if he is asked about his family? There were rumours alleging fraudulent financial transactions and questionable actions done in his name. He had to answer even if he was not directly involved and even if the rumours were false. Social media platforms had been full of tales real and imaginary, from the moment he announced he was forming a party. Questions were being raised about some of his advisers—*Thuglak* editor S. Gurumurthy who belongs to the RSS and Tamilaruvi Manian, who calls himself Gandhian but whose politics are right-leaning. Manian made it clear that his sole wish was to bring an end to the rule of the Dravidian parties.[10]

He will not get a single vote if he aligned with the BJP, said his detractors. In the recent past, there has been a strong resurgence of Tamil nationalism and regionalism among the youth that is vocal and belligerent. This group suspects the agenda of the BJP high command. The open eagerness of the BJP to welcome

---

[8]'Director Bharatiraja on Rajinikanth', *YouTube-Thanthi TV*, 22 May 2017.

[9]'Seeman reaction to Rajinikanth political entry Seeman speech Tamil news', Tamil Live News Red Pix, 31 Dec 2017, available here: https://www.youtube.com/watch?v=gky_YmCPdOI

[10]Manian, 'Rajinikanth my last hope', *Dinamani*, 7 Dec 2008. (Translation by author).

Rajinikanth's entry into politics was definitely an embarrassment to his fan clubs that included members from minority communities. The non–BJP parties would hesitate to align with him. K. Chandru, former Justice of the Madras High Court, says, 'You should not take him lightly. He may become a force to reckon with. There is a strong feeling among a sizeable section of the people wishing to opt for a change. Rajinikanth is known and considered to be a good man. He is an outsider but that is to his advantage. He will not be identified with any caste groups here. He is humble, knows he needs to learn more about the state. He holds regular meetings with various experts at his Kelambakkam farmhouse away from the bustle of the city.'[11]

Gopanna, Secretary, Tamil Nadu Congress Committee says, 'To think that there is a political vacuum is an illusion. M. K. Stalin is a strong contender in the DMK and has been in active politics for more than forty years. And the party has a strong structure [in] the interiors of the state. Rajinikanth's entry will have an impact on the two Dravidian parties but he has a long way to go to take them on.'[12] How long will that take, though? The Superstar was nearing seventy.

'It is a fact that people want a change from the Dravidian party rule,' said senior journalist Maalan. 'He will not win with the first attempt, of course, but will cut into the votes of the Dravidian parties that may lead to a hung assembly.'[13]

There was also Dhinakaran, Sasikala's nephew, to take on. He had won the by-election from the prestigious R. K. Nagar constituency that had been Jayalalithaa's. It appeared corruption was no longer an election issue in Tamil Nadu. The people flock to the politician who is a 'giver'. Someone who is able to fill their pockets or give them appliances for the home. Tellingly, Dhinakaran's election symbol was a cooker.

---

[11]Interview with the author, 20 Mar 2018.
[12]Interview with the author, 21 Mar 2018.
[13]Interview with the author, 26 Mar 2018.

How would Rajinikanth, who was talking of corruption-free spiritual politics, fare in this atmosphere? And how much could he rely on his fan clubs? They had become unruly in the past. Was he aware that they went door to door and collected money to celebrate his birthday?

He is asked difficult questions. What is his ideology—it appears he doesn't have one. What are his views on the effects of Kudankulam nuclear power plant, the farmers' problems, the Sri Lankan Tamils' misery, fishermen's agony, honour killings etc. His position on these matters, among others, is unclear. He had no answer when Seeman, film producer, director, and leader of the Tamil nationalist Naam Thamizhar Katchi, asked, 'Who are you, an outsider who cannot even speak good Tamil, who does not know our culture, heritage, and history, to aspire to rule over us? How dare you? You think the Tamils are fools?'[14]

Rajinikanth was aware that politics was not easy. Especially for a Kannadiga like him in Tamil Nadu.

After three months of intense activity wrapping up film commitments and chalking out his political plans, Rajinikanth needed some time away from the action. In March 2018, he went on a two-week spiritual trip to an ashram in Rishikesh. The Superstar was seen riding a pony on the hills in spotless white attire. His face serene, no security people around. 'I will not speak politics,' he said to the young journalist from India Today TV who stood before him. 'I am on a spiritual journey. Every human being's goal is to realize the self.' He explained to the confused young journalist, 'I am on that path. I want to realize the self. That is my ultimate desire.' He fell silent, refused to say anything more.[15]

In the meantime, politics took a hiatus, as his fans began to look forward to his next big release.

---

[14]'Seeman reaction to Rajinikanth political entry Seeman speech Tamil news'.

[15]'Exclusive: Rajinikanth's visit to Rishikesh ashram made him forget stardom', *India Today*, 15 Mar 2018.

Twenty-one

'Rajinikanth warned of dire consequences. The Karnataka Film Chamber of Commerce decides to ban *Kaala* in Karnataka' screamed the ticker on news channels in Karnataka. Rajinikanth's friends, Raj Bahadur, Ashok, and Raghunandan were disappointed and worried. They had been awaiting the release of this much-hyped film, Rajini's second with the political director Pa. Ranjith. They knew that the story would not revolve around the cult of Rajini. Despite this, their Shivaji would be the hero—he was the Superstar after all. But what sort of hero would the nearly seventy-year-old Rajini play? Did his fans still think he could play the same roles that he did as a young man? Ashok knew this would be a path-breaking film for their friend. It would add another dimension to him—something that Ashok had been telling Shivaji he needed in order to enter politics.

The film had been released in Tamil Nadu on 8 June 2018. Even national news channels had been caught up in the excitement, showing excited fans bursting crackers, dancing and singing outside theatres. Mumbai was also caught up in Rajini mania. Even the heavy monsoon rains did not deter fans from crowding the theatres. But at this time, the Cauvery water troubles had become an issue once again. Karnataka was not happy with the Supreme Court order on 3 May, that Karnataka should release at least 2 tmcft of Cauvery water as directed by the Cauvery Water Tribunals' decision on the release of water to Tamil Nadu.[1] The court did not entertain Karnataka's request for a stay on this order. On 20 May, Rajinikanth

---

[1] 'Cauvery draft scheme delayed because PM, ministers are busy with Karnataka polls, Centre tells SC', *Scroll.in*, 3 May 2018.

had told reporters who asked him for his reaction that it was Karnataka's duty to obey the Supreme Court's order. In response to his remarks, Karnataka Chief Minister H. D. Kumaraswamy had asked Rajinikanth to 'come and check the reservoir levels. Water is not sufficient for our own needs', he said.[2] Kannada chauvinists were up in arms against Rajinikanth. On 29 May, the Karnataka Film Chamber of Commerce decided not to screen *Kaala* after several local organizations demanded a ban on the film over Rajinikanth's comments on the sharing of Cauvery water.

Ashok had heard the hoarse cry from the agitators. 'He is a traitor', they screamed. 'He is a betrayer, concerned only about the success of his films, and his image before the Tamils'.[3]

Shivaji's friends made it a point to see every one of his films as soon as it released and discuss it with him. They never flattered him or held back any criticism. Earlier in the day, Shivaji had called Ashok and asked him if he had seen *Kaala*. Ashok told him that they had not yet watched it because the film had been banned in Karnataka because of the Cauvery water issue. 'What is wrong with my demand?' Shivaji shouted, clearly frustrated with the situation. 'All I said was that we should respect the Supreme Court's order.'

Ashok pacified Shivaji, and told him about their plan to go to Hosur to watch the film. 'We are going to Hosur today,' said Ashok. 'We have bought the tickets, booked our room in a hotel.' Hosur, right across the border from Karnataka, is a district in Tamil Nadu, about 100 kilometres from Bangalore. They had planned it like a holiday. They would stay in a hotel for a few days and watch the movie as many times as they wanted. It was always a pleasure for them to watch him on screen.

'Yes, you must see it somehow. And tell me what you think about it. I hope the film gets released in Karnataka. What fools!'

---

[2] 'Karnataka HC refuses to interfere with ban on 'Kaala', asks state to provide security to theatres', *Scroll.in*, 5 Jun 2018.
[3] Ashok, interview with the author, Bangalore, 10 Jun 2018.

Shivaji grunted. When Ashok called him after watching the film, Shivaji was in Darjeeling for his next film's shoot. 'Super!' Ashok said to him and continued to congratulate Shivaji on the film. Shivaji was ecstatic about Ashok's reaction to the film, Ashok could sense it.[4] He valued his friends' opinion deeply and looked for their appreciation.

Ashok, Raj Bahadur, and Raghunandan watched the film over and over again. Each time, a different aspect of the character became apparent to them. Each facet that seemed more convincing than the previous. He was charming, assertive, ferocious. They marvelled at the changing contours of his face. He moved like a young man. He dominated the screen in every scene. His face had an aged grace with an impish charm. He was Kaala, the dark demon god, Ravana whose heads kept growing as they were cut off. Kaala was invincible. Shivaji was invincible.

Raj Bahadur was a little worried about the film, which was very different from Rajini's usual fare. He was concerned that the philosophy and ideology it was based on might not be appreciated by Rajini fans. But Ashok was thrilled with the message in the film: 'Shivaji should appeal to that section too. They are the most marginalized. Remember he is entering politics.' They agreed that it was a good film and their Shivaji was superb. But will it be a box office hit? That was a different question altogether!

After the release of *Kaala*, journalist G. Pramod Kumar wrote:

When the first publicity material of *Kaala* came out a year ago, besides the star, his black costume and the dark surroundings, what caught the attention of people was the 'throne' in which he was seated—a Mahindra jeep with the number plate displaying MH01 BR 1956. Having seen the Ambedkarite embodiment of Rajinikanth in *Kabali*, including the leader's sartorial philosophy, people were quick to recognize the hidden message: BR denoted B. R. Ambedkar, and 1956 was the year of his passing.

---

[4]Ibid.

> Equally significant was that 1956 was also the year when
> Ambedkar converted to Buddhism as a mark of protest against
> the caste-ridden Hinduism.[5]

Rajini's fans would most likely not have noted any of this. They
had not been initiated into any political or philosophic discourses.
A large number of them were school dropouts and were attracted
to Rajinikanth because he has, in movie after movie, taken them
on a dream ride, allowing them to dream big for their own lives.
Poverty, lack of education, habits such as drinking and smoking—
none of these qualities would hold them back. Their Thalaivar
had these same 'qualifications' but was also blessed with a noble
heart. They could see from his films that they were victims of a
sort because of the powerful corrupt people around them. They
felt vindicated when Rajini gave the villains their due in the story
and fought for the rights of the common man. It felt like *their*
victory. He told them that nothing was impossible. It seemed so
easy—there was no preaching, no reference to any caste. There
were, of course, people from different castes in the fan clubs and
it was natural for the fan clubs to group by caste. But Thalaivar
had no role in that. It gave them a sense of security but did not
cause any friction with other groups. Their bond was stronger
than caste—their love for Thalaiavar.

But they had noticed the change in the language in *Kabaali*.
In that story, Kabaali fought for the rights of the Tamils who
were plantation workers in Malaysia who were from the Dalit
community. *Kaala* was closer to home and more specific. But not
even Dalit fans could understand the symbolism and metaphors
in the film. There were references to the mythological Rama and
Ravana, characters they were familiar with, but to make Thalaivar
a symbol of the dark demon Ravana irked their sensibilities. Of
course, that was not Rajinikanth's outlook, but Ranjith's. But the

---

[5]G. Pramod Kumar, 'After Kaala trailer release, it's clear Rajinikanth will not be
swinging in favour of BJP', *Indian Express*, 2 Jun 2018.

fans were not aware of this.

They knew the story of Ramayana and couldn't understand how Ravana, the symbol of evil, could be played by their hero. But the storyteller of *Kaala* was Ranjith, a proud Dravidian. His Ravana was defiant. His Ravana was the leader of the downtrodden. He was not a rakshasa who abducts a woman. He fights for the land of the poorest and most powerless. The story is not about one man. It is about a people's movement that cannot be conquered. Although there are big special effects in the film, Rajini appears muted, not like the usual larger-than-life characters he plays. In the film, Kaala is a don who protects the people of Dharavi. The fight is between the people who have lived on this land for three generations and a developer who wants to buy the land, turn part of it into a golf course, and provide houses with water and electricity as well, and a school and hospital for the locality.

The story is rife with subtext, very clear for those who can interpret it. Kaala always wears blue or black; the builder who wants to raze the slum is Manu Realty. The politician Hari Dada belongs to the Navbharath Nationalist Party. He wears spotless white clothes, the walls of his house and the soft furnishing are white whereas the slums are blue and black, as is the interior of Kaala's house. One Street is named for Periyar, the leader of the self-respect movement in Tamil Nadu. There is a bust of Ambedkar in a corner. There is no turning away from the Ambedkarite underpinnings of the story. Part of the title song goes like this (G. Pramod Kumar's translation):

> *Win over yourself and these lands*
> *Bring a dream that never ends*
> *Thousand years of silence is enough*
> *Organise, Make Change, Revolt*
> *Educate, Agitate*[6]

---

[6]Ibid.

Rajinikanth, playing the patriarch, does not hide his age like he does in other films. He is a charming old man who can dance better than any of the younger men.

Hari dada, clad in crisp white says, 'I want to make this country clean and pure. The dirt that plagues the slums, the poverty, and the darkness—I want to change it all'. Kaala counters, 'Black is the colour of the proletariat. In my chawl, dust scatters into a rainbow.'

As Rangan points out in his review, this film is curiously lacking in emotion. Kaala doesn't show any anger or grief when his son and wife are killed. Ranjith clearly does not see this as an emotional film. Kaala does not fight when the audience expects he will. The hero doesn't deliver applause-worthy punch lines about exploitation. Rangan says, '[B]ut for the first time Pa. Ranjith brings the Dalit undercurrent to the surface. It's explicit in the scene where the villain refuses to touch the water in Kaala's house.'[7]

But not everyone agrees with this version of Dalit politics. Ravikumar, spokesperson of the Dalit party Viduthalai Chiruthaigal Katchi, says Pa. Ranjith is a half-baked Dalit activist. The party objected to the commercialization of Ambedkar's name in a film that ends up trivializing his philosophy. They felt the whole thing was a sham because Rajinikanth, known to support the right and pro-BJP, was the protagonist of the movie.[8]

Directors like S. P. Muthuraman and Mani Ratnam have talked about how Rajinikanth would never come to the sets without internalizing the scene he had to perform. One wonders if he 'lent himself to Pa. Ranjith's grand idea without internalizing the big picture'[9]. In this role as a proletariat leader, he exhorted his community to use their bodies as weapons to fight against

---

[7]Baradwaj Ranjan, 'Kaala Movie Review', *Film Companion*, 7 Jun 2018.
[8]Phone interview with the author, Jul 2018.
[9]Kumar, 'After Kaala trailer release, it's clear Rajinikanth will not be swinging in favour of BJP'.

exploitation. This was in stark opposition to the recent statements that he had made. The political ideology of *Kaala* was at loggerheads with the politics of Rajinikanth.

So, which is the real Rajinikanth? The working-class mass leader that he portrays on screen or Rajinikanth, the politician, who admonished the young men who disobeyed the police during the IPL cricket match in Chennai, or the one who made statements that anti-social elements had infiltrated the anti-Sterlite agitation after the police opened fire and killed thirteen people in Thoothukudi (Tuticorin) on 22 May 2018.[10]

Since 1 April 2018, the state had been witnessing protests by political parties, pro-Tamil outfits, and voluntary organizations seeking the setting up of the Cauvery Management Board. On 16 February, the Supreme Court had granted six weeks to the centre to formulate a scheme to ensure compliance of its 465-page judgment on the decades-old Cauvery dispute, which modified the CWDT award of 2007. The six-week period ended on 29 March. On 10 April, the 11th edition of the Indian Premier League kicked off in Chennai's Chidambaram stadium. While cricket enthusiasts were jubilant because the Chennai Super Kings had returned to the IPL after three years (they had been suspended for two years on charges of corruption in 2015), Rajinikanth believed it would not be wise to hold the match in Tamil Nadu when the state was embroiled in the Cauvery water dispute. To host the match in Chennai would be an embarrassment, he said. If the matches were played, he suggested that the team and the spectators wear black bands to show solidarity with those who were protesting, demanding the setting up of the Cauvery Management Board as advised by the Supreme Court.[11] Any further delay by Delhi would earn the wrath of Chennai, he roared.[12] His call for banning

---

[10]'Infiltration of anti-social elements into peaceful protest led to Thoothukudi violence, says Rajinikanth', *The Hindu*, 30 May 2018.

[11]'Rajinikanth backs opposition to IPL in Chennai', *Economic Times*, 8 Apr 2018.

[12]'Rajinikanth warns Centre over Cauvery board', *Times of India*, 9 Apr 2018.

the matches did not have any takers in Chennai, especially since the CSK was playing on its home ground.

When the match went on as scheduled, there were protests by pro-Tamil outfits like Naam Thamizhar Katchi headed by Seeman, who had earlier attacked Rajinikanth when he had announced his decision to enter politics. These organizations felt that the IPL matches would divert the attention of the youth from the Cauvery issue and lessen the impact of the state-wide stir. Their protests were marked by the hurling of sandals into the stadium and burning of yellow jerseys, the colour of the CSK uniform. The police resorted to a lathi-charge to quell the agitation. The protestors retaliated and started attacking the police. Three policemen were allegedly shoved and violently attacked by the protestors. There were visuals of them bleeding in a twenty-three-second video that Rajini uploaded on his Twitter handle. In the tweet, Rajinikanth said, 'The worst form of violence...is attack on uniformed personnel.... This form of violence has to be tackled immediately as it poses grave danger to our country. We need more stringent laws to punish the perpetrators....'[13] He sounded authoritarian, giving people an idea what kind of leader he aspired to be.

Soon after was the shooting at the Sterlite agitation. The Sterlite Copper factory had been set up in Thoothukudi in the 90s. For over two decades, the people around the factory have held sporadic protests, claiming that the factory was causing soil, water, and air contamination, leading to health problems. In March 2018, a new wave of protests began when the factory announced its plans to expand the unit. The slogan 'Copper for Sterlite, Cancer for people' was heard in villages around the Sipcot Complex in Thoothukudi. There was, activists claimed, much pent-up anger and frustration over the people's inability to stop the opening of

---

[13]Rajinikanth, Twitter, Tweet available here: https://twitter.com/rajinikanth/status/983933242112815105

new units or expansion of existing ones. They were dissatisfied that the state government had done nothing to assuage their concerns. The agitation slowly attracted people from more than eight villages. Soon the number of protestors, young and old, men and women, grew to thousands. The protest demanding the closure of Sterlite went on peacefully for hundred days but erupted violently in the end. On 22 May, thousands of people defied the Section 144 restrictions that were in place and marched to the district collector's office to submit a petition. Violence broke out between the protestors and the police who opened fire on the crowd. Thirteen people, including a seventeen-year-old-girl, were killed and dozens injured. The state had never seen such an act of mindless firing by the state police. No one seemed willing to answer the question: who gave the order to shoot? The entire nation was shocked when the state government said that anti-social elements, some terrorist groups, had infiltrated the protest and turned it violent.[14] Pon Radhakrishnan, union minister (BJP) of State Shipping, endorsed the government's views that the police was justified in opening fire.[15]

Leaders of opposition parties, joined by actors, condemned the police action and visited the injured in the hospital. Rajinikanth could not avoid speaking about it. But he made a statement that agreed with the government's claim that anti-social elements had infiltrated the protest.[16]

'The government, following the footsteps of Ms. Jayalalithaa should crush the anti-social elements with an iron hand. If not, it will pose a serious threat to Tamil Nadu.' He also appealed to the public 'not to resort to agitation against every industrial investment being made, as it would effectively seal employment generation in Tamil Nadu where farming had already been wiped

---

[14]Anti-Sterlite protest: Police acted against anti-socials, says Tamil Nadu CM', *DaijiWorld*, 25 May 2018.
[15]Ibid.
[16]'Rajinikanth: Anger after actor justifies deadly police firing', *BBC World*, 31 May 2018.

out because of water scarcity. If you keep protesting for everything, Tamil Nadu will become a graveyard,' he added. He mocked the DMK's protest against the state government, saying 'The DMK is politicizing everything and the people, who are closely watching it, will teach it a fitting lesson.'[17]

'When reporters asked Rajinikanth how he blamed anti-social elements, [he] lost his cool: "Don't ask me how I know, I know all of that," he shot back. He went on to declare he would not accept people who harm people in uniform and dismissed protests against police excesses.'[18]

In Thoothukudi, his words touched a raw nerve. His own fans were disturbed and unhappy. There was widespread criticism from opposition party leaders and journalists.

As many actors and political leaders made a beeline to visit the injured in the hospital, Rajinikanth decided to meet the injured to show that he too cared. On 30 May when he visited Thoothukudi Medical College Hospital, one of the injured, a young man, looked Rajinikanth straight in his eyes and asked him, contempt dripping from his voice: 'Who are you?' That video immediately went viral on social media. The families of the victims were not allowed to meet the Thalaivar. Rajinikanth must have been shocked and upset. After he returned to Chennai on the 31st he tweeted to say, 'If any reporter feels hurt, I express my regrets.'[19] He also gave a special recorded video statement in Tamil from his house that was telecast in all the Tamil News channels, saying that he condemned the brutal actions of the police in Thoothukudi.[20]

---

[17]'Continuous protests will turn T.N. into a graveyard: Rajini', *The Hindu*, 31 May 2018.
[18]J. Sam Daniel Stalin, 'Rajinikanth Loses Cool, Blames "Anti-Social Elements" For Sterlite Deaths, NDTV, 31 May 2018.
[19]'Rajinikanth tweets apology after drawing flak for yelling at reporters', *New Indian Express*, 1 Jun 2018.
[20]Sterlite Protest: Rajinikanth condemns Police Action, Thanthi TV, 23 May 2018, available here: https://www.youtube.com/watch?v=8B1TFAiNZT0&vl=ta

These ameliorative actions, however, did not strike a chord with either the victims or his critics, journalists in particular. As has been noted earlier, it was no secret that Rajinikanth was a friend of the BJP. Had it not been Tamil Nadu where he was trying to get into politics, he would likely have declared his allegiance to the right-wing Hindu nationalist party. But in the land of Periyar, this would be political suicide.

By siding with the government in the Sterlite case, he made it clear that he was against agitations. As Kaala, he was a champion of the working class, encouraging them to agitate. Of course, that was when he was mouthing lines conceived and written by someone else, but as far as his fans were concerned, they were his words, his thoughts. So, when they saw that Thailavar didn't support agitations and the demands of the working class and the poor in real life, they were confused.

As these controversies swirled around him, Rajinikanth announced that his next film was with another young director, Karthik Subbaraj. Subbaraj promised that the new film *Petta* (2019) would be an apolitical entertainer.[21] Rangan said, 'I am just glad the two-film deal [between Rajinikanth and Ranjith] is over. Now, Ranjith can go back to being Ranjith, and Rajinikanth... can go back to being Rajinikanth.[22] Raj Bahadur would agree.

---

[21]Rangan, '*Kaala* Movie Review'.
[22]Ibid.

Twenty-two

Rajinikanth was upset with his fan clubs. Even angry. He was yet to formally float his party and already there were disagreements and revolts and threats of resignations en masse. Each fan club leader was behaving like a local satrap, said Surya. Thalaivar expected his fans to be absolutely loyal and obedient to him. There could only be one leader. He was forced to issue a stern warning, saying: 'Fans should stay united to bring about a huge political change in Tamil Nadu. Any sign of discontent will not be tolerated.'[1] The immediate reason for this was the situation that developed in Dindigul. Thalaivar had clear plans about how the RMM—Rajini Makkal Mandram—should be run. The Mandram had a unit in each of the districts of Tamil Nadu (a total of thirty-eight). A secretary was appointed to take care of each unit. His task was to speed up the enrolment.

S. M. Thamburaj, a government employee, had taken voluntary retirement to join Rajinikanth's action group and was made secretary for Dindigul district on 15 March 2018. He was, however, suspended soon after, less than ten days later. On 24 March 2018, a statement was issued by RMM that S. M. Thamburaj, secretary of the RMM, Dindigul district, had been suspended. The reason given later was that he had not followed the guidelines of RMM: 'During the district level executive meeting, Thamburaj did not invite members of the organization, but held one with those loyal to him.' Once Thamburaj was suspended, 107 office bearers in the district unit of the mandram resigned from their posts in

---

[1]Surya, interview with the author, 7 Dec 2020.

protest.[2] Those protesting knew that Thamburaj, an ardent fan, had been working hard for the clubs. 'It seems that Rajinikanth has been misguided by some people.... Hence, to express our unhappiness we are going to resign,' they said.[3]

They thought that the announcement about the suspension had been made without the knowledge of Thalaivar.

V. M. Sudhakar, the administrator of the mandram, issued a statement urging them not to resign from their posts. 'It is an opportunity for us to serve the people following the call of our leader. We should ignore the selfish deeds of a few and join hands to help the cause.'[4] But the fans had no idea what 'cause' they were meant to be working for. They were not political activists or social workers. The only bond that united them was their love for Thalaivar and his movies. For many years, they had pooled together their own money to celebrate the release of his films. They had never asked for a paisa for this expenditure. They also knew that Rajinikanth would retort that he had never asked them to spend their money. This bond of togetherness and their affection for Rajinikanth had given them a sense of power. Now it looked like their devotion of three decades and more had no value.

Sudhakar explained why Thamburaj had been suspended: 'After Thamburaj was appointed district secretary, he convened a meeting without informing the head office in Chennai. He was asked for an explanation. He never responded. He was summoned to attend a meeting in Chennai. He never turned up. The decision to suspend him was taken only with a motive to set things right and with the hope that he would tender an apology. He never did.... All fans and supporters should abide by the decision of Rajinikanth. We should stay together and win over our enemies.'

---

[2]Ibid.

[3]'Rajinikanth's political outfit Rajini Makkal Mandram in trouble even before formal party launch', *Asianet Newsable*, 4 Apr 2018.

[4]Surya, interview with the author, 28 Mar 2018.

He seemed to be saying that the enemies were within the fold. 'This is the last warning from Rajinikanth to those acting against the rules of the organization.'[5]

A few months later, in July, a rumour started doing the rounds—that Rajinikanth had expelled the party secretary Raju Mahalingam over mismanagement of funds and recruitment of members. But RMM denied all rumours of trouble brewing in the star's camp. Rajinikanth had returned to Chennai from Darjeeling after a month-long shooting schedule. Over a telephonic conversation with the *India Today* news channel Mahalingam clarified that the rumours about his expulsion were false.[6]

Then, in August, Samuel Churchill, the state secretary of the youth wing, and Gayathri Duraisamy, secretary of the women's wing, were stripped of their posts and demoted to district level functionaries. 'There is no place for indiscipline,' explained Surya, now an office bearer of RMM. 'Our performance is being closely watched by Thalaivar. Every appointment is based on how we carry forward his ideas among the people. Perform or perish is his mantra. When each member starts acting with a bloated head, Thalaivar has to act tough. The strength of the DMK and the AIADMK is because their leaders ran the affairs of the party with an iron hand.'[7]

Over the past few months, the RMM had been conducting membership drives and was formulating guidelines for the party that was to be formed. But this confused and upset the fans. The new set of rules and Thalaivar's angry statements was distancing them from the current set-up. They had once been a happy lot. What they enjoyed was having their own meetings and celebrations. Once their Thalaivar announced his decision to enter politics, they enthusiastically recruited new members and began

[5]Ibid.
[6]Rajini Makkal Mandram, 'Raju Mahalingam not expelled from Rajini Makkal Mandram, outfit clarifies', *News Minute*, 12 Jul 2018.
[7]Interview with the author over phone, 4 Sep 2018.

expanding the clubs. Did the Thalaivar know how difficult that had been? He would be shocked to know that youngsters were no longer interested in joining Rajini mandrams. They preferred younger actors such as Vijay. The fans had been trying to get more women to join by telling them what they would gain if Thalaivar came to power. What would they gain? Surya was vague. 'We tell them if Thalaivar came to rule, all their miseries will be over. For instance, standing in a queue for long hours at the ration shop.' But the numbers were not encouraging. People were hesitant to join because the party had not yet been formed. There were other problems as well. The fans were saddled with work they had no idea how to do.

RMM struggled to enlist booth committee members for the 65,000 polling stations in the state. Rajinikanth had said very confidently that his party—that still didn't have a name—would contest all 234 seats in the state. How was this going to happen? 'We have just managed to appoint 30 per cent of booth committee members so far,' a district level secretary, requesting anonymity, admitted. They had initially expected that this would be very easy as Rajini fan clubs existed in every village in the state. But the situation on the ground was rather more complicated. While it was true that Rajinikanth had the largest number of fan clubs in the state, many fans who had joined in the early 80s had allegiance to other political parties, like the DMK, AIADMK, or PMK. Others were just not interested in active politics any more. They said they were too old for that. Over the last two decades, the fan clubs had only become active during the release of Rajini films and for celebrations for his birthday. The registration of new clubs had been stopped in the early 1990s. Reviving the clubs was an uphill task for the new office bearers of RMM.

Social media too failed to swell the ranks of Rajini's followers. Many of his fans are school dropouts and don't use social media. The RMM's official Facebook page had a little over 15,000 followers in December 2020.

As has been noted, twenty years ago, Rajinikanth was considered a kingmaker, someone whose words could change the tide of an election. Then his fans had urged him to join politics. Now it's not just him, his fans too have grown old and tired. They were thrilled when he made the announcement that he would contest all the 234 assembly constituencies without an alliance, but they began to wonder how that would be possible.

'How can a person who can be as indecisive as him by procrastinating…for two decades provide good leadership for the state and the country?' asked Professor R. Manivannan, head of the department of politics and public administration, University of Madras, in an interview on Rediff.com. 'I am not certain whether he fully understands his commitment when he says he is plunging into politics. Starting a political party without an ideology is not complete.'[8]

The professor is very clear about the biggest drawback he sees in Rajinikanth—his disconnect from people and their problems. '…he thinks his charisma will help win in politics. He doesn't know that politics is engaging with people. On that count, his experience is nil. He has lived in his own ivory tower, in a world surrounded by his fan clubs and on the cinema circuit. He has to break this barrier and be with the people to be a political leader.' He points out that former film stars MGR, Jayalalithaa, and Vijayakanth have done that—reached out to the masses. MGR and Jayalalithaa were charismatic leaders but they had to work hard to gain the trust of the people. 'Today people are far more critical of film stars and question their relevance in public life…. Yes, there is a vacuum and anyone can fill the vacuum, but then it should be filled by a person who has been working in the political arena, working with people and raising issues. He has not done any of this.'[9]

---

[8]Shobha Warrier, "Except his fans, no one will rally behind Rajinikanth', *Rediff*, 18 Jan 2018.
[9]Ibid.

Harsh words. But true. But perhaps they never reached Rajinikanth's ears. He had been extremely confident on 5 March 2018, when, after unveiling a statue of MGR at Dr M. G. R. Educational and Research Institute in Chennai he said that he would 'rule like MGR'[10] if he was voted to power. He said, 'I know the political journey is not easy. It is a journey through struggles and hurdles, but I can give governance which [MGR] gave to common people and I trust I can do that too.'[11]

On his return from Lucknow where he was shooting his upcoming film *Petta*, produced by Sun Pictures, he said that 90 per cent of the ground work to launch his party had been completed. 'I will announce the date of the party launch at an appropriate time,' he said.[12]

He had been busy shooting two films at that time. So, it was understandable that he had not had the time to work out all the details of his party and fix a launch date. But months later, on 16 October, he explained to his fans, followers, and members of RMM what his style of politics was going to be. Members had noticed that a few big names like Raju Mahalingam and V. M. Sudhakar, who had been active in RMM, no longer figured in any of the mandram meetings or statements. That was perhaps because after Rajinikanth set off to the Himalayas to shoot *Petta*, the activities of RMM had nearly stopped.

A Tamil journalist spread the news via his Twitter handle that Raju Mahalingam was expelled from RMM. But V. M. Sudhakar, administrator of RMM, tweeted denying this. Raju Mahalingam also refuted the news and said he was very much still with Thalaivar. However, there was news from reliable sources in the RMM that both Raju Mahalingam and V. M. Sudhakar were eased

---

[10]Lakshmi Subramanian, 'Rajinikanth's statement exposes his political dilemma', *The Week*, 23 Oct 2018.

[11]'Rajinikanth unveils MGR statue in Chennai; delivers first speech after entry into politics', Sify, 6 Mar 2018.

[12]'90% work for party launch over, says Rajinikanth', *Times of India*, 21 Oct 2018.

out of their official status in the RMM though they continued to be followers of Rajinikanth.[13]

On his return to Chennai in October, in a detailed two-page statement, Rajinikanth explained to the members of RMM what his policy would be: 'In May this year, when I had the fans meeting, I had made it clear that I would not entertain anyone who comes with the intention to make money or look for lucrative positions. I had said that those who had such intentions should go away. It was not just words that I uttered. I want to bring a new political rhetoric in Tamil Nadu and usher in a change in the political scene in the state….'[14]

'He clarified that removing certain people from the RMM was necessary to drive home the need to maintain discipline. "There has been a misinformation campaign that such removals were done without my knowledge. Every action was taken in the RMM with my knowledge and approval."' Political analysts believed that while the statement sent a strong message to his followers that money and power would not play any role in his style of politics, it also revealed that he was still weighing his decisions and questioning 'whether he can make it big in politics like he did in cinema'.[15]

'If someone believes that we can achieve whatever we have dreamt of with just the fan club, he is not mentally stable. Without the support of the people we cannot achieve what we want to,' he said.[16] He made this statement ten months after announcing that he would take the political plunge. But there was still no clear direction about how he was going to engage with the people. He continued, '[E]ven a person associated with the fan club for more than 30-40 years doesn't mean that he can get positions in the Mandram. We need to enrol people and identify those with

---

[13]Lakshmi Subramanian, interview with the author, 3 Nov 2018.
[14]Subramanian, 'Rajinikanth's statement exposes his political dilemma'.
[15]Ibid.
[16]Ibid.

enthusiasm to work by offering them posts.'[17] This caused great disappointment to his long-time fans.

According to RMM rules, members were forbidden from speaking to the media. Ten Cuddalore district office bearers whose photos had appeared in the local papers and online English news portals met with the actor to apologize for making 'out-of-turn' remarks to the media. There were reports that they had been removed for spending lavishly on outfit activities.[18]

His tough talk about bringing about a change in the political scene of Tamil Nadu naturally riled existing political parties. *Murasoli*, the DMK mouthpiece, published a piece attacking the actor on 26 October 2018. Posing questions to him in the name of an 'innocent fan', the piece asked that if the Superstar was really not interested in posts and money and power, should he not have started a movement like the rationalist leader E. V. Periyar Ramasamy had done? It went on to ask: 'Dear leader, if your assertion that posts were not a consideration in your political entry, why did you announce that the party will contest from all [234] seats in the next [assembly] polls?' The piece also pointed out that a certain politician that Rajinikanth had been hobnobbing with had been a bad influence in his earlier stints in other political parties. It went on to say: 'Those who are speaking for you in the media are communal elements who want to divide the Tamil community which exists after transcending caste and religion.... We [fans] trusted you. But you have become a puppet of some persons and are dancing to their tunes....' The innocent fan then asked 'who is the black sheep', referring to a popular dialogue by the actor in his film *Enthiran*.[19]

The piece made a big impact. There were endless debates over it in all forms of media in the state. There were many who agreed

---

[17]Ibid.

[18]'Days after strong words from their leader, Rajini Makkal Mandram members tender apology', *News Minute*, 27 Oct 2018.

[19]*Murasoli*, 26 October 2018. (Translation by the author.)

with the questions and comments posed by the piece, which so
far no one had dared ask Rajinikanth. It was clear why the DMK
mouthpiece had published this piece. The DMK believed that
the party had more than a fair chance to win the next assembly
elections. But many among its cadres were Rajinikanth's fans. The
party was worried that they would be lured away by the RMM.
Of course, the idea that Rajinikanth would win in his very first
attempt was laughable. But if he did contest, he would cut into
the DMK vote share. It could result in a hung assembly, which
would be disastrous.

The article also pointed out to its cadres that Rajinikanth
was likely to be the face of BJP in Tamil Nadu. Products of the
Dravidian movement that upheld rationalism and social justice, they
would not be able to stomach the right-wing party's Hindutva
agenda. If Rajinikanth was upset, he did not show it. He was
shooting for the film *Petta*, under the banner of Sun Pictures, that
was owned by Kalanidhi Maran, the grandnephew of Karunanidhi.
There was also a hushed silence from his fans who would have
otherwise risen up in support of Thalaivar. But Rajinikanth issued
a statement to his fans on his Twitter account: 'I am proud to
have fans like you. No force in this world can break the bond
between me and my fans.'[20]

However, the next day, in the *Murasoli* issue dated 27 October
2018, was published an apology of sorts as a small box item on
the front page. According to sources, Rajinikanth's disappointment
('varuththam' which in Tamil could also mean 'anger') at the
piece had been conveyed to the DMK president Stalin. Published
without a byline, it was an 'Instruction to the editorial team',
which said, 'It has been brought to our notice that an article
published in *Murasoli* about Rajinikanth has hurt a few good
hearts. The Editorial team has been advised to exercise caution

[20]'After outburst against fans, Rajini softens stance', *The Hindu*, 27 Oct 2018.

in publishing such articles in the future.'[21] The article, of course, had been deliberate and, in all likelihood, had the okay of the top leaders of the DMK. It had been rather audacious of Rajinikanth to seek the blessings of Karunanidhi after he announced his entry into politics. When Karunanidhi passed away, he went to pay his respects and personally expressed his condolences to Stalin. Later, he behaved as if the DMK was of no consequence.

Rajinikanth should have been worried that his fans did not react sharply to *Murasoli*'s piece. Because, as Professor Manivannan explained, while there is decay in Dravidian party culture and politics, the social and political foundations of the ideology remain strong. 'Rajinikanth mistakes the decay of Dravidian parties with the decay of Dravidian ideology'. So why did Rajinikanth's unspecified spiritual politics capture the hearts of the people of the state?

Professor Manivannan explained: 'Dravidian politics doesn't say you cannot be spiritual.... Tamil Nadu is not a no-God land; there are 75,000 registered temples in Tamil Nadu which are not run by the RSS or the BJP.'

---

[21]Lokpria Vasudevan, 'Hurt some good hearts: DMK rues Rajinikanth article', *India Today*, 29 Oct 2018.

Twenty-three

....

Rajinikanth walked out of the Arrivals gate at the Chennai Kamaraj Airport on 12 November 2018 looking young and smart. He had dyed his moustache black. He walked out and ran into a group of reporters waving cameras and microphones at him. They always knew his schedules and movements. Rajinikanth cheerfully turned to face them, expecting questions about his forthcoming films.

'What do you think of the release of the seven people, a matter that now hinges on the recommendation of the Governor of Tamil Nadu?' He was caught off guard. He looked absolutely confused. 'Which seven people? I do not know anything about it. I have been away. I do not know anything,' he responded.[1]

'Do you think the BJP is so dangerous that all the opposition parties are joining together opposing it?'

He paused a little and said, 'If so many people oppose, it must definitely be so.' He moved away, thinking he had managed quite well. But it was clear from his words and his bewildered look that he had not handled the questions well. Videos of Rajinikanth asking 'which seven people?' went viral within an hour. It was reminiscent of that other time when the young man in a hospital bed in Thoothukudi had asked him angrily, 'Who are you?'

His fans, members of RMM, were embarrassed. His detractors and Tamil nationalists had a field day taunting him that he had zero knowledge of Tamil Nadu politics, least of all the concerns of the Tamils. Any Tamil worth his salt would know instantly what

---

[1] Janardhan Koushik, 'If opposition parties gang up against one person, who is powerful, asks Rajinikanth', *Indian Express*, 13 Nov 2018.

the question meant. The seven referred to the prisoners lodged in Madras Central Jail for twenty-seven years, convicted for life for the assassination of Rajiv Gandhi. The Supreme Court had decreed that their release was a matter for the Governor of Tamil Nadu to determine. The people were appalled that Rajinikanth could not immediately understand what the questions referred to. The BJP unit of Tamil Nadu was equally embarrassed since it seemed that he was being critical of the party.

He had been away on shoots and had not kept track of the news and events of Tamil Nadu. But how could someone who had announced his entry into politics and who had claimed to be bringing back the times of MGR's rule not keep in touch with what was happening? Once he had decided to take the plunge, he needed to keep himself well informed of what was happening in the state, no matter where he was.

The fact is Rajinikanth needed to learn his script, whether he was acting in a movie or facing the press. He called the press to his residence on 13 November. He came out of his gate and addressed the journalists who stood outside. He said his response to a question on the proposal for premature release of the seven convicts in Rajiv Gandhi assassination case had been misconstrued. Some people were trying to create an impression that he did not know anything on the issue. The question not been clear, he said. He was not such a fool to be ignorant of the seven life convicts. 'They have undergone punishment for the past 28 years. Enough. It is my opinion that they should be released on humanitarian grounds,' he said. He further explained that he had spoken to one of the convicts, Perarivalan, over the phone for ten minutes when he had been out on parole.[2] Perarivalan's lawyer K. Sivakumar confirmed to the *News Minute* that Rajinikanth had indeed spoken to Perarivalan in 2017. 'He

---

[2]'I am not a fool, says Rajini, clarifying on the 7 people issue', *News Today*, 13 Nov 2018.

had also spoken to the convict's mother, Arputhammal, who has been fighting for his release for nearly thirty years…and assured her that her son will be released from jail soon.'[3]

He clarified his answer on the anti–BJP alliance that opposition parties across the country had formed. 'For the opposition parties, BJP is dangerous, right? People should decide whether it is a dangerous party or not. I will not tell my opinion now. I have not entered politics full time. If ten people unite for war against one, who is more powerful? You decide.'[4] The state BJP was jubilant. They felt it was a strong endorsement from the Superstar on the might of their invincible leader, Modi. But Thirumavalavan, leader of Viduthalai Chiruthaigal Katchi, said Rajinikanth's ten against one analogy made no sense. 'When a snake enters a house, 10 people surround it to kill. That doesn't imply the snake is stronger, but that implies it is dangerous and should not be allowed inside.'[5]

A month before these latest attacks on his fitness for a political career, he'd had to rush to Bangalore in the first week of September when news came that his sister-in-law, Kalavathi, his brother Satyanarayana's wife, had died from kidney failure. She had been admitted to Apollo Hospital there, he knew, but did not expect her to die. He was heartbroken for his brother who had lost his partner of so many decades. It must be like losing a part of his life. He could only hug him and pat him on his back. Satyanarayana's sons were there to take care of him—responsible, dignified men, who asked for nothing from their uncle.

Even as Rajinikanth was having to deal with this loss, there were other matters crowding in. Tamil Nadu's film world was all agog at the release of the young Vijay-starrer *Sarkar* (2018) directed by A. R. Murugadoss. There had been so much hype

---

[3]Manasa Rao, 'Rajini clarifies stand on Rajiv Gandhi case, says convicts should be released', *News Minute*, 13 Nov 2018.
[4]'Rajinikanth hints Modi is more powerful than Opposition', *The Hindu*, 21 Nov 2018.
[5]'National-level solidarity of secular forces need of the hour: Thirumavalavan', *The Hindu*, 16 Nov 2018.

surrounding this movie. It felt like Rajinikanth's reign was over and Thalapathy Vijay was taking over. Produced by Sun TV Network chairman Kalanithi Maran for Sun Pictures, *Sarkar* had run into trouble before its release over the copyright of the story. Writer Varun Rajendran had alleged that the director had plagiarized his story *Sengol*. The case was settled out of court and the film was released.[6]

The movie released in theatres on 6 November, showing on around 3,400 screens worldwide; in the first couple of days, it was reported to have entered the ₹100 crore club. But the bigger news around the film was the controversy that it had provoked. Tamil Nadu information minister Kadambur C. Raju who watched the movie on the first day of its release took exception to some of the scenes. 'There are a few scenes in the film which give room for political misgivings. This is not good for a growing star like Vijay,' he said to the reporters outside the theatre. It sounded like a veiled threat to the actor and to the producer.

He demanded that those scenes be removed and warned that the state government would be forced to intervene if the makers of the film did not comply. 'I shall consult with the Chief Minister to decide on the next course of action.'[7]

Soon, all the other ministers followed suit, protesting that their revered leader, Amma, was being insulted for her welfare measures that had helped raise the standard of living of lakhs of poor people. A character in the movie, played by the director Murugadoss himself, breaks a laptop and throws it into the dustbin, calling it evil. The antagonist in the film is called Komalavalli, which was Jayalalithaa's name at birth. Members of the AIADMK were deeply hurt. They accused Sun Pictures of having used the movie to push their political agenda.

---

[6]'Sarkar plagiarism row: AR Murugadoss settles with writer Varun Rajendran but claims unfair treatment', *Hindustan Times*, 30 Oct 2018.
[7]D. Govardan, 'Vijay-starrer Sarkar courts controversy with scenes on AIADMK govt schemes', *Times of India*, 7 Nov 2018.

The film was cleared by the Censor Board, so what was the problem? The fact was the AIADMK leaders saw the film as a blatant attack on their Thalaivi's welfare measures. Encouraged by the ministers, the AIADMK cadres went berserk. They went round shouting slogans, tearing down posters of *Sarkar* and destroying banners that were erected at the theatres, burnt cut-outs of Vijay, and ransacked movie theatres. Even ministers were seen tearing down banners. Some film theatres stopped shows. Thanks to the protests, a film that received mixed reviews from critics became a box office hit and is said to have made ₹260 crores worldwide.[8]

It had long been rumoured that the forty-five-year-old Vijay was looking to make his entrance into politics. His previous film *Mersal* (2017) had become controversial as it attacked demonetization and GST. *Sarkar* was an attack on the governing style of the Dravidian parties who had, for many years, been luring people with freebies. In *Sarkar*, Vijay plays a corporate CEO in the US who comes to India just to cast his vote during an election. He finds that someone else has already cast his vote. He files a complaint in court and stalls the counting until he is able to cast his vote. The root cause for the corruption is traced to the freebies—grinders, mixies, laptops—given in the name of welfare measures. In the process, both the Dravidian parties that have ruled Tamil Nadu for fifty years get a beating through the political statements made by Vijay's character, who says that the old order should make way for a young, modern, self-reliant new order. Following the controversy, Sun Pictures released a statement that the controversial scenes had been deleted in the interest of the public good and to safeguard the life and property of people who come to watch the movie.[9]

Rajinikanth was outraged about the way events had developed.

[8] Lata Jha, 'Protests notwithstanding, Tamil film Sarkar emerges as a Diwali blockbuster', *Livemint*, 12 Nov 2018.
[9] '*Sarkar* makers reveal why controversial scenes were chopped off from Vijay's film', *India Today*, 10 Nov 2018.

He said it was absolutely unreasonable on the part of the government to object and obstruct the screening of the movie when it had obtained official clearance from the Censor Board. At that time, he was shooting a film with Sun Pictures. He didn't worry about the fact that Vijay could turn out to be his rival in the political arena. He didn't believe that the young man could be a threat to his ambitions. He said, 'A film should not be re-censored to satisfy the whims and fancies of a political party.'[10]

Chief Minister Palaniswami lashed out at the Superstar and told the media, 'Amma had provided household items normally associated with the rich to be distributed among the poorest of the poor. Filmmakers spend up to 900 crores to make a film. Where do they get the money from? By selling ₹100 tickets illegally for ₹1000, they suck the moviegoers' blood![11] What have those actors who earned ₹50 crore for acting in a film done for the people?'[12]

Kamal Haasan too criticized the ruling party for encouraging violence over a film that had been cleared by the Censor Board. Palaniswami responded to Kamal Haasan as well. He questioned what these stars could know about the lives, pains, and aspirations of the ordinary people. About two crore people had benefited from the freebies that made their lives more comfortable. He also justified the actions of the AIADMK workers who had allegedly vandalized *Sarkar* posters. He said when schemes brought about by political leaders are belittled, party men would respond.[13]

Rajinikanth decided there was no need to carry on the dialogue. He had made his point, and that was it. The release of the trailer of his much-awaited film *2.0* was due in a few days.

---

[10]Jha, 'Protests notwithstanding, Tamil film *Sarkar* emerges as a Diwali blockbuster'.

[11]'Film Industry 'Sucking the Blood of Movie-Goers', Says CM Palanisamy After Forcing Cuts in Vijay's *Sarkar*', *News18*, 11 Nov 2018.

[12]'How filmmakers get crores to make movies: TN CM', *Deccan Chronicle*, 11 Nov 2018.

[13]Akshaya Nath, 'Sarkar row: Tamil Nadu CM defends AIADMK protests, hits out at Kamal Haasan for supporting movie', *India Today*, 11 Nov 2018.

But he did make a note of what the chief minister had said about the ₹100 tickets sold for ₹1,000. He was most likely talking about Rajini's films. He had to do something about this—so far, he had not bothered to address this problem.

Twenty-four

Rajinikanth was seething over the chief minister's remarks. It was a direct attack on him and his integrity. He could not let this go unanswered especially as one of his political planks was the promise of corruption-free rule. He had to deal with this right away. There were complaints—they were not new—that the tickets sold to fans were resold at exorbitant rates on the black market.[1] He had not bothered to address the issue because part of the booty was shared by the distributors, publicity units, and the fans. This was illegal and corrupt, but perhaps as it was to the advantage of the fan clubs, he hadn't involved himself. But now that the paradigm had changed from entertainment to politics, this was something that could derail him.

Rajinikanth had to show that he was blemishless. Although when he was young, he too used to buy tickets in black for the first shows of Rajkumar's films, he had no option now but to put out a harsh statement warning fans against selling tickets for his upcoming film *2.0* in black. According to reports, tickets for the movie were going to be sold for exorbitant prices from ₹2,000 to ₹4,000 on the black market. The message came in the form of a letter from R. Sudhakar, the executive manager of RMM. 'Tickets purchased for mandrams should not be sold to anyone outside, and also the club members should not be charged a paisa more than the rates fixed by the government.'[2] After seeing this message, the fans fell into a pall of gloom, but Surya kept

[1] 'Kabali: Tickets for Rajinikanth-starrer being sold by "fan clubs" for exorbitant prices', *India Today*, 22 Jul 2016.
[2] 'Wow! Rajinikanth takes the first step to eradicate Black Tickets', *India Glitz*, 18 Nov 2018.

shaking his head that the allegations were not true. 'Maybe a few greedy members indulge in such activities, spoiling our names. Our devotion to Thalaivar is above all this pettiness,' he mumbled.[3]

Sometimes Surya thinks it would be better if Thalaivar did not enter politics. He believes, of course, that if Rajinikanth were to become the chief minister, he would bring about change and do much good for the people. But he's heartbroken when politicians, especially those in power, taunt his leader.

Surya's hope at that time was that *2.0* would be a hit and revive the fans' spirits. This film is all magic and fantasy and will be a lot more entertaining than the last two films—*Kabaali* and *Kaala*. None of his friends wanted to watch a story about protestors from a particular class or caste. It was not all that entertaining and made them uncomfortable. When Thalaivar spoke his lines in the movie, it didn't sound like him. The films flopped because no one wanted to go and watch them over and over again. Surya remembered how many times he and his friends had watched *Muthu, Annaamalai, Padayappa, Baashha*. They had such a good time, felt so much pride repeating the lines over and over and clapping and whistling each time as if they were watching it for the first time.[4]

The fans and the rest of the world were eagerly awaiting *2.0*, which marked the reunion of Shankar and Rajinikanth. Produced on a lavish budget of nearly ₹600 crore,[5] the movie was being called Shankar's magnum opus[6]. On Saturday, 3 November 2018 the trailer was released. The sci-fi adventure, touted to be the most expensive Indian project ever made, had Thalaivar locking horns with Bollywood star Akshay Kumar. Kumar plays a mysterious supervillain who has the ability to control crows and mobile

[3]Interview with the author over phone, 10 Dec 2018.
[4]Ibid.
[5]'2.0 Made On A Lavish Budget Of ₹600 Crore: Rajinikanth', *Outlook*, 3 Nov 2018.
[6]Haricharan Pudipeddi, '2.0: Rajinikanth, Shankar's magnum opus expected to collect ₹20 cr in Telugu states, say trade pundits', *Firstpost*, 25 Nov 2018.

phones. He quickly takes over the world, which now needs a superhero who can counter him. Since no human being could stand up to him, Chitti, the robot from *Enthiran*, is rebooted.

The launch of the trailer saw a celebration more lavish than hundreth day celebrations during the days of MGR. The entire film crew was present and Rajinikanth thanked each one of them, the press, and the fans who intermittently cheered him and applauded his every utterance. Rajini's brother, Satyanarayana, who had lost his wife just a month ago, had come from Bangalore to attend the event. Deeply touched, Rajinikanth said, 'I am glad my philosopher brother is here.'[7]

He said there was a message in the movie to the international audience: '*2.0* is a thriller, entertainer, but has a message that the planet is not just for human beings but for other creatures as well. The film cost a good deal, almost ₹600 crore but it is not about that. It is about the magic. I am sure it happened in the project. Mark my words, *2.0* will be a super duper hit.'[8] The fans went delirious and the walls reverberated with the sound of applause for a long time.

Shankar attributed the magic to 'Rajini sir's' dedication. 'We shot the climax scenes in Delhi but Rajini sir was not keeping well. Five hundred people were involved, and we had invested a lot of money and we were concerned about his well-being. His knee was also hurt. But he came undaunted and worked full swing. Such was his dedication.'[9]

The marketing department left no stone unturned to make the movie a success. Luckily, the Censor Board gave the film U/A certificate. The film would be released the world over in 7,500 theatres in the US, Canada, Europe, Singapore, Malaysia, the Philippines, and Japan. The Telugu and Hindi versions would also

---

[7]'Rajnikanth Speech at 2.0 Trailer Launch', *YouTube*, available here: https://www.youtube.com/watch?v=Q0Ul52t5LTk
[8]Ibid.
[9]Ibid.

be screened simultaneously. In the US alone, it was set to release in 800 theatres of which 550 had 3D facilities. The price of the ticket was about $30. That would be a pittance for a hard-core Rajini fan living abroad. The producers—Lyca Productions— hoped they would see a bumper collection in return.

Despite all the hype, the trailer was not universally loved. 'The trailer has been released to mixed response with apparently many disappointed with the visual effects,' reported *The Hindu*'s Friday Review. 'Rajini has confessed that the film cost 600 crores making it the most expensive Indian film. Some sniggered and sympathized with the solemn-looking producer, Subaskaran, who didn't manage even a smile during the entire elaborate audio release of the film widely watched on TV.'[10]

The release date was finally fixed for 29 November 2018. Ram Gopal Verma's big budget Telugu film, *Bhairava Geetha,* was also to be released on the same day. A worried Ram Gopal tweeted teasingly in Telugu about *2.0* in Telugu, 'It is a film made for children by a big director whereas *Bhairava Geetha* has been directed by a young director [Siddarth Thatholu] for adults.'[11] Ram Gopal Verma knew that both Rajinikanth's and Shankar's films had large markets in Telugu-speaking states. 'Their previous films *Shivaji* and *Enthiran* did exceptionally well in Telugu when there was hardly any market for dubbed Telugu films from Tamil industry,' said Telugu film distributor Jayatheertha.[12] The timing of the release of a mega budget film was crucial, though the success of the film depended on the reaction of the public. Smaller producers never dared to clash with the release of Rajini's films.

However, the public's attention was diverted by more important things. Tamil Nadu was rocked by an unprecedented natural disaster—the cyclone Gaja that hit the coastal areas

[10]S. Shiva Kumar, 'What is in store for Rajnikanth's 2.0?', *The Hindu*, 23 Nov 2018.
[11]Ram Gopal Verma, Twitter, Tweet available here: https://twitter.com/rgvzoomin/status/1066193461194371072?lang=en
[12]Interview with the author, Bangalore, 27 Jun 2018.

between Nagapattinam and Vedaranyam on 16 November, killing sixty-three people and leaving a trail of destruction behind. It unexpectedly spread to the interior regions of Nagapattinam, Thanjavur, Tiruvarur, and Pudukkottai districts. Gaja uprooted thousands of trees, damaged homes and boats, creating incredible damage and loss to the farmers, fishermen, and the public in general. Around 3.7 lakh people were rendered homeless. The pre-cyclone warnings and instructions given by the government were commendable and appreciated even by the opposition parties, but it soon became evident that the government machinery was ill-prepared for the urgent rehabilitation work that needed to be addressed. The officials handled the criticism that the government faced with the usual alacrity that Tamil Nadu officialdom has always shown during such times.

Kamal Haasan was the first to react among the actors. The members of his Makkal Needhi Maiam were everywhere to lend a hand with relief work. Kamal Haasan himself was seen with those affected. He handed over a cheque for ₹50 lakh to the Chief Minister's Relief Fund and that was broadcast on all news channels. Rajinikanth's RMM was asked to distribute food and clothing and other essentials worth ₹50 lakhs according to reports.[13]

'Let us rise above politics,' Kamal Haasan tweeted. 'Let us join together and lend a hand.'[14] He was, however, vociferous in criticizing the government's inefficiency. Rajinikanth did not want to join the opposition parties, DMK in particular, in blaming the government for insufficient relief work. Unlike Kamal, Rajini did not visit the cyclone hit areas. There were rumours that he had fallen seriously ill and had been hospitalized. These rumours were promptly rubbished by the RMM.

On 24 November came the tragic news of the death of his

---

[13]Gopi, 'Cyclone Gaja: Tamil actors Rajinikanth, Vijay, Suriya donate to relief fund', *Social News*, 20 Nov 2018.
[14]PTI, 'Cyclone Gaja: Rise above politics and extend support, Kamal Haasan urges Pinarayi Vijayan', *The Hindu*, 27 Nov 2018.

dear friend, fellow actor turned politician Ambarish. The news shook him. The Kannada actor was a good friend of his for forty years. Ambarish was diabetic, suffered from kidney problems, but was reckless and ignored his doctor's advice. There were stories about his drinking and rumours that he was often drunk right from the morning.[15] But he went about life cheerfully, as if nothing bothered him. Rajini appreciated how Ambarish brought good cheer wherever he went. But he was concerned about his state and its people. He joined the Congress and was part of the cabinet in the state under Siddaramaiah and in the centre during Manmohan Singh's regime. Rajinikanth remembered what a nice person he was and a great actor. Back in the day, Ambarish was one of the reasons that Rajinikanth had decided to leave Bangalore and try his luck in Tamil films. He knew he could not compete with the likes of Ambarish in Kannada films. As soon as he heard the news of the Kannada actor's death, Rajinikanth flew to Bangalore to pay his respects. As he stood before the body, he broke down. Kannada TV channels broadcast the funeral.[16]

Just a day after his return, during the early hours of 26th came the news of another death that grieved him deeply. Rajam, the wife of his mentor, Balachander, had passed away. He thought of her as a gentle soul, always smiling. She had been the silent pillar of strength behind her husband. The couple suffered together when their fifty-four-year-old son Bala Kailasam passed away in 2014. Balachander could not have borne the loss alone. Rajini felt like the old world was slipping away slowly like grains of sand between his fingers.

---

[15]Jagadish Angadi, 'The Ambareesh you didn't know', *Deccan Herald*, 5 Jan 2019.
[16]'Superstar Rajinikanth Sheds Tears & Mourns the Death of Rebel Star Ambareesh', *YouTube*, available here: https://www.youtube.com/watch?v=TfRlsJwebdw

Twenty-five

What the lady said was disturbing. Rajinikanth wondered if he could trust her words. She worked for a leading national English paper and was based in the North. She had not come to his Poes Garden residence to interview him. He had firmly refused to meet journalists and avoided interviews ever since he had announced he would enter politics. She was a close relative of a very dear friend who had recently passed away. She was on a visit to Chennai and wished to see him to condole his friend's demise.

The lady said, 'The BJP is no longer popular among the people in the North. There is a lot of discontent. They may lose power in the Hindi heartland during the coming assembly elections in Madhya Pradesh, Rajasthan, and Chhattisgarh.'

That was in response to what he had said: 'I think the BJP is the answer to India's future.' She had asked him about his political preferences.

But it seemed like he truly believed that the BJP was the right party to lead the country. His right-leaning friends all must have assured him that it was the only national party strong enough to win the second time and lead the country onto the right path. She was silent for a minute and then spoke those words. She went on: 'People are angry. So many things have gone wrong. Demonetization, GST, most importantly, the hate speeches, cow vigilantism, cases of mob lynching, the governments apathy to the whole thing siding with the vigilantes, ignoring the real issues like the farmers' unrest....' The list was long.

'Do you think BJP will lose the 2019 elections?' he asked.

'I am not sure of that, but it will be tough,' she said.

She had asked him if he was serious about entering politics, if he knew that the surveys said he would get not more than 10 per cent votes. He had laughed. 'I am certainly contesting the state assembly elections. It will not be just 10 per cent. If I come it will be one big sweep, nothing less,' he said with confidence. Nevertheless, the conversation would have given him something to think about.

She smiled but didn't seem convinced. Perhaps she thought he was being naïve. But that didn't bother him. He knew that it was possible for him to win. He and his well-wishers—he had a group of advisers, prominent among them were Tamilaruvi Manian, Karate Thiagarajan, S. Gurumurthy and Rangaraj Pandey, former editor-in-chief of Thanthi TV—had made a detailed study of the situation. But what the lady had said was playing on his mind.

By temperament, he felt in tune with the Bharatiya Janata Party's Hindutva ideology. But when he heard the hate-filled speeches that some BJP leaders made, he must have been upset and bothered that those who indulged in mob lynching were going unpunished. He was truly secular and inclusive in spirit. When he spoke of spiritualism, he didn't mean the type of spiritualism that discriminated against some. He had grown up in Bangalore, one of the most cosmopolitan cities in the country, where people of different faiths lived in harmony, each following her own dharma. He had close friends who were Muslim and Christian.

His friend, Cho Ramaswamy, had urged him to enter politics. Why? 'Because we need good people to be at the helm. He is a good man'.[1] Cho was very persuasive and had convinced him that he was indeed the man to be at the helm. Now Cho was dead and other advisors who had taken his place were also telling him that he was the man to be in charge. We will see that you win, they told him. You have a ready vote bank.

He had often felt like throwing his up hands and walking away. 'Politics is a very big game and very dangerous too. I have

---

[1] Interview with the author, 1996.

to play it very cautiously. Timing is very important,' he had said to the lady journalist.

While shooting a scene, his sense of timing was impeccable. In politics as well, he had to wait and strike at the right moment. He had felt very strongly that the BJP was the right party for the country. Now he was not all that sure. He knew that to bring order into society, a strong leader was needed. Lord Krishna had said as much to the vacillating Arjuna in the battleground of Kurukshetra. But unlike a film set, where he had a script to follow, politics was complicated. It had to be a script that he wrote, needed courage to write.

The much-awaited sci-fi blockbuster *2.0* was released to mixed reviews. One reviewer said '*2.0* is dull as ditchwater in the first half, perking up a little in the second, with a half-way watchable Akshay, and a Rajinikanth coming into his own right towards the end, for a bit. There are some oh-wow moments, but on the whole, the film is not worth all the sound and fury.'[2] It was disappointing to read this. He heard that his fans were disappointed as well. He had made a fool of himself by turning into a robot for the film. He sported a lush head of hair and Elvis Presley sideburns and a Batman-like costume. He had decided to go with the idea of a director who was obsessed with technology and digital graphics. It was not a Rajinikanth film. It was the director Shankar's film. Why did he demean himself? Any actor could have played the role. He had agreed because his name sold tickets. And, of course, he was paid handsomely. And it was his name that would make a movie worth it. Without it, would any producer be willing to invest ₹600 crore on a project? There were conflicting reports about how much the film did at the box office. Inside the walls of the mandrams they spoke worriedly about whether the movie would magnify his superstar status and

[2]Shubhra Gupta, '2.0 review: Not worth all the sound and fury', *Indian Express*, 30 Nov 2018.

boost his electoral appeal or puncture his stardom and with it his promise of entering Tamil Nadu politics in a big way. They vowed that they would not let the latter happen. But they did not want to watch the film more than twice. They would wait for his next film, *Petta*. In the posters, Thalaivar looks unbelievably dashing and even younger than before.

But Thalaivar didn't seem to think that the film's reception would impact his political career. In a rare interview to *India Today*, he insisted that he would never bank on his films to promote his political agenda. 'My films are different and my life is entirely different. Why should I merge the two? I am paid as an actor for films, whether I like the role or not. If I enter politics, I will be myself.... I want to introduce a new and different kind of politics. Otherwise, I am 67, my health too is in check-up stage (chuckles). It is not easy to enter politics at this age, it is not a path of flowers. Still, you have to change things, change that will make a difference in politics.'[3] But he didn't elaborate on how he was going to bring about this change.

K. Hariharan, film director and former professor of Film Studies at Ashoka University, was severe in his critique. 'Rajinikanth seems to be telling us that this "system" has atrophied and rotted to such an extent that when he takes on a new political avatar, a real war will have to be waged. ...he declares that when he does step into the arena, "god willing" he will ensure that all the corrupt elements shall be eliminated. How does he plan to do that? Does he have any means other than a "democratic" platform to come into a position of leadership? Is he in the process of authoring a new political credo called "Rajinikanthism" for his beloved masses?'[4]

Hariharan goes on, 'Rajinikanth needs to recognize that Tamil Nadu is actually in the forefront when it comes to primary

[3]Amarnath K. Menon and Raj Chengappa, 'Politics is a dangerous game: Rajinikanth', *India Today*, 10 Dec 2018.

[4]K. Hariharan, 'The Robotic Politics of Rajinikanth', *Open*, 25 May 2017.

health services being offered across India, the noon-meal schemes, women's education, industrial growth especially in the IT sector and efficiency in the state's intra-regional transport connectivity. The MGNREGA scheme in Tamil Nadu has successfully empowered women and Dalit communities in appreciable ways.... Though this sounds like the victorious climax scene from an earlier Rajinikanth film *Yejmaan*, it could not have happened if the system was totally rotten.... He is now more of a mascot for the quixotic lumpen from the 70s, dreaming loud and rebelling louder against all establishments.'

And on the question of whether Rajini will enter politics or not, Hariharan doesn't believe we need to worry about that. 'He has been giving false alarms such as this for the last ten years and Tamilians have learned to sleep happily with this alarm clock.'

⟋

Rajinikanth was travelling and he saw the news that the BJP had lost the most important states in the assembly elections in the Hindi heartland and that the Congress had come to power. Though it had lost by a very slim margin, it was a defeat, a loss of face. He was shocked but remembered what the journalist had told him about the BJP losing its popularity in the Hindi heartland. She had been right after all. When his flight landed in Chennai, sure enough, reporters from various TV channels were waiting for his remarks.

'What do you think, what do you think about the election results, sir?'

He looked away and said what was uppermost in his mind. 'It is proof that the BJP has lost its popularity.'[5]

Until a month ago he had been saying nearly the opposite. He had said that that the BJP was so strong that ten parties had to join together to oppose it. But he never shied away from

---

[5]Vikram Venkateswaran, 'BJP Losing Popularity: What Rajnikanth's Comment Means for 2019', *The Quint*, 11 Dec 2018.

saying what he felt. It was a warning to the Tamil Nadu BJP leaders who were trying to get him to put his weight behind them during the 2019 Lok Sabha elections.

Sometime later he received an invitation from the DMK to attend the unveiling of Karunanidhi's statue at Arivalayam, the DMK headquarters. Several leaders of the Opposition from various southern states and Sonia and Rahul Gandhi had also been invited. Rajinikanth attended and graciously shook hands with the DMK president, Stalin, and other leaders. He avoided the press after the event and soon after left for the US.

Twenty-six

Surya had not stopped smiling for weeks. Over the last ten days he'd had no time to breathe, eat or sleep. This was how it always was before the release of Thalaivar's film. In a span of seven months, three of Rajini's films had been released—*Kaala* in June 2018, *2.0* in November 2018 and the latest, *Petta,* in mid-January 2019. It was like the early days when the Superstar had films releasing one after the other, two or three in a year. The fan clubs had been working day and night and every member was exhausted. They had been feeling the stress of it all, worrying if the film would be a hit. Their job, as always, was to hype the film among the fans as well as the general public. Many of the fans had been disappointed with *2.0* even though the film was said to have had a good collection worldwide. They didn't understand the economics of it and didn't really care about that. All they wanted was a wholesome entertainer, and *Petta* promised to be just that. The trailer showed a Thalaivar who thrilled with his speed, energy, and dialogue delivery. He looked like he had gone back in time to the days when Surya and his friends had first been enthralled by him. Surya had heard that Rajini's youthful appearance was due to a make-up artist called Banu who had had special training abroad. The film reminded them of the blockbusters of yesteryears, with all the punch lines, political allusions, and action scenes. Surya knew that *Petta* would be a hit but there was a small spanner in the works in the form of Ajith's *Viswasam* (2019) that was meant to be released the same day. But, as it turned out, both films became big hits, which was rare in film history. Surya and the other fans were relieved. *Petta* was not a big budget film but is reported to have grossed nearly ₹200 crore within 23 days.[1]

Film critic Baradwaj Rangan wrote: 'Superstar is in super form and it is a thrill to be reminded—in this age of disposable stardom—of enduring screen charisma. To hook you with a look at this age, at this stage of his career you can forgive any number of *Baba*s and *Lingaa*s. He is lit beautifully and the heightened pace of his movement (something we missed in his recent films) brings to mind the Rajinikanth of old, when he spoke so fast that the words sometimes tumbled and merged into one another.

'The talented young director Karthik Subbaraj takes us back to that iconic first "Rajini moment" when he enters by flinging open the gates in *Apoorva Raagangal* by having a similar scene in *Petta* where, as the hostel warden, Rajini flings open the gate. The cigarette toss too is back to the thrill of the whistling fans.'[2]

Subbaraj knew that the fans were nostalgic and thirsting for just such callbacks. Rajini's loyal audience was ready to forgive his worst lapses in exchange for just such a blockbuster. 'You don't direct Rajinikanth,' says Kavithalayaa Krishnan, who worked with director Balachander, 'He happens to you. The story is incidental. The title, the fight scenes and the punch dialogues are the key to cracking the market.'[3]

People in the industry marvel at the energy and passion he exudes in films today just as he did forty years ago, capturing the imagination of a new generation of teenagers and young men. In the interview with *India Today*, he explained: 'In the beginning, I took to acting for a livelihood. Thereafter, I met the needs of my life.... It is not like a profession. Now it is like a game, it is relaxing. That is probably where I get my energy from—from

[1]Sreedhar Pillai, '*Viswasam* to *Petta*: a look at Kollywood in the first quarter', *The Hindu*, 2 Apr 2019.

[2]Baradwaj Rangan, 'Petta Movie Review: A Treat for Fans of the Star Makes You Wish it had also been One for Fans of the Director', *Film Companion*, 10 Jan 2019.

[3]Interview with the author, 28 Mar 2018.

the thought'[4]—that it is just entertainment.

Of course, there is more to it than that. He acts with a passion that has never diminished. Now it comes more easily but he has never forgotten how important it is for an actor to do a great job in an important business that involves profit and loss, success and failure at the box office. And Rajinikanth is very aware of this and deeply concerned about it. He is not naïve, he is street smart and extremely intelligent as Mani Ratnam said. He is meticulous in his planning—he rehearses his scenes and works with them for a long time. He internalizes every act, every scene, before he faces the camera, Muthuraman said about his method. That is his nature and that is the secret of his success. So, he could not be different when it came to politics, could he?

By the time *Petta* released, it had been more than a year since his announcement about entering politics. The world had changed a great deal in that time. The BJP, the party he was rumoured to be close to had lost its hold in three large states in the Hindi heartland. In Tamil Nadu, the DMK had suddenly, and surprisingly, loomed large after the demise of its stalwart leader Karunanidhi. His heir and the now party leader, Stalin, made an aggressive declaration of the DMK's alliance with the Congress in the ensuing Lok Sabha elections of 2019. He did not stop with that. Taking a leaf from his father's political statesmanship book, he declared that the DMK's choice for the prime minister's chair was Rahul Gandhi, leader of the Congress. The DMK–Congress combine in the state now seemed formidable. Poll surveys had been predicting a clean sweep for them. Rajinikanth was not even a factor in the survey. So perhaps there was no vacuum after all.

During this year, rather than firm up his political party and electoral plans, there were reports that he signed new films. Two years after the announcement, he seemed to be in no hurry and was being very cautious.

---

[4]Chengappa and Menon, 'Politics is a dangerous game'.

He had in any case bought two years by announcing that his party would only contest the assembly elections in 2021. He had not made any commitments about the parliamentary elections in 2019. When he had made this announcement, both the Dravidian parties appeared weak—Karunanidhi, the leader of the DMK, was ailing, and the ruling AIADMK had lost its charismatic leader. The shameful jockeying for power within the party had come out into the open. He knew that a section of Tamil society was keen for a change from the sixty years of Dravidian rule.

Chennai-based RSS ideologue and editor of *Thuglak*, S. Gurumurthy, welcomed the entry of Rajinikanth into politics and endorsed the Superstar's brand of 'spiritual politics' as a potential game changer, liberating the state 'from the anti-god politics concealing within it the Dravidian anti-Hindu sentiments which has become outdated and counterproductive in Tamil Nadu's increasingly pervasive religiosity'.[5] Gurumurthy's argument was flawed, however, as neither the AIADMK (under Jayalalithaa in particular), nor the DMK from the time of Annadurai, who came to power in 1967, was anti-god. Jayalalithaa openly demonstrated her faith while Annadurai famously defined the DMK's ideology as 'onre kulam, oruvane devan'—one community, one god. If the Dravidian parties had followed an anti-god policy, Tamil Nadu would not have witnessed an increasingly pervasive religiosity.

The BJP had no presence in Tamil Nadu and desperately wanted to piggyback on his popularity and the strength of his fan club. But when BJP spokespersons and RSS ideologues openly welcomed him to politics and claimed that 'Tamil Nadu politics will undergo a paradigm shift if he came to power',[6] he must have felt embarrassed. His fans who followed different faiths and were influenced by the Dravidian movement would be suspicious of such statements.

---

[5]S. Gurumurthy, 'Will Rajini change the paradigm of Tamil Nadu politics? *New Indian Express*, 8 Jan 2018.
[6]Ibid.

Pushpa Kandasamy, Balachander's daughter, was quite intrigued when Rajini announced that he was entering politics. She remembered what her father had said to him many years ago when the question of the Superstar joining politics had come up. A lot had changed since then, but her father's words were still relevant. Pushpa says she asked Rajinikanth about his decision and he explained to her that everyone around him was asking him to enter. 'I will give it a try. If they put me on the seat, I will do good for the people. If I don't succeed, I will say that I did try, didn't I?'[7]

She, like many others, felt that he was under pressure to take up the challenge. But others who know him well don't think he is the sort of person to be so influenced by others. They think he makes his own decisions based on his assessment of the situation. He had a team of advisers, among them media persons, professionals, right-wingers, and disgruntled persons from the two Dravidian parties. Each had his own agenda, he knew that. He listened to them very attentively. He hardly commented. Journalists who were reportedly close to him said Rajinikanth had his own intelligence inputs from the centre, one reason why he hadn't plunged headlong into politics like Kamal Haasan. He waited and watched. From the time he made his announcement, there had been many who criticized his move, questioned his qualifications. Even those from his own film fraternity had made sarcastic comments, asking him to pack up and leave. He knew he had work to do before he won the confidence of the people. He didn't want to start too early and lose steam before the elections. He knew that getting the public to vote for him was a very different proposition from entertaining moviegoers. He was focused on quietly revitalizing the RMM—his state-wide network of fans—and building a cadre of political workers and leaders at the grassroots level. He believed that the RMM could

[7]Interview with the author, 2 Jan 2019.

be leveraged to help him take the plunge at an appropriate time. RMM members were instructed to scrupulously follow the thirty-six-page manual that he released that outlined how they should conduct themselves in politics. On the cover was the photograph of a reflective Rajinikanth and a hand in apaana mudra, popularized by his flop film *Baba*. The manual spelt out ideals and values that RMM must follow. It may not have had the approval of his left-leaning friend, Ashok, but the latter would not comment on it. He and his friends in Bangalore were a little worried about Rajinikanth's political plans. Ashok was concerned that Shivaji's age was against him, and that his health was not good.[8] Perhaps Ashok was aware of the kidney transplant his friend had undergone in 2016. Rajinikanth made this information public only in October 2020.[9]

Rajinikanth asked members of RMM to use social media, go all out to draw in the younger generation and first-time voters. He wanted his fans to be part of his campaign for a 'total revolution' along with RMM members who hail from different age groups. The website when it was first launched got 300,000 registrations in the first twenty-four hours according to Surya[10] but some months later the momentum was lost. Poll surveys did not show more than 9 per cent vote share for Rajinikanth. He would need 35 per cent of the votes to form the government if there was a three-way split among parties. Subsequent poll surveys showed that the vote share of the AIADMK had not reduced drastically despite the absence of Jayalalithaa. The government, contrary to all speculations, has not crumbled. Much of what the RMM was doing in organization-building was similar to what the BJP has done successfully to capture power in several states. To quote *India Today*, 'Rajinikanth's political strategy team

---

[8]Interview with the author, Jun 2018.
[9]'Rajinikanth breaks silence, says doctors advised him against joining politics', *Mint*, 29 Oct 2020.
[10]Interview with the author, 28 Mar 2018.

seems to be working on several imponderables starting with the purported uncertainties in the AIADMK ranks, the perceived dwindling of the DMK cadre strength and possible churn in the equally strong ranks of non-committed voters, who play a decisive factor in Tamil Nadu elections. Whether they will vote for him because of that is another question.'[11]

But no matter what the DMK tried to drum up, it did not manage to pull the government down. The AIADMK had 37 members in the Lok Sabha and the BJP at the centre realized that the AIADMK's support in the Parliament was essential for it to face the passing of resolutions that were opposed by the Opposition. The BJP had lost three states in the Hindi heartland and when Rajinikanth openly distanced himself from the BJP, it became imperative to help the AIADMK remain in power. The DMK and the other opposition parties must have believed that the BJP had a secret pact with the AIADMK to help it survive. The government in Tamil Nadu was in fact stronger and more confident than it had been before.

---

[11]Amarnath K. Menon and Raj Chengappa, 'Rajinikanth: The One Man Army', *India Today*, 10 Dec 2018.

Twenty-seven

The incumbent BJP government returned with a greater majority in the 2019 Lok Sabha elections, winning 303 out of 543 seats on its own. Not only had it managed to retain its support base of 2014, but it had also expanded geographically and socially. It expanded its support base in states like West Bengal, Tripura, Odisha, and Telangana, while its social support base expanded in UP, Bihar, Karnataka, Maharashtra, and Jharkhand.[1]

While it looked like a success story for the BJP all over the country, it suffered a severe drubbing in Tamil Nadu, having lost even the one seat—Kanyakumari—it had won in 2014. And once again, the BJP failed to gain a foothold in the state despite its desperate attempts. In 2014, the state gave a huge victory to the AIADMK, keeping the BJP at bay, and in 2019 it voted in the DMK-led front, clearly signalling that the saffron brigade was not welcome. 'Hours before the results were being announced, Tamil Twitter trended #GoBackModi yet again; only with the results it emerged that the trend was more than just a hashtag,' commented *The Wire*.[2] Out of the 38 constituencies that went to the polls (elections in Vellore were cancelled due to complaints of corruption), the DMK alliance won 37, leaving just one to AIADMK, which was won by O. P. Ravindran, son of OPS, the deputy chief minister.[3]

[1]Sanjay Kumar, 'Here's how BJP earned the massive mandate: Explained in numbers', *Economic Times*, 28 May 2019.

[2]Kavitha Muralidharan, 'Why Tamil Nadu Voted the Way It Did', *The Wire*, 24 May 2019.

[3]E. T. B. Sivapriyan, 'Anti-Modi wave in TN; DMK alliance wins 37 of 38 seats', *Deccan Herald*, 23 May 2019.

It must have become clear to Rajinikanth that the anti-Modi wave in Tamil Nadu was no myth. But he had never shied away from praising Modi, so it was no surprise that he tweeted: 'Respected dear @narendramodi ji hearty congratulations....You made it!!! God bless' as soon as the results were announced on 23 May. He told reporters outside his Poes Garden residence, 'This victory is for an individual called Modi.... While the rest of India experienced pro-Modi wave, Tamil Nadu voted out the BJP due to anti-Modi wave.' He felt the 'intense campaign' by the Opposition was the reason for the defeat.[4]

The anti-Modi feeling became clearer in the by-polls to 22 assembly constituencies (18 had fallen vacant with AIADMK members having resigned, voicing grievance against the chief minister) that were held at around the same time. There was a neck-to-neck race between the DMK and the AIADMK. The DMK won 13 seats and the AIADMK 9, clearly indicating that in an election in Tamil Nadu, the fight would only be between the two Dravidian parties even after the demise of their respective charismatic leaders.

The 2019 Lok Sabha election in Tamil Nadu was a game-changer. It was the first major election in many years not led by DMK's Karunanidhi and AIADMK's Jayalalithaa. The DMK front's stupendous victory clearly showed that M. K. Stalin, son of Karunanidhi, had come into his own, emerging as a strong 'regional leader who stopped the BJP juggernaut from setting foot in Tamil Nadu'. His victory seemed to prove 'that the Hindi-Hindutva BJP would not be kosher' in the state.[5] The local BJP leaders were indeed shamefaced by the party's debacle in the state.

It became imperative on their part to aggressively pursue ways to improve the party's presence in the state. Doing it on their

---

[4] E. T. B. Sivapriyan, 'This victory is for an individual called Modi: Rajini', *Deccan Herald*, 28 May 2019.
[5] R. Kannan, 'How MK Stalin has emerged on his own and vindicated himself with Lok Sabha 2019', *News Minute*, 24 May 2019.

own was now near impossible, it seemed. Even as Rajinikanth kept himself busy with his film shoots, members of the BJP and journalists who were pro-BJP said in media debates that they were confident that Rajinikanth would align with or support the BJP. Arjun Sampath, founder of Hindu Makkal Katchi, an ally of the BJP, said in many TV debates that he was confident that Rajinikanth, with his mass appeal and fan base, would sweep the polls, indicating that Rajinikanth would help the lotus bloom in Tamil Nadu. 'Rajini's will not be a political party—it will be a movement,' he said.[6]

Ravindran Doraiswamy, political commentator and a strong supporter of Rajinikanth, said that Tamil Nadu was in search of its next mass leader. 'It is my opinion that Stalin, while he has filled the leadership gap in his party, has not filled the vacuum in the hearts of the people. And Rajinikanth is in prime position to do that. Since Rajinikanth cannot be identified with any caste, he is a supra-caste icon who, like NTR in 1982, wants to enter the fray at a later stage so that the election becomes about him.' Ravindran, who claims to know Rajinikanth well, is sure that Rajinikanth will never align with the BJP. 'Superstar knows it will be suicidal.'[7]

But there were a number of instances where his confused fans and observers got a different impression. He seemed to signal that he was gravitating towards the right. He briefly distanced himself from the right in November 2019 when there was an uproar from the anti-BJP front when Thiruvalluvar, the iconic saint poet of Tamil Nadu, appeared in saffron robes in the tweet from the Tamil Nadu BJP handle. When reporters rushed to Rajinikanth's gates and asked for his reaction, he said that there have been attempts to saffronize him. 'But neither Thiruvalluvar

---

[6]'Arjun Sampath's Speech on Rajinikanth Political Entry, Makkal Mandram, Thanthi TV, 12 Jan 2018, available here: https://www.youtube.com/watch?v=4vftvmDAZlQ
[7]Phone interview with the author.

nor I would get into any saffron trap.'[8] His followers heaved a sigh of relief.

At an event on 14 January 2020 to mark fifty years of the Tamil magazine *Thuglak*, he launched a bitter verbal attack on the Dravidian movement. He talked about how Cho Ramaswamy, when he had been editor of *Thuglak*, had been bold enough to attack Periyar for parading naked figures of Hindu gods on the streets of Salem in 1971. He added sarcastically that this had happened during the reign of the DMK under Karunanidhi. Rajini's remarks at this event caused a controversy. But he refused to apologize when members of the Dravidar Kazhagam demanded it. Rajinikanth's comments on Periyar were, in fact, intended as a direct jibe at the DMK. He had begun his speech with 'People who read *Murasoli* [the DMK's mouthpiece] can be identified as DMK. Those who carry *Thuglak* can be identified as intellectuals.'[9]

Not only was this attack deliberate, it was also in bad taste. So why did he do that? The BJP had identified that the DMK was the strong party in Tamil Nadu that needed to be weakened. It is difficult to say if Rajinikanth was testing the waters or if it was the BJP using him to do so. He had been quite open about supporting the centre's actions and Tamil Nadu BJP leaders were pleased with his endorsements and made no effort to hide it.

On 5 August 2019, the BJP government at the centre had revoked the special status or limited autonomy granted under Article 370 of the Indian Constitution to Jammu and Kashmir. The state was divided into two union territories to be governed by a lieutenant governor. Cutting off all communication effectively silenced reaction in the valley. International human rights groups condemned the revocation and so did the Opposition parties, including the J&K National Congress, J&K People's Democratic

---

[8]'Neither Tiruvalluvar nor I can be saffronised: Rajinikanth', *Deccan Chronicle*, 9 Nov 2019.
[9]Kavitha Muralidharan, 'Reaction to Rajinikanth's Periyar Remark Mirrors Shifting Political Dynamics in Tamil Nadu', *The Wire*, 24 Jan 2020.

Party, the Indian National Congress, Trinamool Congress, Janata
Dal, and the DMK. Constitutional expert opinion is still divided
on whether the revocation is legally sound.

Later that same month, on 10 August, Vice President Venkaiah
Naidu's book on his two years in office was released by Home
Minister Amit Shah in Chennai. Rajinikanth was invited as a special
guest. At the event, Rajinikanth congratulated Prime Minister
Narendra Modi and Home Minister Amit Shah for how they
handled the Kashmir issue. 'Really, my heartfelt congratulations
for your mission Kashmir operations, sir. The way you conducted
it, hats off, especially the speech you delivered in Parliament,
fantastic, sir, fantastic.'[10]

He repeated his admiration for the way the Kashmir issue had
been handled when he met reporters outside his home the next
day. 'It is a huge issue related to our country's security. Kashmir
is like a mother's house for terrorists and extremists…. It is like
a gateway to India for them.' He also praised the planning and
execution of the move as 'raja thanthiram' (king's strategy). When
asked about the opposition to this move, he said, 'Some leaders
should know what issues can be politicized and what should not,
since this is an issue related to the country's security.'[11] Political
analysts accused him of being the BJP's proxy in Tamil Nadu.

When the Citizenship Amendment Act (CAA) was passed in
Parliament on 11 December 2019, he similarly showed his support
for the Act. The Act grants citizenship to undocumented members
of six minority communities—Hindus, Sikhs, Christians, Jains,
Buddhists, and Parsis—from Pakistan, Bangladesh, and Afghanistan
who had migrated to India on account of religious persecution
before 31 December 2014. Though the bill was passed in both

---

[10]See Rajinikanth Latest Speech, Puthiyathalaimurai TV, 10 Aug 2019, available
here: https://www.youtube.com/watch?v=2HlD0kaTZUI&feature=emb_title and
'Rajinikanth praises Modi, Amit Shah for scrapping Article 370, compares them to
Krishna and Arjuna', *Scroll.in*, 11 Aug 2019.
[11]Ibid.

the houses of Parliament amidst severe debate by the Opposition over the hidden agenda—its exclusion of Muslims from the list who could seek citizenship—there were widespread protests all over the country in which the student community joined in large numbers. The demonstrators argued that by excluding Muslims, the CAA violates the country's secular principles and risks turning India into a majoritarian state. The police retaliated by cracking down on demonstrators. Several protesters were injured and some died.[12] Following this, Muslim women in an area called Shaheen Bagh in Delhi went on a massive sit-in peaceful protest. It became a symbol of protest for every citizen's rights and in an amazing show of solidarity several Shaheen Baghs sprang up in various cities including Chennai's Old Washermanpet—a Muslim dominated area.

Speaking to reporters in front of his Poes Garden residence on 4 February 2020 Rajinikanth explained that there was no reason for any Indian Muslims to feel threatened. 'They [the government] have explained clearly that because of the CAA there won't be any problem for Indian citizens or their citizenship.' He went on with a smile: 'The Muslims who stayed back during Partition did so with the thought that this is my country, this is my birthplace, this is my soil and if I die here, I will die here and are living with these thoughts. How will they send these Muslims outside? If anything like that happens, I, Rajinikanth, will be the first person to stand up for those Muslims.' He sounded sincere, and full of belief in his own words. He said that some political parties were provoking Muslims for their own benefit.

Political analysts felt that Rajinikanth appeared naïve in an atmosphere that was increasingly becoming volatile. The protests had started with students, but soon was joined by Muslim groups, as well as writers and activists in large numbers all over the country.

[12]Aditi Malik, Shivaji Mukherjee, and Ajay Verghese, 'In India, thousands are protesting the new citizenship law. Here are 4 things to know', *Washington Post*, 31 Dec 2019.

The narrative that troubled many was that the combination of CAA, NPR, and NRC was aimed at one particular community.

In Delhi, the protests that had remained peaceful, turned into communal clashes in mid-February. Over 20 people died and 150 were injured. Congress President Sonia Gandhi held the central government and the Delhi's AAP responsible for the situation. 'Many BJP leaders have been spreading an atmosphere of fear and hate by making inflammatory speeches,' she said, without naming anyone in particular.[13]

Rajinikanth, who was busy shooting for his upcoming film *Annaatthe*, hit out at the central government, saying, 'Intelligence failure means Home Ministry's failure'. Opposition parties had also demanded the home minister's resignation for failing to contain the violence.[14] The BJP must have been surprised by his outburst.

It was then that the members of the Muslim outfit, Tamil Nadu Jamathul Ulama Sabai (TNJUS) decided to meet the actor. It was high time that they explained to him why Muslim women who had never stepped out of their houses were sitting in the narrow lanes of Old Washermanpet, armed with copies of the Constitution, demanding the repeal of the CAA.

They met him at his Poes Garden residence and apprised him of issues Muslims would face due to the Citizenship Amendment Act, the National Population Register, and the National Register of Citizens. They told him that all these laws were interconnected and went against the Constitution by deciding citizenship on the basis of religion. The fear is deep that it is a move to tear apart the secular fabric of the nation and turn India into a Hindu Rashtra. The fear was not without basis. Muslims, even those who have lived here for generations, were being asked to prove their nationality. If they didn't have the paperwork to prove it, and

---

[13]Prabhash K. Dutta, 'Delhi violence: A story of politics, police and riot-ready mob', *India Today*, 26 Feb 2020.
[14]'Reporter's diary: Rajini outburst catches saffron camp off guard', *DT Next*, 28 Feb 2020.

this is the case for millions in the country, they could, with one stroke of the pen, become stateless, declared illegal immigrants. The members of TNJUS reminded the actor about cases of lynching of Muslims in the northern states.

They explained that this was not just a protest by the Muslim community alone. It was a spontaneous nationwide protest that was not politically motivated or sponsored by the opposition parties as the government claims.[15] Soon after the meeting, Rajinikanth tweeted: I am willing to play any role in order to maintain peace in the country. I too agree with their [Muslim leaders] comment that a country's prime objective should be love unity and peace.[16]

Political analysts knew that if Rajinikanth did indeed contest the elections, there was real danger that the votes of the main Dravidian parties would be split. The disgruntled in the DMK and AIADMK may join him. This will be to the advantage of the BJP. For more than fifty years, Tamil Nadu has seen and acknowledged Dravidian politics that is based on the philosophy of social justice and equality. And Tamil pride is something that is ingrained in its soul. How would Rajinikanth fit into the scheme of things?

---

[15]Interview with Priyan, also see 'Tamil Nadu Jamathul Ulama Sabai delegation meets actor Rajinikanth', ANI, 1 Mar 2020.
[16]'Ready to play any role to maintain peace in country: Rajinikanth on Delhi violence', *Indian Express*, 2 Mar 2020.

Epilogue

....

From the time that Rajnikanth announced that he would definitely stand for elections, there have been changes and setbacks. On 12 March 2020, Rajinikanth met briefly with the mandram chiefs and then left for the Leela Palace where his fans were gathered to hear his latest announcement. As his black Audi approached the hotel's entrance, frenzied fans rushed forward shouting, 'Superstar vaazga! Varungaala mudalvar vaazga! (Long live the Superstar! Long live the future chief minister!)'. Once inside, the seventy-year-old actor, clad in his trademark white kurta-pyjama, walked briskly onto the dais and stood before the microphone. As the thunderous applause subsided, he began to speak. It was a thirty-minute monologue, emotional and defensive. He outlined 'three novel proposals'—'limited number of party posts to curb corruption, bringing youngsters and clean people to politics and place them in pole positions in the corridor of power and him not being the Chief Minister....' He asked the people to 'please stop projecting me as the next chief minister. Tell people about my ideas and let there be a resurgence.... I will come then.'[1]

'There was not a hint on when he would launch his political party and gave enough indications that he may not be a true–blue political material,' wrote the *Deccan Herald*. 'Rajinikanth said he can't imagine sitting in the Assembly, giving speeches even while making it clear that he just wants to play the role of a "facilitator" to usher in the change, which Tamil Nadu has been "yearning"

---

[1] E. T. B. Sivapriyan, 'Reluctant on political plunge, Rajinikanth says not interested in Chief Minister's post', *Deccan Herald*, 12 Mar 2020.

for decades.'[2] There was supposed to be an interaction with the media but he left the venue without taking any questions.

It became clear from his announcement what the crux of the matter was. It appeared that he had come to realize what unbiased political observers had been saying for a long time—that it was just not possible to win an election banking on his fan base that was not homogeneous in nature. He said: 'I can just be a vote splitter with 10 or 20% votes. Tell me, at this age of mine should I come just to split votes? I will turn seventy-one next year. I can't wait for the next election to win.'[3] Members of RMM and his admirers were dismayed. After all these years of waiting, and days of hard work they had put in hoping that Thalaivar would become the next chief minister, he said that he does not want the chief minister's post but wants change to happen. Through posters, public meetings, and door-to-door visits they had been projecting him as the icon of change. Why would any member of RMM continue working if Thalaivar was not going to contest the election? RMM existed because of their love for him. He had promised on 31 December 2017 that he would bring back MGR's rule if he came to power. Now how can he say that he has never desired to be the chief minister?

On the film front as well, things were not going smoothly. *Darbar* (2020), directed by A. R. Murugadoss, released on 9 January, turned out to be a big disappointment at the box office. 'Made on a budget of ₹200 crore which included ₹108 crore salary of Rajinikanth, *Darbar* was adjudged a disaster despite collecting around ₹250 crore worldwide.' The distributors who suffered heavy losses were planning to meet Rajinikanth to ask for compensation for the losses.[4]

Over the three years since Rajinikanth's announcement about

---

[2]Ibid.

[3]Reported in *Dinamani,* 13 Mar 2020.

[4]Karthik Kumar, 'Darbar box office: Film ends up as a colossal flop, distributors plan to approach Rajinikanth', *Hindustan Times,* 31 Jan 2020.

standing for elections, the landscape had changed greatly. His plans for a grand entry had vanished. But he still had to assuage the long waiting fans. But by mid-March 2020, the country and the entire world was reeling from the novel coronavirus pandemic, putting everything on pause. On 1 December 2020, he convened a meeting with RMM members and informed them that the doctors had forbidden him from entering the electoral fray—it was too risky with his health problems and low immunity (after his kidney transplant in 2016). The fans understood. Their Thalaivar's health was more important than anything else.

Two days later he said that he would announce the party name on 31 December and float the party in January 2021. 'I am ready to sacrifice even my life for the sake of Tamil people,' he said,[5] flanked by his political advisers—Arjuna Murthy (formerly a member of the BJP) and Tamilaruvi Manian. The fans were deeply moved by his sense of commitment but wondered what had made him change his mind. They also wondered about his choice of advisers. Once again political analysts concluded he was under pressure from the BJP.

He left soon after for Hyderabad to proceed with the shooting of his latest film *Annaatthe* produced by Sun Pictures. Within a week, four of the crew members were found to be COVID-19 positive. That was a scare, but even more worrying was the news that Rajinikanth had been admitted in the hospital with severe fluctuations in blood pressure. He was discharged after two days, and the doctors advised him to take complete bed rest for a week. They also seem to have warned the seventy-year-old actor against campaigning in the midst of COVID-19, given his health condition, especially due to the kidney transplant he had had a few years ago. On 29 December in a three-page statement released on social media, he announced that he will not be starting his

[5]J. Sam Daniel Stalin, '"Willing To Die For Tamil People": Rajinikanth Party Arrives In January', NDTV, 3 Dec 2020.

political party—his health scare having come as 'a warning from the Gods'[6].

He had always said that if it was God's will that he should enter politics, nobody could prevent that from happening. Now it appears that it is not God's will. Journalists who had always said that his decision to enter politics was because of pressure from the BJP were now puzzled about his withdrawal. Arjuna Murthy, in an interview on Thanthi TV denied that there was any pressure from the BJP. 'Rajinikanth takes his own decisions. Now it was the doctor's decision that he had to heed though he was pained to do so.'[7]

'He has betrayed his fans,' exclaimed senior journalist, Kolakala Srinivas, who had fervently supported Rajinikanth's entry into politics. He is of the firm belief that Rajinikanth would have won, with his charisma and mass support, and would have definitely brought about the change that a large section of Tamil Nadu desired. He went on to attack the actor of having cheated fans who had waited for him like undertaking a penance—'thavam'—for thirty years.[8]

That is rather harsh, since the actor does indeed have health problems. He had been ignoring that in his desire to enter politics, but had to finally accept the reality and throw in the towel. But even before the pandemic, he must have seen that the party he wanted to launch lacked a clear ideology that could attract people, and a strong structure to compete with the two Dravidan giants.

Most people who made public statements, including Kamal Haasan, supported Rajini's decision, saying that one's health was the most important thing to take care of. Now speculations are on if he might 'lend his voice' in support of any party. His

---

[6]'Rajinikanth announces he will not start a political party after warning from God', *India Today*, 29 Dec 2020.

[7]Interview on Thanthi TV, 2 Jan.

[8]Kolakala Srinivas, '30 years penance destroyed', Chanakyaa, available here: https://youtu.be/JRay2FLiHts

detractors say he has lost his credibility.

'His retreat from the fray removes a key unknown factor that had promised to turn the election into a more exciting and unpredictable event,' said the *Indian Express* in its editorial. 'In his absence, the main contest would be, as it has been, between the two major Dravidian parties, the ruling AIADMK and the DMK.'[9] It must surely be a relief to both the parties whose respective vote share might have been dented had he contested, perhaps resulting in a hung assembly.

His announcement of contesting elections had sent tremors through the political arena for three years, generating speculation and discussion. But that had all ended anticlimactically.

But for those three years, the actor who had come to Chennai as a young man with nothing but the clothes on his back, nervous and hungry, had become a force to reckon with in Tamil Nadu politics. Certain things about him remain unchanged from those days: his commitment and passion for cinema and his closeness and affection for his friends in Bangalore. These are his friends who let him feel normal. They tease him, chide and advise him. His fame, stardom, and wealth had made no difference to them. It was their selfless love that made him seek out their company when he was overwhelmed by the pressures he had to face. Even the mind-boggling affection of the fans constantly reminded him that he was indebted to them and had to pay them back in some way. Perhaps he thought that attaining political power and changing the 'corrupt system' was the only way to do it. He and his friends seem to have deluded themselves that this was achievable, and some friends from political parties fueled the idea. He was aware of course that they had their own agenda. But he had made a commitment to his fans. He had made promises, had kept the carrot dangling. Now he had to walk away from the promises. They might well say that this was a betrayal. He is

---

[9]'Editorial: Rajini can't', *Indian Express*, 31 Dec 2020.

deeply pained at having let them down.

He knows one person who would have been happy about his decision—his mentor, S. Balachander sir. How could he forget his words? 'I would be happy if you don't enter politics,' he had said. 'Your temperament is not suited for politics.' How true that was. And so it will be. Back to cinema, his first love. It was this love for cinema that made the fans flock to him. They will understand his pain. Such is their love.

Life has led him to unexpected turns and twists. And what a life it has been! For the moment there are still the films. 'I will continue doing films for as long as people ask for, and want to see Rajinikanth,' he said. 'Till I have the energy, I will do films.'[10] And he is still a box office star who has had many more successes than flops. A superstar who seems not to have lost his lustre in these forty-odd years. Whatever the political situation will be, for the time being, his fans are bursting crackers, anticipating his next film as if welcoming a new dawn.

---

[10]Menon and Chengappa, 'Rajinikanth: The One Man Army'.

Acknowledgements

Writing the biography of Rajnikanth was more complex than I thought it would be. He was a phenomenon, larger than life. The more I tried to decipher the character, the more enigmatic he became.

My thanks to David Davidar, publisher of Aleph Book Company, for giving me the assignment and for his faith and trust in my ability to write the amazing, fascinating life of the actor who remains the supreme entertainer for over four decades in Tamil Nadu.

I am indebted to many for their encouragement and assistance in the pursuit of this project that entailed several trips to Chennai and Bangalore. My special thanks to my friend K. S. Radhakrishnan, whose generous hospitality enabled me to stay in his house during my month-long visits to Chennai. He helped me fix interviews with Tamilaruvi Manian, Karate Thiagarajan and also got me the contact numbers of persons I had to meet. Thiagarajan introduced me to Surya, Rajinikanth's ardent fan from age twenty to this day at sixty.

My heartfelt thanks to Sadanand Menon for sharing with me his insights into Tamil cinema and the reasons for the star's spectacular appeal to Tamil audiences. Thanks to Baradwaj Rangan for allowing me to quote from his blogs and reviews of Rajanikanth's films. My thanks to Mani Rathnam and S. P. Muthuraman for their valuable inputs about their experience directing Rajinikanth in their productions. I thank Y. G. Mahendran, Pushpa Kandasamy, and Kavithalayaa Krishnan for sharing with me their intimate observations and knowledge of Rajinikanth as a person. I thank actor Sivakumar and Retired Justice K. Chandru for sharing their thoughts about the actor.

Journalists Priyan, Maalan, D. I. Aravindan, Manaa, Ravindran Duraisamy, Lakshmi Subramanian, Nirupama Subramanian, Arun Janardhanan, and many others helped me understand the importance of Rajinikanth in Tamil Nadu politics. I thank Thuglak Ramesh for sending me Xeroxed copies of Rajinikanth's articles that had appeared in *Thuglak* weekly in the nineties.

My thanks to my brother Shekar and his wife, Sujatha, for their affection and loving care when I stayed with them in Bangalore for more than a month. My friend, journalist Imran Qureshi, introduced me to veteran Kannada journalist Bhaskar Rao, who had known Rajinikanth from his bus conductor days. Rao in turn took me to Ashok, Kannada actor, who was Rajinikanth's classmate at the Madras Film Institute and remains the latter's close friend. I thank actor Raghunandan, also a classmate from the institute who remains close to Rajinikanth, for the long chat we had when he shared with me his fond memories of his friend. Rohini, journalist, took the trouble of taking me to Gangadheeshwar temple to meet the priest Somasundara who had been Rajinikanth's schoolmate. I would like to thank Malavika Avinash for her inputs on Rajinikanth's interest in Kannada literature.

I thank Professors S. V. Srinivas and M. K. Raghavendra for their academic analysis of Rajinikanth's phenomenal success in Tamil Nadu and Theodore Baskaran for explaining the difference between MGR's fan clubs and those of Rajinikanth in the context of electoral politics of Tamil Nadu.

I have used as a resource the Tamil translation of Gayathri Sreekant's biography *The Name is Rajinikanth* for incidents from the actor's early life in Bangalore. The book was endorsed by Rajinikanth and released by the actor's close friend Cho Ramaswamy and attended by his daughter Soundarya in March 2008. I have also used as a reference Naman Ramachandran's *Rajinikanth: The Definitive Biography*.

My regret is I could not get an appointment to meet the Superstar though I kept trying through various sources close to him. I had interviewed him in 1993 (he had produced and released his film *Valli* with the intention of helping his less fortunate friends) when I was the editor of *India Today* Tamil edition. He seemed a little reserved.

My special thanks to my editor Pujitha Krishnan for her meticulous attention to detail, insisting on references where she found they were needed, crosschecking them, and the graceful editing that resulted in the end. Thank you, Pujitha, for the care you took to shape the book.

Finally, my son Ravi Sundaram and his wife Ranjani who were a source of great encouragement that sustained me through this work. I am grateful to all of them.

INDEX

Rao, Bhaskar, 13, 14, 15, 26, 34, 35, 37, 46, 62, 120, 122, 256
Rao, C. Vidyasagar, 175
Rao, Nageswara A., 21
Rao, P. V. Narasimha, 99–101, 103
Rao, T. Rama, 76
Ratnam, Mani, 77, 78, 80, 93, 94, 108, 116, 173, 198, 235
Ratnam, S. G., 78
Ravikumar, K. S., 112, 145, 149, 155, 198
Ravindranath, 22, 25, 69, 71
Rockline Entertainment, 155
Roy, Reena, 76

Saajan Chale Sasural (1996), 90
Saint Raghavendra, 10, 23, 31, 72, 185, 186, 187
Saint Vallalar, 37
Saravanan, 130
Saravanan, A. V. M., 46, 131, 132
Sarkar (2018), 216
Sasikala, 166, 167, 168, 174, 175, 176, 182, 191
Satchidananda, Swami, 73, 96, 115, 116, 117, 118, 147
Sathya (1988), 95
Sathyaraj, 127
Sathyamurthy Bhavan, 100
Satyanarayana (brother), 1, 3–8, 11, 12, 17, 20, 28, 34, 62, 88, 146, 223
Satyanarayana (fan club aide), 82, 106, 122
self-respect movement, 197
Sengottaiyan, K. A., 81
Seshan, T. N., 94
Shankar, S., 73, 131
Shanti Kranti (1991), 46
Shivappa, Justice C., 104
Shobana, 149

Siddaramaiah, 226
Sivaji: The Boss (2007), 73, 131, 132-136, 163
Sivakumar, P., 40, 41, 55, 62, 63, 215, 255
Sivan, Santosh, 78
Soundarya, 73, 149, 256
South Indian Film Chamber of Commerce, 19
Sripriya, 51, 52, 62
Sri Ramachandra Medical Centre, 146
Srividya, 32
Stalin, 162, 169, 181, 182, 189, 191, 202, 212, 213, 232, 235, 241, 242, 250
St Isabel's Hospital, 145
Subaskaran, 224
Subbaraj, Karthik, 203, 234
Sudha, 32
Sundarrajan, Major, 32
Surya, 54, 55, 58, 59, 78, 80, 101, 189, 204, 205, 206, 207, 221, 222, 233, 238, 255
Swamy, Subramanian, 95, 156

Tamil Maanila Congress (TMC), 101, 102, 107, 108, 112
Tamil Nadu Congress Committee (TNCC), 99, 100, 191
Thalaivar, ix, xii, 54, 56, 58, 59, 75, 85, 86, 101, 108, 113, 115, 134, 135, 143, 149, 150, 178, 187, 189, 196, 202, 204, 205, 206, 207, 209, 212, 222, 230, 233, 249, 250
Thalapathi (1991), 78
Thambidurai, M., 111
'Thamizh engkal moochu' (Tamil is our breath), ix
Thiagarajan, Karate R., 98, 100–103, 114, 146, 154, 188, 228, 255